Practical Internet of Things Security

A practical, indispensable security guide that will navigate you through the complex realm of securely building and deploying systems in our IoT-connected world

Brian Russell

Drew Van Duren

[PACKT] open source *
PUBLISHING   community experience distilled

BIRMINGHAM - MUMBAI

Practical Internet of Things Security

First published: June 2016

Production reference: 1230616

Published by Packt Publishing Ltd.
Livery Place
35 Livery Street
Birmingham B3 2PB, UK.

ISBN 978-1-78588-963-9

www.packtpub.com

Credits

Authors
Brian Russell
Drew Van Duren

Reviewer
Aaron Guzman

Commissioning Editor
Kartikey Pandey

Acquisition Editor
Prachi Bisht

Content Development Editor
Arshiya Ayaz Umer

Technical Editor
Siddhi Rane

Copy Editor
Safis Editing

Project Coordinator
Kinjal Bari

Proofreader
Safis Editing

Indexer
Hemangini Bari

Graphics
Kirk D'Penha

Production Coordinator
Shantanu N. Zagade

Cover Work
Shantanu N. Zagade

About the Authors

Brian Russell is a chief engineer focused on cyber security solutions for Leidos (https://www.leidos.com/). He oversees the design and development of security solutions and the implementation of privacy and trust controls for customers, with a focus on securing Internet of Things (IoT). Brian leads efforts that include security engineering for Unmanned Aircraft Systems (UAS) and connected vehicles and development security systems, including high assurance cryptographic key management systems. He has 16 years of information security experience. He serves as chair of the Cloud Security Alliance (CSA) Internet of Things (IoT) Working Group, and as a member of the Federal Communications Commission (FCC) Technological Advisory Council (TAC) Cybersecurity Working Group. Brian also volunteers in support of the Center for Internet Security (CIS) 20 Critical Security Controls Editorial Panel and the Securing Smart Cities (SSC) Initiative (http://securingsmartcities.org/).

Join the Cloud Security Alliance (CSA) IoT WG @ https://cloudsecurityalliance.org/group/internet-of-things/#_join.

You can contact Brian at https://www.linkedin.com/in/brian-russell-65a4991.

I would like to thank my wife, Charmae, and children, Trinity and Ethan. Their encouragement and love during my time collaboration on this project has been invaluable. I would also like to thank all the great volunteers and staff of the Cloud Security Alliance (CSA) Internet of Things (IoT) Working Group, who have worked with me over the past few years to better understand and recommend solutions for IoT security. Lastly, I would like to thank my parents, without whom I would not have the drive to complete this book.

Drew Van Duren currently works at Leidos as a senior cryptographic and cybersecurity engineer, highlighting 15 years of support to commercial, US Department of Defense, and US Department of Transportation (USDOT) customers in their efforts to secure vital transportation and national security systems. Originally an aerospace engineer, his experience evolved into cyber-physical (transportation system) risk management, secure cryptographic communications engineering, and secure network protocol design for high assurance DoD systems. Drew has provided extensive security expertise to the Federal Aviation Administration's Unmanned Aircraft Systems (UAS) integration office and supported RTCA standards body in the development of cryptographic protections for unmanned aircraft flying in the US National Airspace System. He has additionally supported USDOT Federal Highway Administration (FHWA) and the automotive industry in threat modeling and security analysis of connected vehicle communications design, security systems, surface transportation systems, and cryptographic credentialing operations via the connected vehicle security credential management system (SCMS). Prior to his work in the transportation industry, Drew was a technical director, managing two of the largest (FIPS 140-2) cryptographic testing laboratories and frequently provided cryptographic key management and protocol expertise to various national security programs. He is a licensed pilot and flies drone systems commercially, and is also a co-founder of Responsible Robotics, LLC, which is dedicated to safe and responsible flight operations for unmanned aircraft.

You can reach Drew at https://www.linkedin.com/in/drew-van-duren-33a7b54.

I would first like to thank my wife, Robin, and children, Jakob and Lindsey, for their immense love, humor, and patience that shone brightly as I collaborated on this book. They were always keen to provide the diversions when I needed them the most. I would also like to thank my parents for their unceasing love, discipline, and encouragement to pursue diverse interests—model making, engineering, aviation, and music—in my formative years. More than anything, playing the cello has enriched and centered me amid life's demands. Lastly, my gratitude goes to my departed grandparents, especially my maternal grandfather, Arthur Glenn Foster, whose unquenchable scientific and engineering inquisitiveness provided just the footsteps I needed in my young life.

About the Reviewer

Aaron Guzman is a principal penetration tester from the Los Angeles area with expertise in application security, mobile pentesting, web pentesting, IoT hacking, and network penetration testing. He has previously worked with established tech companies such as Belkin, Symantec, and Dell, breaking code and architecting infrastructures. With Aaron's years of experience, he has given presentations at various conferences, ranging from Defcon and OWASP AppSecUSA to developer code camps across America. He has contributed to many IoT security guideline publications and open source community projects around application security. Furthermore, Aaron is a chapter leader for the Open Web Application Security Project (OWASP), Los Angeles, Cloud Security Alliance SoCal (CSA SoCal), and High Technology Crime Investigation Association of Southern California (HTCIA SoCal). You can follow Aaron's latest research and updates on Twitter at `@scriptingxss`.

www.PacktPub.com

eBooks, discount offers, and more

Did you know that Packt offers eBook versions of every book published, with PDF and ePub files available? You can upgrade to the eBook version at `www.PacktPub.com` and as a print book customer, you are entitled to a discount on the eBook copy. Get in touch with us at `customercare@packtpub.com` for more details.

At `www.PacktPub.com`, you can also read a collection of free technical articles, sign up for a range of free newsletters and receive exclusive discounts and offers on Packt books and eBooks.

`https://www2.packtpub.com/books/subscription/packtlib`

Do you need instant solutions to your IT questions? PacktLib is Packt's online digital book library. Here, you can search, access, and read Packt's entire library of books.

Why subscribe?

- Fully searchable across every book published by Packt
- Copy and paste, print, and bookmark content
- On demand and accessible via a web browser

Table of Contents

Preface

Only a few people would contest the assertion that the phenomenon of the Internet of Things poses problems related to security, safety, and privacy. Given the remarkable industrial and consumer diversity of the IoT, one of the principal challenges and goals we faced when electing to write this book was determining how to identify and distill the core IoT security principles in as useful, but industry-agnostic a way as possible. It was equally important to balance real-world application with background theory, especially given the unfathomable number of current and forthcoming IoT products, systems, and applications. To end this, we included some basic security (and safety) topics that we must adequately, if minimally, cover as they are needed as a reference point in any meaningful security conversation. Some of the security topics apply to devices (endpoints), some to communication connections between them, and yet others to the larger enterprise.

Another goal of this book was to lay out security guidance in a way that did not regurgitate the vast amounts of existing cybersecurity knowledge as it applies to today's networks, hosts, operating systems, software, and so on, though we realized some is necessary for a meaningful discussion on IoT security. Not wanting to align with a single industry or company selling products, we strove to sufficiently carve out and tailor useful security approaches that encompass the peculiarities and nuances of what we think both distinguishes and aligns IoT with conventional cybersecurity.

A wide range of both legacy industries (for example, home appliance makers, toy manufacturers, automotive, and so on) and startup technology companies are today creating and selling connected devices and services at a phenomenal and growing rate. Unfortunately, not all are terribly secure—a fact that some security researchers have unrelentingly pointed out, often with a sense of genuine concern. Though much of the criticism is valid and warranted, some of it has unfortunately been conveyed with a certain degree of unhelpful hubris.

Interestingly, however, is how advanced some of the legacy industries are with regard to high-assurance safety and fault-tolerant design. These industries make extensive use of the core engineering disciplines—mechanical, electrical, industrial, aerospace, and control engineering—and high-assurance safety design to engineer products and complex systems that are, well, pretty safe. Many cybersecurity engineers are frankly ignorant of these disciplines and their remarkable contributions to safety and fault-tolerant design. Hence, we arrive at one of the serious obstructions that IoT imposes to achieving its security goals: poor collaboration between safety, functional, and security engineering disciplines needed to design and deploy what we term **cyber-physical systems (CPS)**. CPS put the physical and digital engineering disciplines together in ways that are seldom addressed in academic curricula or corporate engineering offices. It is our hope that engineers, security engineers, and all types of technology managers learn to better collaborate on the required safety and security-assurance goals.

While we benefit from the IoT, we must prevent, to the highest possible degree, our current and future IoT from harming us; and to do this, we need to secure it properly and safely. We hope you enjoy this book and find the information useful for securing your IoT.

What this book covers

Chapter 1, A Brave New World, introduces you to the basics of IoT, its definition, uses, applications, and its implementations.

Chapter 2, Vulnerabilities, Attacks, and Countermeasures, takes you on a tour where you will learn about the various threats and the measures that we can take to counter them.

Chapter 3, Security Engineering for IoT Development, teaches you about the various phases of the IoT security lifecycle.

Chapter 4, The IoT Security Lifecycle, explores the operational aspects of the IoT security lifecycle in detail.

Chapter 5, Cryptographic Fundamentals for IoT Security Engineering, provides a background on applied cryptography.

Chapter 6, Identity and Access Management Solutions for the IoT, dives deep into identity and access management for the IoT.

Chapter 7, Mitigating IoT Privacy Concerns, explores IoT privacy concerns. It will also help you to understand how to address and mitigate such concerns.

Chapter 8, Setting Up a Compliance Monitoring Program for the IoT, helps you explore setting up an IoT compliance program.

Chapter 9, Cloud Security for the IoT, explains the concepts of cloud security that are related to the IoT.

Chapter 10, IoT Incident Response, explores incident management and forensics for the IoT.

What you need for this book

You will need SecureITree version 4.3, a common desktop or laptop, and a Windows, Mac, or Linux platform running Java 8.

Who this book is for

This book targets IT security professionals and security engineers (including pentesters, security architects, and ethical hackers) who would like to ensure the security of their organization's data when connected through the IoT. Business analysts and managers will also find this book useful.

Conventions

In this book, you will find a number of text styles that distinguish between different kinds of information. Here are some examples of these styles and an explanation of their meaning.

Code words in text, database table names, folder names, filenames, file extensions, pathnames, dummy URLs, user input, and Twitter handles are shown as follows: "Smart light switches in which the switch sends a PUT command to change the behavior (state, color) of each light in the system."

New terms and **important words** are shown in bold.

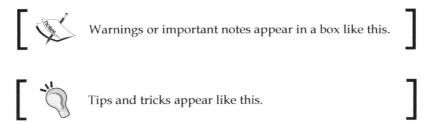

Warnings or important notes appear in a box like this.

Tips and tricks appear like this.

Reader feedback

Feedback from our readers is always welcome. Let us know what you think about this book—what you liked or disliked. Reader feedback is important for us as it helps us develop titles that you will really get the most out of.

To send us general feedback, simply e-mail feedback@packtpub.com, and mention the book's title in the subject of your message.

If there is a topic that you have expertise in and you are interested in either writing or contributing to a book, see our author guide at www.packtpub.com/authors.

Customer support

Now that you are the proud owner of a Packt book, we have a number of things to help you to get the most from your purchase.

Errata

Although we have taken every care to ensure the accuracy of our content, mistakes do happen. If you find a mistake in one of our books—maybe a mistake in the text or the code—we would be grateful if you could report this to us. By doing so, you can save other readers from frustration and help us improve subsequent versions of this book. If you find any errata, please report them by visiting http://www.packtpub.com/submit-errata, selecting your book, clicking on the **Errata Submission Form** link, and entering the details of your errata. Once your errata are verified, your submission will be accepted and the errata will be uploaded to our website or added to any list of existing errata under the Errata section of that title.

To view the previously submitted errata, go to https://www.packtpub.com/books/content/support and enter the name of the book in the search field. The required information will appear under the **Errata** section.

Piracy

Piracy of copyrighted material on the Internet is an ongoing problem across all media. At Packt, we take the protection of our copyright and licenses very seriously. If you come across any illegal copies of our works in any form on the Internet, please provide us with the location address or website name immediately so that we can pursue a remedy.

Please contact us at copyright@packtpub.com with a link to the suspected pirated material.

We appreciate your help in protecting our authors and our ability to bring you valuable content.

Questions

If you have a problem with any aspect of this book, you can contact us at questions@packtpub.com, and we will do our best to address the problem.

1
A Brave New World

"When the winds of change blow, some people build walls and others build windmills."

— *Chinese proverb*

The Internet of Things is changing everything. Unfortunately, many industries, consumer and commercial technology device owners, and infrastructure operators are fast discovering themselves at the precipice of a security nightmare. The drive to make all devices "smart" is creating a frenzy of opportunity for cyber-criminals, nation-state actors, and security researchers alike. These threats will only grow in their potential impact on the economy, corporations, business transactions, individual privacy, and safety. Target, Sony Pictures, insurance providers such as Blue Cross, and even the White House **Office of Personnel and Management (OPM)** provide vivid, not-so-pleasant newsflashes about major vulnerabilities and security breaches in the traditional cybersecurity sense. Some of these breaches have led to the tarnishing or downfall of companies and CEOs, and most importantly, significant damage to individual citizens. Our record in cybersecurity has proven to be substandard. Now consider the world of the Internet of Things, or IoT, things such as Linux-embedded smart refrigerators, connected washing machines, automobiles, wearables, implantable medical devices, factory robotics systems, and just about anything newly *connected* over networks. Historically, many of these industries never had to be concerned with security. Given the feverish race to be competitive with marketable new products and features, however, they now find themselves in dangerous territory, not knowing how to develop, deploy, and securely operate.

While we advance technologically, there are ever-present human motivations and tendencies in some people to attempt, consciously or unconsciously, to exploit those advancements. We asserted above that we are at the precipice of a security nightmare. What do we mean by this? For one, technology innovation in the IoT is rapidly outpacing the security knowledge and awareness of the IoT. New physical and information systems, devices, and connections barely dreamed of a decade ago are quickly stretching human ethics to the limit. Consider a similar field that allows us to draw analogies—bioethics and the new, extraordinary genetic engineering capabilities we now have. We can now biologically synthesize DNA from digitally sequenced nucleotide bases to engineer new attributes into creatures, and humans. Just because we can do something doesn't mean we always should. Just because we can connect a new device doesn't mean we always should. But that is exactly what the IoT is doing.

We must counterbalance all of our dreamy, hopeful thoughts about humanity's future with the fact that human consciousness and behavior always has, and always will, fall short of utopian ideals. There will always be overt and concealed criminal activity; there will always be otherwise decent citizens who find themselves entangled in plots, financial messes, blackmail; there will always be accidents; there will always be profiteers and scammers willing to hurt and benefit from the misery of others. In short, there will always be some individuals motivated to break in and compromise devices and systems for the same reason a burglar breaks into your house to steal your most prized possessions. Your loss is his gain. Worse, with the IoT, the motivation may extend to imposing physical injury or even death in some cases. A keystroke today can save a human life if properly configuring a pacemaker; it can also disable a car's braking system or hobble an Iranian nuclear research facility.

IoT security is clearly important, but before we can delve into practical aspects of securing it, the remainder of this chapter will address the following:

- Defining the IoT
- IoT uses today
- The cybersecurity, cyber-physical, and IoT relationship
- Why cross-industry collaboration is vital
- The *things* in the IoT
- Enterprise IoT
- The IoT of the future and the need to secure it

Defining the IoT

While any new generation prides itself on the technological advancements it enjoys compared to its forebears, it is not uncommon for each to dismiss or simply not acknowledge the enormity of thought, innovation, collaboration, competition, and connections throughout history that made, say, smartphones or unmanned aircraft possible. The reality is that while previous generations may not have enjoyed the realizations in gadgetry we have today, they most certainly did envision them. Science fiction has always served as a frighteningly predictive medium, whether it's Arthur C. Clarke's envisioning of Earth-orbiting satellites or E.E. "Doc" Smith's classic sci-fi stories melding the universe of thought and action together (reminiscent of today's phenomenal, new brain-machine interfaces). While the term and acronym IoT is new, the ideas of today's and tomorrow's IoT are not.

Consider one of the greatest engineering pioneers, Nikola Tesla, who in a 1926 interview with Colliers magazine said:

> *"When wireless is perfectly applied the whole earth will be converted into a huge brain, which in fact it is, all things being particles of a real and rhythmic whole and the instruments through which we shall be able to do this will be amazingly simple compared with our present telephone. A man will be able to carry one in his vest pocket."*

Source: http://www.tfcbooks.com/tesla/1926-01-30.htmv

In 1950, the British scientist Alan Turing was quoted as saying:

> *"It can also be maintained that it is best to provide the machine with the best sense organs that money can buy, and then teach it to understand and speak English. This process could follow the normal teaching of a child."*

Source: A. M. Turing (1950) Computing Machinery and Intelligence. Mind 49: 433-460

No doubt, the incredible advancements in digital processing, communications, manufacturing, sensors, and control are bringing to life the realistic imaginings of both our current generation and our forebears. Such advancements provide us a powerful metaphor of the very ecosystem of the thoughts, needs, and wants that drive us to build new tools and solutions we both want for enjoyment and need for survival.

We arrive then at the problem of how to define the IoT and how to distinguish the IoT from today's Internet of, well, computers. The IoT is certainly not a new term for mobile-to-mobile technology. It is far more. While many definitions of the IoT exist, we will primarily lean on the following three throughout this book:

- The ITU's member-approved definition defines the IoT as "A global infrastructure for the information society, enabling advanced services by interconnecting (physical and virtual) things based on existing and evolving, interoperable information and communication technologies."

  `http://www.itu.int/ITU-T/recommendations/rec.aspx?rec=y.2060`

- The IEEE's small environment description of the IoT is "An IoT is a network that connects uniquely identifiable "things" to the Internet. The "things" have sensing/actuation and potential programmability capabilities. Through the exploitation of the unique identification and sensing, information about the "thing" can be collected and the state of the "thing" can be changed from anywhere, anytime, by anything."

  `http://iot.ieee.org/images/files/pdf/IEEE_IoT_Towards_`
  `Definition_Internet_of_Things_Revision1_27MAY15.pdf`

- The IEEE's large environment scenario describes the IoT as "Internet of Things envisions a self-configuring, adaptive, complex network that interconnects things to the Internet through the use of standard communication protocols. The interconnected things have physical or virtual representation in the digital world, sensing/actuation capability, a programmability feature, and are uniquely identifiable. The representation contains information including the thing's identity, status, location, or any other business, social or privately relevant information. The things offer services, with or without human intervention, through the exploitation of unique identification, data capture and communication, and actuation capability. The service is exploited through the use of intelligent interfaces and is made available anywhere, anytime, and for anything taking security into consideration."

  `http://iot.ieee.org/images/files/pdf/IEEE_IoT_Towards_`
  `Definition_Internet_of_Things_Revision1_27MAY15.pdf`

Each of these definitions is complementary. They overlap and describe just about anything that can be dreamed up and physically or logically connected to anything else over a diverse, Internet-connected world.

Cybersecurity versus IoT security and cyber-physical systems

IoT security is not traditional cybersecurity, but a fusion of cybersecurity with other engineering disciplines. It addresses much more than mere data, servers, network infrastructure, and information security. Rather, it includes the direct or distributed monitoring and/or control of the state of physical systems connected over the Internet. In other words, a large element of what distinguishes the IoT from cybersecurity is what many industry practitioners today refer to as cyber-physical systems. Cybersecurity, if you like that term at all, generally does not address the physical and security aspects of the hardware device or the physical world interactions it can have. Digital control of physical processes over networks makes the IoT unique in that the security equation is not limited to basic information assurance principles of confidentiality, integrity, non-repudiation, and so on, but also that of physical resources and machines that originate and receive that information in the physical world. In other words, the IoT has very real analog and physical elements. IoT devices are physical things, many of which are safety-related. Therefore, the compromise of such devices may lead to physical harm of persons and property, even death.

The subject of IoT security, then, is not the application of a single, static set of meta-security rules as they apply to networked devices and hosts. It requires a unique application for each system and system-of-systems in which IoT devices participate. IoT devices have many different embodiments, but collectively, an IoT device is almost anything possessing the following properties:

- Ability to communicate either directly on, or indirectly over the Internet
- Manipulates or monitors something physical (in the device or the device's medium or environment), that is, the thing itself, or a direct connection to a thing

Cognizant of these two properties, anything physical can be an IoT device because anything physical today can be connected to the Internet with the appropriate electronic interfaces. The security of the IoT device is then a function of the device's use, the physical process or state impacted by or controlled by the device, and the sensitivity of the systems to which the device connects.

Cyber-physical systems (CPS) are a huge, overlapping subset of the IoT. They fuse a broad range of engineering disciplines, each with a historically well-defined scope that includes the essential theory, lore, application, and relevant subject matter needed by their respective practitioners. These topics range from engineering dynamics, fluid dynamics, thermodynamics, control theory, digital design, and many others. So, what is the difference between the IoT and **CPSs**? Borrowing from the IEEE, the principal difference is that a CPS comprising connected sensors, actuators, and monitoring/control systems do not necessarily have to be connected to the Internet. A CPS can be isolated from the Internet and still achieve its business objective. From a communications perspective, an IoT is comprised of things that, necessarily and by definition, are connected to the Internet and through some aggregation of applications achieve some business objective.

Note that CPS, even if technically air-gapped from the Internet, will almost always be connected in some way to the Internet, whether through its supply chain, operating personnel, or out-of-band software patch management system.

```
http://iot.ieee.org/images/files/pdf/IEEE_IoT_Towards_
Definition_Internet_of_Things_Revision1_27MAY15.pdf
```

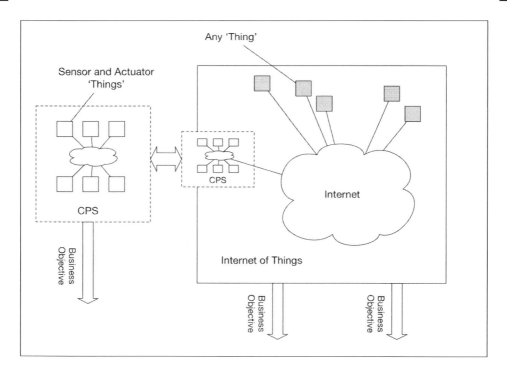

In other words, it is worthwhile to think of the IoT as a superset of CPS, as CPS can be enveloped into the IoT simply by connectivity to the Internet. A CPS is generally a rigorously engineered system designed for safety, security, and functionality. Emergent enterprise IoT deployments should take lessons learned from the engineering rigor associated with CPS.

Why cross-industry collaboration is vital

We will cover IoT security engineering in the following chapters, but for now we would like to emphasize how cross-discipline security engineering is in the real world. One struggles to find it covered in academic curricula outside of a few university computer science programs, network engineering, or dedicated security programs such as SANS. Most security practitioners have strong computer science and networking skills but are less versed in the physical and safety engineering disciplines covered by core engineering curricula. So, the cyber-physical aspects of the IoT face a safety versus security clash of cultures and conundrums:

- Everyone is responsible for security
- The IoT and CPS expose huge security problems crisscrossing information computing and the physical world
- Most traditional, core engineering disciplines rarely address security engineering (though some address safety)
- Many security engineers are ignorant of core engineering disciplines (for example, mechanical, chemical, electrical), including fault-tolerant safety design

Because the IoT is concerned with connecting physically engineered and manufactured objects—and thus may be a CPS—this conundrum more than any other comes into play. The IoT device engineer may be well versed in safety issues, but not fully understand the security implications of design decisions. Likewise, skilled security engineers may not understand the physical engineering nuances of a *thing* to ascertain and characterize its physical-world interactions (in its intended environment) and fix them. In other words, core engineering disciplines typically focus on functional design, creating things to do what we want them to do. Security engineering shifts the view to consider what the thing can do and how one might misuse it in ways the original designer never considered. Malicious hackers depend on this. The refrigeration system engineer never had to consider a cryptographic access control scheme in what was historically a basic thermodynamic system design. Now, designers of connected refrigerators do, because malicious hackers will look for unauthenticated data originating from the refrigerator or attempt to exploit it and pivot to additional nodes in a home network.

Security engineering is maturing as a cross-discipline, fortunately. One can argue that it is more efficient to enlighten a broad range of engineering professionals in baseline security principles than it is to train existing security engineers in all physical engineering subjects. Improving IoT security requires that security engineering tenets and principles be learned and promulgated by the core engineering disciplines in their respective industries. If not, industries will never succeed in responding well to emergent threats. Such a response requires appropriating the right security mitigations at the right time when they are the least expensive to implement (that is, the original design as well as its flexibility and accommodation of future-proofing principles). For example, a thermodynamics process and control engineer designing a power-plant will have tremendous knowledge concerning the physical processes of the control system, safety redundancies, and so on. If she understands security engineering principles, she will be in a much better position to dictate additional sensors, redundant state estimation logic, or redundant actuators based on certain exposures to other networks. In addition, she will be in a much better position to ascertain the sensitivity of certain state variables and timing information that network, host, application, sensor, and actuator security controls should help protect. She can better characterize the cyber-attack and control system interactions that might cause gas pressure and temperature tolerances to be exceeded with a resultant explosion. The traditional network cybersecurity engineer will not have the physical engineering basis on which to orchestrate these design decisions.

Before characterizing today's IoT devices and enterprises, it should be clear how cross-cutting the IoT is across industries. Medical device and biomedical companies, automotive and aircraft manufacturers, the energy industry, even video game makers and broad consumer markets are involved in the IoT. These industries, historically isolated from each other, must learn to collaborate when it comes to securing their devices and infrastructure. Unfortunately, there are some in these industries who believe that most security mitigations need to be developed and deployed uniquely in each industry. This isolated, turf-protecting approach is ill-advised and short-sighted. It has the potential of stifling valuable cross-industry security collaboration, learning, and development of common countermeasures.

IoT security is an equal-opportunity threat environment; the same threats against one industry exist against the others. An attack and compromise of one device today may represent a threat to devices in almost all other industries. A smart light bulb installed in a hospital may be compromised and used to perform various privacy attacks on medical devices. In other words, the cross-industry relationship may be due to intersections in the supply chain or the fact that one industry's IoT implementations were added to another industry's systems. Real-time intelligence as well as lessons learned from attacks against industrial control systems should be leveraged by all industries and tailored to suit. Threat intelligence, defined well by Gartner, is: *evidence-based knowledge, including context, mechanisms, indicators, implications and actionable advice, about an existing or emerging menace or hazard to assets that can be used to inform decisions regarding the subject's response to that menace or hazard* (http://www.gartner.com/document/2487216).

The discovery, analysis, understanding and sharing of how real-world threats are compromising ever-present vulnerabilities needs to be improved for the IoT. No single industry, government organization, standards body or other entity can assume to be the dominant control of threat intelligence and information sharing. Security is an ecosystem.

As a government standards body, NIST is well aware of this problem. NIST's recently formed CPS Public Working Group represents a cross-industry collaboration of security professionals working to build a framework approach to solving many cyber-physical IoT challenges facing different industries. It is accomplishing this in meta-form through its draft Framework for Cyber-Physical Systems. This framework provides a useful reference frame from which to describe CPS along with their security and physical properties. Industries will be able to leverage the framework to improve and communicate CPS designs and provide a basis on which to develop system-specific security standards. This book will address CPS security in more detail in terms of common patterns that span many industries.

Like the thermodynamics example we provided above, cyber-physical and many IoT systems frequently invoke an intersection of safety and security engineering, two disciplines that have developed on very different evolutionary paths but which possess partially overlapping goals. We will delve more into safety aspects of IoT security engineering later in this volume, but for now we point out an elegantly expressed distinction between safety and security provided by noted academic Dr. Barry Boehm, Axelrod, W. C., Engineering Safe and Secure Software Systems, p.61, Massachussetts, Artech House, 2013. He poignantly but beautifully expressed the relationship as follows:

- **Safety**: The system must not harm the world
- **Security**: The world must not harm the system

Thus it is clear that the IoT and IoT security are much more complex than traditional networks, hosts and cybersecurity. Safety-conscious industries such as aircraft manufacturers, regulators, and researchers have evolved highly effective safety engineering approaches and standards because aircraft can harm the world, and the people in it. The aircraft industry today, like the automotive industry, is now playing catch-up with regard to security due to the accelerating growth of network connectivity to their vehicles.

IoT uses today

It is a cliché to declare how fast Moore's law is changing our technology-rich world, how connected our devices, social networks, even bodies, cars, and other objects are becoming.

Another useful way to think of the IoT is what happens when the network extends not to the last mile or last inch endpoint, but the last micron where virtual and digital become physical. Whether the network extends to a motor servo controller, temperature sensor, accelerometer, light bulb, stepper motor, washing machine monitor, or pacemaker, the effect is the same; the information sources and sinks allow broad control, monitoring, and useful visibility between our physical and virtual worlds. In the case of the IoT, the physical world is a direct component of the digital information, whether acting as subject or object.

IoT applications are boundless. Volumes could be written today about what is already deployed and what is currently being planned. The following are just a few examples of how we are leveraging the IoT.

Energy industry and smart grid

Fast disappearing are the days of utility companies sending workers out in vans to read the electrical and gas meters mounted to the exterior of your house. Some homes today and all homes tomorrow will be connected homes with connected smart appliances that communicate electrical demand and load information with the utilities. Combined with a utility's ability to reach down into the home's appliance, such demand-response technology aims to make our energy generation and distribution systems much more efficient, resilient, and more supportive of environmentally responsible living. Home appliances represent just one Home Area Network component of the so-called **smart grid**, however. The distribution, monitoring, and control systems of this energy system involve the IoT in many capacities. Ubiquitous sensing, control, and communications needed in energy production are critical CPS elements of the IoT. The newly installed **smart meter** now attached to your home is just one example, and allows direct two-way communication between your home's electrical enclave and the utility providing its energy.

Connected vehicles and transportation

Consider a connected automobile that is constantly leveraging an onboard array of sensors that scan the roadway and make real-time calculations to identify potential safety issues that a driver would not be able to see. Now, add additional **vehicle-to-vehicle (V2V)** communication capabilities that allow other cars to message and signal to your vehicle. Preemptive messages allow decisions to be made based on information that is not yet available to the driver's or vehicle's line-of-sight sensors (for example, reporting of vehicle pile-up in dense fog conditions). With all of these capabilities, we can begin to have confidence in the abilities of cars to eventually drive themselves (autonomous vehicles) safely and not just report hazards to us.

Manufacturing

The manufacturing world has driven a substantial amount of the industrial IoT use cases. Robotic systems, assembly lines, manufacturing plan design and operation; all of these systems are driven by myriad types of connected sensors and actuators. Originally isolated, now they're connected over various data buses, intranets, and the Internet. Distributed automation and control requires diverse and distributed devices communicating with management and monitoring applications. Improving the efficiency of these systems has been the principal driver for such IoT enablement.

Wearables

Wearables in the IoT include anything strapped to or otherwise attached to the human body that collects state, communicates information, or otherwise performs some type of control function on or around the individual. The Apple iWatch, FitBit, and others are well-known examples. Wearable, networked sensors may detect inertial acceleration (for example, to evaluate a runner's stride and tempo), heart rate, temperature, geospatial location (for calculating speed and historic tracks), and many others. The enormous utility of wearables and the data they produce is evident in the variety of wearable applications available on today's iTunes proprietary application stores. The majority of wearables have direct or indirect network connectivity to various cloud service providers typically associated with the wearables manufacturer (for example, Fitbit). Some organizations are now including wearables in corporate fitness programs to track employee health and encourage health-conscious living with the promise of lowering corporate and employee healthcare expenses.

New advancements will transform wearables, however, into far more sophisticated structures and enhancements to common living items. For example, micro devices and sensors are being embedded into clothing; virtual reality goggles are being miniaturized and are transforming how we simultaneously interface with the physical and virtual worlds. In addition, the variety of new consumer-level medical wearables promises to improve health monitoring and reporting. The barriers are fast disappearing between the machine and the human body.

Implantables and medical devices

If wearable IoT devices don't closely enough bridge the physical and cyber domains, implantables make up the distance. Implantables include any sensor, controller, or communication device that is inserted and operated within the human body. While implantable IoT devices are typically associated with the medical field (for example, pacemakers), they may also include non-medical products and use cases such as embedded RFID tags usable in physical and logical access control systems. The implant industry is no different than any other device industry in that it has added new communication interfaces to implanted devices that allow the devices to be accessed, controlled, and monitored over a network. Those devices just happened to be located subcutaneously in human beings or other creatures. Both wearables and implantable IoT devices are being miniaturized in the form of **micro-electrical mechanical systems (MEMS)**, some of which can communicate over **radio frequency (RF)**.

The IoT in the enterprise

Enterprise IoT is also moving forward with the deployment of IoT systems that serve various business purposes. Some industries have matured their concepts of IoT more than others. In the energy industry, for example, the roll-out of advanced metering infrastructures (which include smart meters with wireless communications capabilities) has greatly enhanced the energy use and monitoring capabilities of the utility. Other industries, such as retail, for example, are still trying to determine how to fully leverage new sensors and data in retail establishments to support enhanced marketing capabilities, improved customer satisfaction, and higher sales.

The architecture of IoT enterprise systems is relatively consistent across industries. Given the various technology layers and physical components that comprise an IoT ecosystem, it is good to consider an enterprise IoT implementation as a **system-of-systems**. The architecting of these systems that provide business value to organizations can be a complex undertaking, as enterprise architects work to design integrated solutions that include edge devices, gateways, applications, transports, cloud services, diverse protocols, and data analytics capabilities.

Indeed, some enterprises may find that they must utilize IoT capabilities typically found in other industries and served by new or unfamiliar technology providers. Consider a typical Fortune 500 company that may own both manufacturing and retail facilities. This company's **Chief Information Officer (CIO)** may need to consider deploying smart manufacturing systems, including sensors that track industrial equipment health status, robotics that perform various manufacturing functions, as well as sensors that provide data used to optimize the overall manufacturing process. Some of the deployed sensors may even be embedded right in their own products to add additional benefits for their customers.

This same company must also consider how to leverage the IoT to offer enhanced retail experiences to their customers. This may include information transmitted to smart billboards. In the near future, through direct integration with a connected vehicle's infotainment system, customized advertisements to consumers as they pass by a retail establishment will be possible. There are also complex data analytics capabilities required to support these integrations and customizations.

Elaborating on the Fortune 500 company example, the same CIO may also be tasked with managing fleets of connected cars and shipping vehicles, drone systems that support the inspection of critical infrastructure and facilities, agricultural sensors that are embedded into the ground to provide feedback on soil quality, and even sensors embedded in concrete to provide feedback on the curing process at their construction sites. These examples only begin to scratch the surface of the types of connected IoT implementations and deployments we will see by 2020 and beyond.

This complexity introduces challenges to keeping the IoT secure, and ensuring that particular instances of the IoT cannot be used as a pivoting point to attack other enterprise systems and applications. For this, organizations must employ the services of enterprise security architects who can look at the IoT from the big picture perspective. Security architects will need to be critically involved early in the design process to establish security requirements that must be tracked and followed through during the development and deployment of the enterprise IoT system. It is much too expensive to attempt to integrate security after the fact. Enterprise security architects will select the infrastructure and backend system components that can easily scale to support not only the massive quantities of IoT-generated data, but also have the ability to make secure, actionable sense of all of that data. The following figure provides a representative view of a generic enterprise IoT system-of-systems, and showcases the IoT's dynamic and diverse nature:

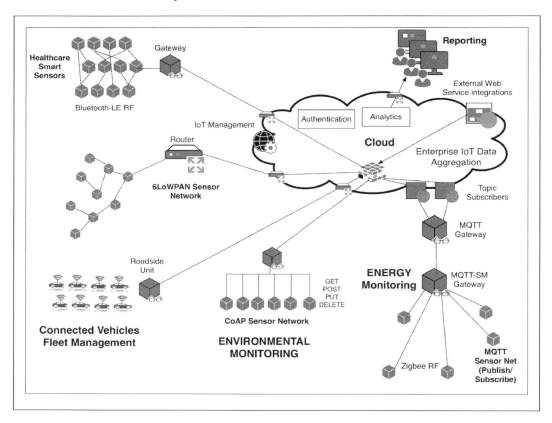

Generically, an IoT deployment can consist of smart sensors, control systems and actuators, web and other cloud services, analytics, reporting, and a host of other components and services that satisfy a variety of business use cases. Note that in the preceding figure, we see energy IoT deployments connected to the cloud along with connected vehicle roadside equipment, healthcare equipment, and environmental monitoring sensors. This is not accidental—as previously discussed, one principal feature of IoT is that anything can be connected to everything, and everything to anything. It is perfectly conceivable that a healthcare biosensor both connects to a hospital's monitoring and data analytics system and simultaneously communicates power consumption data to local and remote energy monitoring equipment and systems.

As enterprise security architects begin to design their systems, they will note that the flexibility associated with today's IoT market affords them significant creative ability, as they bring together many different types of protocols, processors, and sensors to meet business objectives. As designs mature, it will become evident that organizations should consider a revision to their overall enterprise architecture to better meet the scaling needs afforded by the large quantities of data that will be collected. Gartner predicts that we will begin to see a shift in the design of transport networks and data processing centers as the IoT matures:

> *"IoT threatens to generate massive amounts of input data from sources that are globally distributed. Transferring the entirety of that data to a single location for processing will not be technically and economically viable. The recent trend to centralize applications to reduce costs and increase security is incompatible with the IoT. Organizations will be forced to aggregate data in multiple distributed mini data centers where initial processing can occur. Relevant data will then be forwarded to a central site for additional processing."*

Source: http://www.gartner.com/newsroom/id/2684616

In other words, unprecedented amounts of data will be moved around in unprecedented ways. Integration points will also play a significant role in an enterprise's IoT adoption strategy. Today's ability to share data across organizational boundaries is large, but dwarfed by the justifications and ability to do so in the near future. Many of the data analytics capabilities that support the IoT will rely on a mix of data captured from sensors as well as data from third parties and independent websites.

Consider the concept of a microgrid. Microgrids are self-contained energy generation and distribution systems that allow owner-operators to be heavily self-sufficient. Microgrid control systems rely on data captured from the edge devices themselves, for example, solar panels or wind turbines, but also require data collected from the Internet. The control system may capture data on energy prices from the local utility through an **application programming interface (API)** that allows the system to determine the optimal time to generate versus buy (or even sell back) energy from the utility. The same control system may require weather forecast feeds to predict how much energy their solar panel installations will generate during a certain period of time.

Another example of the immense data collection from IoT devices is the anticipated proliferation of **Unmanned Aerial Systems (UAS)** — or drones — that provide an aerial platform for deploying data-rich airborne sensors. Today, 3D terrain mapping is performed by inexpensive drones that collect high-resolution images and associated metadata (location, camera information, and so on) and transfer them to powerful backend systems for photogrammetric processing and digital model generation. The processing of these datasets is too computationally intensive to perform directly on a drone that faces unavoidable size, weight, and power constraints. It must be done in backend systems and servers. These uses will continue to grow, especially as the countries around the world make progress at safely integrated unmanned aircraft into their national airspace systems.

From a security perspective, it is interesting to examine an enterprise IoT implementation based on the many new points of connection and data types. These integration points can significantly heighten the attack surface of an enterprise; therefore, they must be thoroughly evaluated to understand the threats and most cost-effective mitigations.

Another IoT challenge facing enterprise engineers is the ability to securely automate processes and workflows. One of the greatest strengths of the IoT its emphasis on automating transactions between devices and systems; however, we must ensure that sufficient levels of trust are engineered into the systems supporting those transactions. Not doing so will allow adversaries to leverage the automation processes for their own purposes as scalable attack vectors. Organizations that heavily automate workflows should spend adequate time designing their endpoint hardening strategies and the cryptographic support technologies that are vitally important to enabling device and system trust. This can often include infrastructure build-outs such as **Public Key Infrastructure (PKI)** that provision authentication, confidentiality, and cryptographic credentials to each endpoint in a transaction to enable confidentiality, integrity, and authentication services.

The things in the IoT

There are so many different types of "things" within the IoT that it becomes difficult to prescribe security recommendations for the development of any one particular thing. To aid in doing this, we must first understand the definition of devices and things. ITU-T Y.2060 prescribes the following definitions:

- **Device**: A piece of equipment with the mandatory capabilities of communication and the optional capabilities of sensing, actuation, data capture, data storage, and data processing
- **Thing**: An object of the physical world (physical things) or the information world (virtual things), which is capable of being identified and integrated into communication networks

An intrinsic capability of a thing, as it applies to the IoT, is its capability to communicate. The communication methods and layers, especially as they apply to security, are therefore given special attention in this book. Other aspects, such as data storage, sophisticated processing, and data capture, are not present in all IoT devices, but will be addressed in this book as well.

The definition of a *thing* is especially interesting as it refers to both physical and virtual devices. In practice, we have seen the concept of virtual things in the context of cloud provider solutions. For example, the **Amazon Web Services (AWS)** IoT Cloud service includes elements known as **thing shadows**, virtual representations of physical things. These thing shadows allow the enterprise to track the state of physical things even when network connectivity is disrupted and they are not observably online.

Some common IoT things include smart home appliances, connected vehicles (onboard equipment as well as roadside-mounted units), RFID systems used in inventory and identification systems, wearables, wired and wireless sensor arrays and networks, local and remote gateways (mobile phones, tablets), **Unmanned Aircraft Systems (UAS)**, and a host of typically low-power embedded devices. Next, we decompose common elements of IoT devices.

The IoT device lifecycle

Before delving into the basic constitution of an IoT device, we first need to clarify aspects of the IoT lifecycle. IoT security ultimately depends on the entire lifecycle, therefore this book aims to provide security guidance across most of it. You will see certain terms in this book used to specify different IoT lifecycle phases and the relevant actors in each.

IoT device implementation

This includes all aspects of IoT device design and development. At times, we simply refer to it as *implementation*. It includes the actual, physical, and logical designers of an IoT device in its manufacturing and patching supply chain. Organizations included in this phase include the following:

- **Original Equipment Manufacturer** (or just "manufacturer") (**OEM**): OEMs will typically procure off-the-shelf hardware and firmware and tailor a device with unique physical characteristics, enclosure, and/or applications. They package and distribute the products to end operators.
- **Board Support Package** (**BSP**) vendors: This vendor typically provides to the OEM customized or off-the-shelf firmware, APIs, and drivers between the hardware and operating systems.
- **Original Design Manufacturers** (**ODM**): ODMs will typically provide custom operating systems and OS APIs to OEMs. They may also include hardware sub-assemblies that OEMs make use of.

IoT service implementation

This phase refers to the service organizations who support IoT deployments through enterprise APIs, gateways, and other architectural commodities. Organizations supporting this phase include the following:

- **Cloud service provider (CSP)**: These organizations typically provide, at a minimum, infrastructure as a service
- **OEMs**: In some cases, IoT device manufacturers (for example, Samsung) operate and manage their own infrastructure

IoT device and service deployment

This lifecycle phase refers to the end deployment of the IoT devices using IoT infrastructure. IoT deployment typically involves IoT application providers, end service providers, and other businesses. Some of these businesses may operate their own infrastructures (for example, some OEMs), but some make use of existing infrastructure offerings as provided by Amazon AWS, Microsoft Azure, and others. They typically provide service layers on top of what the infrastructure supports.

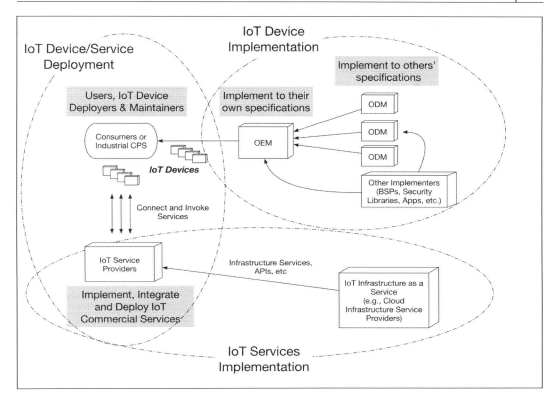

This book jumps around the three simplified lifecycle categories described above depending on the security topic at hand. Each has an indispensible impact on the end security of the devices and their tailored usage.

The hardware

There are a number of IoT development boards that have become popular for prototyping and provide various levels of functionality. Examples of these boards come from Arduino, Beagle Board, Pinoccio, Rasberry Pi, and CubieBoard, among others. These development boards include **microcontrollers (MCUs)**, which serve as the brains of the device, provide memory, and a number of both digital and analog **General Purpose Input/Output (GPIO)** pins. These boards can be modularly stacked with other boards to provide communication capabilities, new sensors, actuators, and so on to form a complete IoT device.

There are a number of MCUs on the market today that are well suited for IoT development and included within various development boards. Leading developers of MCUs include ARM, Intel, Broadcom, Atmel, **Texas Instruments (TI)**, Freescale, and Microchip Technology. MCUs are **integrated circuits (IC)** that contain a processor, **Read Only Memory (ROM)**, and **Random Access Memory (RAM)**. Memory resources are frequently limited in these devices; however, a number of manufacturers are IoT-enabling just about anything by augmenting these microcontrollers with complete network stacks, interfaces, and RF and cellular-type transceivers. All of this horsepower is going into system-on-chip configurations and miniaturized daughter boards (single board computers).

In terms of sensor types in the IoT, the sky is the limit. Examples include temperature sensors, accelerometers, air quality sensors, potentiometers, proximity sensors, moisture sensors, and vibration sensors. These sensors are frequently hardwired into the MCU for local processing, responsive actuation, and/or relay to other systems.

Operating systems

Although some IoT devices do not require an operating system, many utilize **real time operating system (RTOS)** for process and memory management as well as utility services supporting messaging and other communications. The selection of each RTOS is based on needed performance, security and functional requirements of the product.

The selection of any particular IoT component product needs to be evaluated against the requirements of a particular IoT system. Some organizations may require more elaborate operating systems with additional security features such as separation kernels, high assurance process isolation, information flow control, and/or tightly integrated cryptographic security architectures. In these scenarios, an enterprise security architect should look to procure devices that support high-assurance RTOSes, such as Green Hills IntegrityOS or Lynx Software's LynxOS. Some popular IoT operating systems include TinyOS, Contiki, Mantis, FreeRTOS, BrilloOS, Embedded Linux, ARM's mbedOS, and Snappy Ubuntu Core.

Other critical security attributes pertain to security configuration and the storage of security sensitive parameters. In some instances, configuration settings that are applied to an operating system are lost upon power cycle without battery-backed RAM or some other persistent storage. In many instances, a configuration file is kept within persistent memory to provide the various network and other settings necessary to allow the device to perform its functions and communicate. Of even greater interest is the handling of the root password, other account passwords, and cryptographic keys stored on the devices when the device is power-cycled. Each of these issues has one or more security implications and requires the attention of security engineers.

IoT communications

In most deployments, an IoT device communicates with a gateway that in turn communicates with a controller or a web service. There are many gateway options, some as simple as a mobile device (smart phone) co-located with the IoT endpoint and communicating over an RF protocol such as Bluetooth-LE, ZigBee, or Wi-Fi. Gateways such as this are sometimes called edge gateways. Others may be more centrally located in data centers to support any number of dedicated or proprietary gateway IoT protocols, such as **message queuing telemetry transport (MQTT)** or **representational state transfer (REST)** communications. The web service may be provided by the manufacturer of the device, or it may be an enterprise or public cloud service that collects information from the fielded edge devices.

In many situations, the end-to-end connectivity between a fielded IoT device and web service may be provided by a series of field and cloud gateways, each aggregating larger quantities of data from sprawled-out devices. Dell, Intel, and other companies have recently introduced IoT gateways to the market. Companies such as Systech offer multi-protocol gateways that allow for a variety of IoT device types to be connected together, using multiple antennas and receivers. There are also consumer-focused gateways, also called hubs, available in the commercial market, that support smart home communications. The Samsung SmartThings hub (`https://www.smartthings.com/`) is one example of this.

IoT devices may also communicate horizontally, enabling some powerful interactive features. Enabling connected workflows requires the ability to interface via an API to many diverse IoT product types. Consider the example of the smart home for illustrative purposes. As you wake in the morning, your wearable autonomously transmits the wake-up signal over the Wi-Fi network to subscribing devices. The smart television turns on to your favorite news channel, the window blinds automatically rise, the coffee maker kicks off, the shower starts and your car sets a timer to warm up before you leave your home. All of these interactions are enabled through device-to-device communications and illustrate the immense potential of applying the IoT to business enterprises.

Within an IoT device and its host network, a wide array of protocols may be used to enable message transfer and communication. The selection of the appropriate stack of messaging and communication protocols is dependent upon the use cases and security requirements of any specific system; however, there are common protocols that each serve valuable purposes:

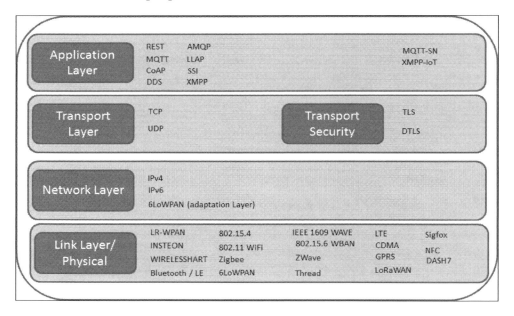

This figure provides a view into some of the better-known protocols that can be implemented by IoT devices to form a complete communications stack.

It is worth noting that at this time, many products' design and security requirements are purely up to the manufacturer due to the infancy of the IoT. In many cases, security professionals may not be included this early in the development phase. Although some organizations may provide guidelines, suggestions and checklists, it is important to note that industry regulations strictly pertaining to IoT devices are almost non-existent. The industry for which the device is intended may have its own requirements for privacy, transport communications, and so on, but they are typically based on existing regulatory or compliance requirements such as HIPAA, PCI, SOX, and others. The industrial IoT will probably lead the way in developing much-needed security standardizations before consumer-oriented organizations. For the time being, early efforts to secure IoT implementation and deployment are akin to stuffing square pegs into round holes. The IoT simply has different needs.

Messaging protocols

At the top of the IoT communication stack live the protocols that support the exchange of formatted message data between two endpoints, typically clients and servers, or client-to-client. Protocols such as the MQTT, the **Constrained Application Protocol (CoAP)**, the **Data Distribution Service (DDS)**, the **Advanced Message Queuing Protocol (AMQP)**, and the **Extensible Messaging and Presence Protocol (XMPP)** run on top of lower-layer communication protocols and provide the ability for both clients and servers to efficiently agree upon data to exchange. RESTful communications can also be run very effectively within many IoT systems. As of today, REST-based communications and MQTT seem to be leading the way.

(`http://www.hivemq.com/blog/how-to-get-started-with-mqtt`)

MQTT

MQTT is a publish/subscribe model whereby clients subscribe to topics and maintain an always-on TCP connection to a broker server. As new messages are sent to the broker, they include the topic with the message, allowing the broker to determine which clients should receive the message. Messages are pushed to the clients through the always-on connection.

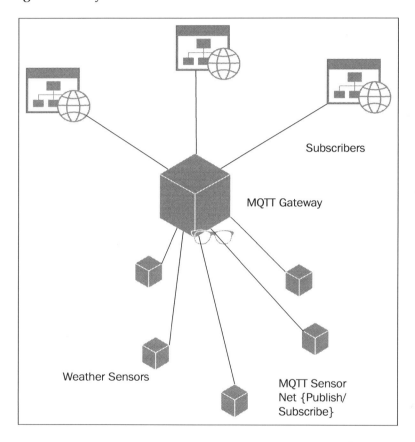

This neatly supports a variety of communication use cases, wherein sensors MQTT-publish their data to a broker and the broker passes them on to other subscribing systems that have an interest in consuming or further processing the sensor data. Although MQTT is primarily suited for use over TCP-based networks, the **MQTT For Sensor Networks (MQTT-SN)** specification provides an optimized version of MQTT for use within **wireless sensor networks (WSN)**.

Stanford-Clark and Linh Truong. **MQTT For Sensor Networks (MQTT-SN)** protocol specification, Version 1.2. International Business Machines (IBM). 2013. URL: http://mqtt.org/new/wp-content/uploads/2009/06/MQTT-SN_spec_v1.2.pdf.

MQTT-SN is well suited for use with battery-operated devices possessing limited processing and storage resources. It allows sensors and actuators to make use of the publish/subscribe model on top of ZigBee and similar RF protocol specifications.

CoAP

CoAP is another IoT messaging protocol, UDP-based, and intended for use in resource-constrained Internet devices such as **WSN** nodes. It consists of a set of messages that map easily to HTTP: GET, POST, PUT, and DELETE.

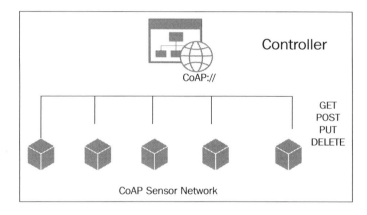

Source: http://www.herjulf.se/download/coap-2013-fall.pdf

CoAP device implementations communicate to web servers using specific **Uniform Resource Indicators (URIs)** to process commands. Examples of CoAP-enabled implementations include smart light switches in which the switch sends a PUT command to change the behavior (state, color) of each light in the system.

XMPP

XMPP is based on **Extensible Markup Language (XML)** and is an open technology for real-time communications. It evolved from the **Jabber Instant Messaging** (IM) protocol: http://www.ibm.com/developerworks/library/x-xmppintro/.

XMPP supports the transmission of XML messages over TCP transport, allowing IoT developers to efficiently implement service discovery and service advertisements.

XMPP-IoT is a tailored version of XMPP. Similar to human-to-human communication scenarios, XMPP-IoT communications begin with friend requests: `http://www.xmpp-iot.org/basics/being-friends/`.

Upon confirmation of a friend request, the two IoT devices are able to communicate with each other regardless of their domains. There also exist parent-child device relationships. Parent nodes within XMPP-IoT offer a degree of security in that they can provide policies dictating whom a particular child node can trust (and hence become friends with). Communication between IoT devices cannot proceed without a confirmed friend request between them.

DDS

DDS is a data bus used for integrating intelligent machines. Like MQTT, it also uses a publish/subscribe model for readers to subscribe to topics of interest.

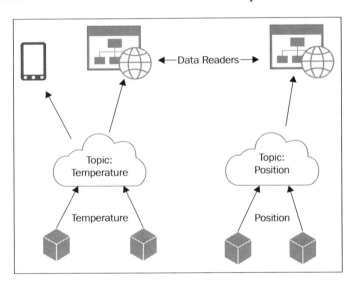

Source: `http://www.slideshare.net/Angelo.Corsaro/applied-opensplice-dds-a-collection-of-use-cases`

DDS allows communications to happen in an anonymous and automated fashion, since no relationship between endpoints is required. Additionally, **Quality of Service (QoS)** mechanisms are built into the protocol. DDS is designed primarily for device-to-device communication and is used in deployment scenarios involving wind farms, medical imaging systems, and asset-tracking systems.

AMQP

AMQP was designed to provide a queuing system in support of server-to-server communications. Applied to the IoT, it allows for both publish/subscribe and point-to-point based communications. AMQP IoT endpoints listen for messages on each queue. AMQP has been deployed in numerous sectors, such as transportation in which vehicle telemetry devices provide data to analytics systems for near-real-time processing.

Gateways

Most of the message specifications discussed so far require the implementation of protocol-specific gateways or other devices to either re-encapsulate the communications over another protocol (for example, if it needs to become IP-routable) or perform protocol translation. The different ways of fusing such protocols can have enormous security implications, potentially introducing new attack surfaces into an enterprise. Protocol limitations, configuration, and stacking options must be taken into account during the design of the enterprise architecture. Threat modeling exercises by appropriately qualified protocol security engineers can help in the process.

Transport protocols

The Internet was designed to operate reliably using the **Transmission Control Protocol (TCP)**, which facilitates the acknowledgement of TCP segments transmitted across a network. TCP is the protocol of choice for today's web-based communications as the underlying, reliable transport. Some IoT products have been designed to operate using TCP (for example, those products robust enough to employ a full TCP/IP stack that can speak HTTP or MQTT over a secure (TLS) connection). TCP is frequently unsuitable for use in constrained network environments suffering from high latency or limited bandwidth.

The **User Datagram Protocol (UDP)** provides a useful alternative, however. UDP provides a lightweight transport mechanism for connectionless communications (unlike session-based TCP). Many highly constrained IoT sensor devices support UDP. For example, MQTT-SN is a tailored version of MQTT that works with UDP. Other protocols, such as CoAP, are also designed to work well with UDP. There is even an alternative TLS design called **Datagram TLS (DTLS)** intended for products that implement UDP-based transport.

Network protocols

IPv4 and IPv6 both play a role at various points within many IoT systems. Tailored protocol stacks such as **IPv6 over Low Power Wireless Personal Area Networks (6LoWPAN)** support the use of IPv6 within network-constrained environments common to many IoT devices. 6LoWPan supports wireless Internet connectivity at lower data rates to accommodate highly constrained device form factors: `http://projets-gmi.univ-avignon.fr/projets//proj1112/M1/p09/doc/6LoWPAN_overview.pdf`.

6LoWPAN builds upon the 802.15.4 -**Low Rate Wireless Personal Area Networks (LRWPAN)** specification to create an adaptation layer that supports IPv6. The adaptation layer provides features that include IPv6 with UDP header compression and support for fragmentation, allowing constrained sensors, for example, to be used in building automation and security. Using 6LoWPAN, designers can take advantage of link encryption offered within IEEE 802.15.4 but can also apply transport layer encryption such as DTLS.

Data link and physical protocols

If you examine the many communication protocols available within the IoT, you notice that one in particular, IEEE 802.15.4, plays a significant role as the foundation for other protocols—providing the **Physical (PHY)** and **Medium Access Control (MAC)** layers for protocols such as ZigBee, 6LoWPAN, WirelessHART, and even thread.

IEEE 802.15.4

802.15.4 is designed to operate using either point-to-point or star topologies and is ideal for use in low-power or low-speed environments. 802.15.4 devices operate in the 915 MHz and 2.4 GHz frequency ranges, support data rates up to 250 kb/s and communication ranges of roughly 10 meters. The PHY layer is responsible for managing RF network access, while the MAC layer is responsible for managing transmission and receipt of frames onto the data link.

ZWave

Another protocol that operates at this layer of the stack is ZWave. ZWave supports the transmission of three frame types on a network – unicast, multicast, and broadcast. Unicast communications (that is, direct) are acknowledged by the receiver; however, neither multicast nor broadcast transmissions are acknowledged. ZWave networks consist of controllers and slaves. There are variants of each of these, of course. For example, there can be both primary and secondary controllers. Primary controllers have responsibilities such as the ability to add/remove nodes form the network. ZWave operates at 908.42 MHz (North America)/868.42 MHz (Europe) frequency with data rates of 100 kb/s over a range of about 30 meters.

Bluetooth/Bluetooth Smart (also known as Bluetooth Low Energy or BLE) is an evolution of Bluetooth designed for enhanced battery life. Bluetooth Smart achieves its power saving capability by defaulting to sleep mode and only waking when needed. Both operate in the 2.4 GHz frequency range. Bluetooth Smart implements a high-rate frequency-hopping spread spectrum and supports AES encryption.

Reference: `http://www.medicalelectronicsdesign.com/article/bluetooth-low-energy-vs-classic-bluetooth-choose-best-wireless-technology-your-application`

Power Line Communications

In the energy industry, WirelessHART and **Power Line Communications (PLC)** technologies such as Insteon are additional technologies that operate at the link and physical layers of the communication stack. PLC-enabled devices (not to be confused with Programmable Logic Controller) can support both home and industrial uses and are interesting in that their communications are modulated directly over existing power lines. This communications method enables power-connected devices to be controlled and monitored without secondary communication conduits.

Reference: `http://www.eetimes.com/document.asp?doc_id=1279014`

Cellular communications

The move towards 5G communications will have a significant impact on IoT system designs. When 5G rolls out with higher throughput and the ability to support many more connections, we will begin to see increased movement for direct connectivity of IoT devices to the cloud. This will allow for new centralized controller functions to be created that support multitudes of geographically dispersed sensors/actuators with limited infrastructure in place. More robust cellular capabilities will further enable the cloud to be the aggregation point for sensor data feeds, web service interactions, and interfaces to numerous enterprise applications.

IoT data collection, storage, and analytics

So far, we have talked extensively about the endpoints and the protocols that comprise the IoT. Although there is great promise in device-to-device communication and coordination, there are even more opportunities to streamline business processes, enhance customer experiences, and increase capabilities when the power of connected devices is paired with the ability to analyze data. The cloud offers a ready-made infrastructure to support this pairing.

Many public **CSPs** have deployed IoT services that are well integrated with their other cloud offerings. **AWS**, for example, has created the AWS IoT service. This service allows IoT devices to be configured and connect to the AWS IoT gateway using MQTT or REST communications. Data can also be ingested into AWS through platforms such as Kinesis or Kinesis Firehose. Kinesis Firehose, for example, can be used to collect and process large streams of data and forward on to other AWS infrastructure components for storage and analysis.

Once data has been collected within a CSP, logic rules can be set up to forward that data where most appropriate. Data can be sent for analysis, storage, or to be combined with other data from other devices and systems. Reasons for the analysis of IoT data run the gamut from wanting to understand trends in shopping patterns (for example, beacons) to predicting whether a machine will break down (predictive maintenance).

Other CSPs have also entered the IoT marketplace. Microsoft's Azure offering now has a specific IoT service in addition to IBM and Google. Even **Software as a Service (SaaS)** providers have begun offering analytics services. Salesforce.com has designed a tailored IoT analytics solution. Salesforce makes use of the Apache stack to connect devices to the cloud and analyze their large data streams. Salesforce's IoT Cloud relies upon Apache's Cassandra database, the Spark data-processing engine, Storm for data analysis, and Kafka for messaging.

Reference: `http://fortune.com/2015/09/15/salesforce-com-iot-cloud/`

IoT integration platforms and solutions

As new IoT devices and systems continue to be built by diverse organizations, we're beginning to see the need for improved and enhanced integration capabilities. Companies such as Xively and Thingspeak are now offering flexible development solutions for integrating new things into enterprise architectures. In the domain of smart cities, platforms such as Accella and SCOPE, a "smart-city cloud-based open platform and ecosystem", offer the ability to integrate a variety of IoT systems into enterprise solutions.

These platforms provide APIs that IoT device developers can leverage to build new features and services. Increasingly, IoT developers are incorporating these APIs and demonstrating ease-of-integration into enterprise IT environments. The Thingspeak API, for example, can be used to integrate IoT devices via HTTP communications. This enables organizations to capture data from their sensors, analyze that data, and then take action on that data. Similarly, AllJoyn is an open source project from the AllSeen Alliance. It is focused heavily on interoperability between IoT devices even when the devices use different transport mechanisms. As IoT matures, disparate IoT components, protocols, and APIs will continue to be glued together to build powerful enterprise-wide systems. These trends beg the question of just how secured these systems will be.

The IoT of the future and the need to secure

While today's IoT innovations continue to push the envelope identifying and establishing new relationships between objects, systems, and people, our imaginations continuously dream up new capabilities to solve problems at unprecedented scale. When we apply our imaginative prowess, the promises of the IoT becomes boundless. Today, we are barely scratching the surface.

The future – cognitive systems and the IoT

The computer-to-device and device-device IoT is poised for staggering growth today and over the coming years, but what about brand new research that is on the brink of consumerization? What will need to secure in the future, and how will it depend on how we secure the IoT today? Cognitive systems and research provides us a valuable glimpse into the IoT of tomorrow.

Over a decade ago, Duke University researchers demonstrated cognitive control of a robotic arm by translating neural control signals from electrodes embedded into the parietal and frontal cortex lobes of a monkey's brain. The researchers converted the brain signals to motor servo actuator inputs. These inputs allowed the monkey — through initial training on a joystick — to control a non-biological, robotic arm using only visual feedback to adjust its own motor-driving thoughts. So-called **brain-computer interfaces (BCI)**, or **brain-machine interfaces (BMI)**, continue to be advanced by Dr. Miguel Nocolelis' Duke laboratory and others. The technology promises a future in which neuroprosthetics allow debilitated individuals to regain physical function by wearing and controlling robotic systems merely by thought. Research has also demonstrated brain-to-brain functioning, allowing distributed, cognitive problem-solving through brainlets.

Digital conversion of brain-sensed (via neuroencaphalography) signals allows the cognition-ready data to be conveyed over data buses, IP networks, and yes, even the Internet. In terms of the IoT, this type of cognitive research implies a future in which some types of smart devices will be smart because there is a human or other type of brain controlling or receiving signals from it across a BMI. Or the human brain is made hyper-aware by providing it sensor feeds from sensors located thousands of kilometers away. Imagine a pilot flying a drone as though it were an extension of his body, but the pilot has no joystick. Using only thought signals (controls) and feedback (feeling) conveyed over a communications link, all necessary flight maneuvers and adjustments can be made. Imagine the aircraft's airspeed, as measured by its pitot tube, conveyed in digital form to the pilot's BMI interface and the pilot "feeling" the speed like wind blowing across his skin. That future of the IoT is not as far off as it may seem.

Now imagine what type of IoT security may be needed in such cognitive systems where the things are human brains and dynamic physical systems. How would one authenticate a human brain, for example, to a device, or authenticate the device back to the brain? What would digital integrity losses entail with the BMI? What could happen if outgoing or incoming signals were spoofed, corrupted, or manipulated in timing and availability? The overarching benefits of today's IoT, as large as they are, are small when we consider such future systems and what they mean to the human race. So too are the threats and risks.

Summary

In this chapter, we saw how the world is developing and advancing towards a better future with the help of the IoT. We also looked at various uses of the IoT in today's world and then had a brief look at its concepts.

In the next chapter, we will learn about the various threats and the measures that we can take to avoid/overcome them.

Vulnerabilities, Attacks, and Countermeasures

This chapter elaborates on attack methods against IoT implementations and deployments, how attacks are organized into attack trees, and how IoT cyber-physical systems complicate the threat landscape. We then rationalize a systematic methodology for incorporating countermeasures to secure the IoT. We will explore both typical and unique vulnerabilities seen within various layers of the IoT technology stack and describe new ways in which electronic and physical threats interact. We provide a tailored approach to threat modeling to show the reader how to perform usable IoT threat modeling in their own organizations.

We explore vulnerabilities, attacks, and countermeasures, and methods of managing them through the following chapter subsections:

- Primer on threats, vulnerability, and risk
- Primer on attacks and countermeasures
- Today's IoT attacks
- Lessons learned—the use of systematic approaches

Primer on threats, vulnerability, and risks (TVR)

A substantial amount of academic wrangling has evolved competing definitions for the concepts of threats, vulnerability, and risks. In the interest of keeping this volume practical and usable, we will first revisit in this section what the information assurance industry has termed the five pillars of information assurance. These pillars, or domains, of information assurance represent the highest-level categories of assurance in an information system. Next, we will introduce two additional pillars that are critically important in cyber-physical systems. Once introduced, we will then explore IoT threats, vulnerabilities and risks.

The classic pillars of information assurance

It is nearly impossible to discuss practical aspects of threat, vulnerability, and risk without identifying the essential components of **information assurance (IA)**, an important subdomain of IoT security. Succinctly, they are as follows:

- **Confidentiality**: Keeping sensitive information secret and protected from disclosure

- **Integrity**: Ensuring that information is not modified, accidentally or purposefully, without being detected

- **Authentication**: Ensuring that the source of data is from a known identity or endpoint (generally follows identification)

- **Non-repudiation**: Ensuring that an individual or system cannot later deny having performed an action

- **Availability**: Ensuring that information is available when needed

Satisfying an information security goal does not necessarily imply that an organization has to keep all of the preceding assurances in place. Not all data requires confidentiality, for example. Information and data categorization is a complex topic in itself and not all information is critically sensitive or important. Proper threat modeling of a device and its hosted applications and data requires an organization to identify the sensitivities of both individual data elements and data in aggregate form. Aggregation risks of large, seemingly benign IoT datasets pose some of the most difficult challenges. Well-defined data categories and combinational constraints enable specific assurances such as confidentiality or integrity to be defined for each data element or complex information type.

The five pillars of IA each apply to the IoT because the IoT blends information with a device's environment, physicality, information, data sources, sinks, and networks. Beyond the pillars of IA, however, we must introduce two additional assurances that relate to cyber-physical aspects of the IoT, namely, resilience and safety. Resilience and safety engineering are closely related; we define and distinguish them in this section.

Resilience in the cyber-physical IoT relates to resilience of a cyber-physical control system:

> *"A resilient control system is one that maintains state awareness and an accepted level of operational normalcy in response to disturbances, including threats of an unexpected and malicious nature."*

Source: Rieger, C.G.; Gertman, D.I.; McQueen, M.A. (May 2009), Resilient Control Systems: Next Generation Design Research, Catania, Italy: 2nd IEEE Conference on Human System Interaction.

Safety in the cyber-physical IoT is defined as:

> *"The condition of being safe from undergoing or causing hurt, injury, or loss."*

Source: http://www.merriam-webster.com/dictionary/safety

The IoT's convergence of the five pillars of IA with resilience and safety implies that cyber-physical engineers adhere to security and safety approaches that simultaneously address both failure (fault) trees for safety and attack trees for security. Safety design decisions and security controls comprise the solution space wherein engineers must simultaneously address the following:

- Fault tree best practices to avoid common mode failures
- Appropriate risk-based security controls that help inhibit an adversary from compromising the system and wreaking havoc on safety controls and systems impacted by safety controls

An engineering approach is needed in the IoT that merges both attack and fault tree analysis to identify and resolve common mode failures and attack vectors. Isolated inspection of either tree may no longer be sufficient.

Threats

It is important to distinguish between a threat and threat source (or threat actor). Each threat has a threat actor. For example, in the case of the burglar invading your home, it is tempting to consider the burglar as the actual threat, but it is more accurate and useful to consider him the threat source (or actor). He is the actor, who may attack your house for a variety of malicious purposes, most notably his self-serving desire to separate you from your valued assets. In this context, the threat is actually the potential for the burglary to be performed, or more generally represents the **exploit potential**.

Threats may therefore come in a variety of types, both natural and man-made. Tornados, floods, and hurricanes can be considered natural threats; in these cases, the Earth's weather serves as the threat actor (or *acts of God* in the lingo of many insurance policies).

IoT threats include all of the information assurance threats to management and application data sent to and from IoT devices. In addition, IoT devices are subject to the same physical security, hardware, software quality, environmental, supply chain, and many other threats inherent in both security and safety domains. IoT devices in CPS (for example, actuation, physical sensing, and so on) are subject to physical reliability and resilience threats beyond just the compromise and degradation of the computing platform. Additional engineering disciplines are at play in CPS, such as classical control theory, state estimation and control, and others that use sensors, sensor feedback, controllers, filters, and actuation devices to manipulate physical system states. Threats can also target control system transfer functions, state estimation filters (such as Kalman filters), and other inner control loop artifacts that have direct responses and consequences in the physical world.

Vulnerability

Vulnerability is the term we use to identify a weakness, either in the design, integration, or operation of a system or device. Vulnerabilities are ever-present, and countless new ones are discovered every day. Many online databases and web portals now provide us with automated updates on newly discovered vulnerabilities. The following diagram provides a view into the relationships between each of these concepts:

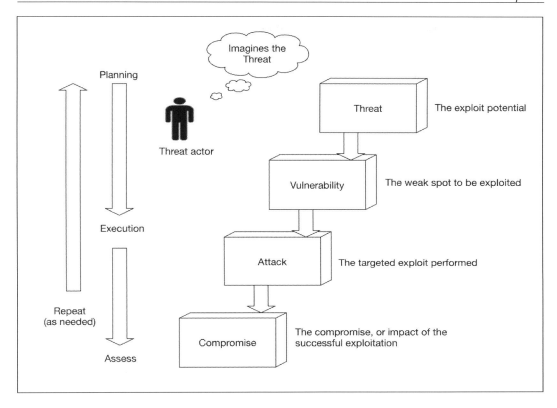

Vulnerabilities may be deficiencies in a device's physical protection (for example, weaknesses in a device's casing that allow the ability to tamper), software quality, configuration, suitability of protocol security for its environment, or appropriateness of the protocols themselves. They can include just about anything in the device, from design implementation deficiencies in the hardware (for example, allowing tampering with FPGA or EEPROM), to internal physical architecture and interfaces, the operating system, or applications. Attackers are well aware of the vulnerability potentials. They will typically seek to unearth the vulnerabilities that are easiest, least costly, or fastest to exploit. Malicious hacking drives a for-profit marketplace of its own in *dark web* settings; malicious hackers understand the concept of **return-on-investment (ROI)** well. While the threat is the potential for exploit, the vulnerability is the target of the actual exploit from the threat actor.

Risks

One can use qualitative or quantitative methods for evaluating risk. Simply put, risk is *one's exposure to loss*. It is different from vulnerability, because it depends on the probability of a particular event, attack, or condition and has a strong link to the motivations of an attacker. It also depends on how large the impact is of a single, atomic compromise or a whole campaign of attack/compromise events. Vulnerability does not directly invoke impact or probability, but is the innate weakness itself. It may be easy or hard to exploit, or result in a small or large loss when exploited. For example, a desktop operating system may have a serious vulnerability in its process isolation logic allowing an untrusted process to access the virtual memory of another application. This vulnerability may be exploitable and most certainly represents a weakness, but if the system is air-gapped and never connected directly or indirectly to the Internet, the vulnerability may invoke little if any risk—exposure. If, on the other hand, the platform is connected to the Internet, the risk level may jump due to an attacker finding a practical means of injecting hostile shell code that exploits the process isolation vulnerability and allows the attacker to assume ownership of the machine.

Risk can be managed through threat modeling, which helps ascertain the following:

- Impact and overall cost of a compromise
- How valuable the target may be to attackers
- Anticipated skill and motivations of the attackers (based on threat modeling)
- A priori knowledge of a system's vulnerabilities (for example, those discovered during threat modeling, public advisories, penetration testing, and so on)

Risk management relies on judicious application of mitigations against the types of vulnerabilities that are known to be present and that may be targeted by the potential exploits (threats). Naturally, not all vulnerabilities will be known ahead of time; these we call zero-days or 0 days. We know that certain OS vulnerabilities are in our Windows operating system; therefore, we apply well-selected anti-malware and network monitoring equipment to reduce the exposure. Because mitigating security controls are never perfect, we are still left with some smaller remaining amount of risk, typically called residual risk. Residual risk is often accepted as is, or offset by the application of other risk offset mechanisms such as insurance.

Primer on attacks and countermeasures

Now that we have briefly visited threats, vulnerabilities, and risk, let's dive into greater detail on the types and compositions of attacks present in the IoT and how they can be put together to perform attack campaigns. In this section, we also introduce attack trees (and fault trees) to help readers visualize and communicate how real-world attacks can happen. It is also our hope that they gain wider adoption and use in broader threat modeling activities, not unlike the threat model example later in the chapter.

Common IoT attack types

There are many attack types to cover in this book; however, the following list provides some of the most significant as they relate to the IoT:

- Wired and wireless scanning and mapping attacks
- Protocol attacks
- Eavesdropping attacks (loss of confidentiality)
- Cryptographic algorithm and key management attacks
- Spoofing and masquerading (authentication attacks)
- Operating system and application integrity attacks
- Denial of service and jamming
- Physical security attacks (for example, tampering, interface exposures)
- Access control attacks (privilege escalation)

The preceding attacks are only a small sample of what exists in the wild. In the real world, however, most attacks are highly customized to a specific, known vulnerability. A vulnerability that is not yet publicly known, and for which an exploit has typically been developed, is called a zero-day (or O-day) vulnerability. Any number of attacks may exploit such vulnerabilities, and any number of attacks may be publicly shared over the Internet to do so. Well-placed security controls are vital to reducing either the likelihood or severity of an attack's exploitation of a vulnerability. The following diagram shows the ecosystem of attacks, vulnerabilities, and controls:

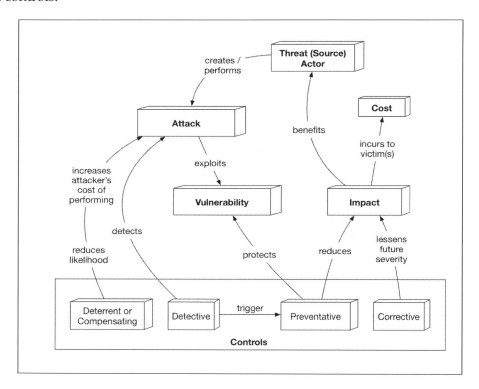

The types of attacks on IoT systems will grow over time and in some cases will follow profit motive trends similar to what we see in the evolving cybersecurity industry. For example, today there is a disturbing trend in the malware business whereby attackers employ cryptographic algorithms to encrypt a victim's personal hard drive data. The attackers then offer to return the data, decrypted, for a fee. Called ransomware, the potential for such an attack in the IoT realm is frightening. Consider a malicious hacker performing ransom attacks on physical infrastructure or medical equipment. One receives a note that one's pacemaker was unknowingly compromised, the victim receives a short, non-lethal jolt to prove it, then is instructed to immediately wire funds to a destination account or risk a full-fledged, potentially lethal attack. Consider automobiles, garage doors opening (while on vacation), and other potential activities usable by malicious actors for ransom. The IoT must take these types of attacks seriously and not dismiss them as the musings of pundits. The greatest challenge in the security industry is finding methods today of defending against tomorrow's attacks.

Attack trees

It is easy in the security industry to be drawn to the latest and greatest exploits and attack methodologies. We frequently speak of attack vectors and attack surfaces without any real specificity or rigor. If it is specific, it is usually in the form of news reports or publications from security researchers about new zero-days discovered in the wild and how they may have been deployed against a target. In other words, many of our discussions about attack vectors and attack surfaces are simply undisciplined.

It is possible for a single attack on a device or application to yield substantial value to an attacker, either in information compromised, manipulation of the device for physical effect, or opportunities for pivoting elsewhere in the device's network. In practice, however, an attack is usually part of a campaign of grouped and/or sequenced subattacks or other activities, each carefully chosen from a variety of intelligence methods (for example, human social engineering, profiling, scanning, Internet research, familiarity with the system, and so on). Each activity designed to accomplish its immediate goal has some level of difficulty, cost, and probability of success. Attack trees help us model these characteristics in devices and systems.

Attack trees are conceptual diagrams showing how an asset, or target, might be attacked (https://en.wikipedia.org/wiki/Attack_tree). In other words, when it is time to really understand a system's security posture and not just knee-jerk worry about the latest, sensational reported attack vectors du jour, it is time to build an attack tree. An attack tree can help your organization visualize, communicate, and come to a more realistic understanding of the sequence of vulnerability that can be exploited for some end effect.

Building an attack tree

If you haven't done it before, building an attack tree can seem like a daunting task, and it is difficult to know where to start. To begin, a tool is needed to both build the model and run analysis against it. One example is SecurITree, a capabilities-based attack tree modeling tool built by the Canadian company Amenaza (the Spanish word for threat) (http://www.amenaza.com/). Building an attack tree is perhaps best described with a simple example.

Suppose an attacker wishes to accomplish the overarching goal of re-directing an **Unmanned Aircraft Systems (UAS)**, that is, a drone, while in flight. The following diagram shows the top-level activities of the attack tree to accomplish this:

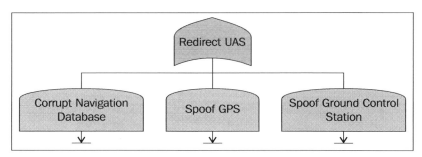

You will notice the two well-known logic operator symbols for AND (smooth and rounded top) and OR (pointy top). The root node, entitled **Redirect UAS** represents the end objective and is made up of an OR operator. This means that any one of its children can satisfy the end goal. In this case, the attacker may redirect the aircraft by any of the following methods:

- **Corrupting its navigation database**: A navigation database maps named locations to positions in space (latitude, longitude, and typically, altitude above mean sea level). In practice, there are many potential ways to compromise a navigation database, for example, either directly on the aircraft, its ground control station, or even in the navigation and mapping supply chain (this is true of manned aviation as well, as commercial airliners' flight computers have extensive navigation databases).

- **Spoofing GPS**: In this case, the attacker could choose to perform an active RF-based GPS attack in which they generate and transmit false GPS timing data that the drone interprets as a false location. In response, the drone (if under autonomous flight) navigates unknowingly, based on its falsely perceived location, and follows a path maliciously designed by the attacker. (Note, we assume there is no machine vision or other passive navigation system in use.)

- **Spoofing the ground control station (GCS)**: In this option, the attacker can find a way to spoof the drone's legitimate operator and attempt to send malicious routing commands.

Now, let's expand the attack tree a bit (the tiny arrow pointing to a horizontal line at the bottom of each node indicates the node is expandable). Specifically, let's expand the **Corrupt Navigation Database** goal node:

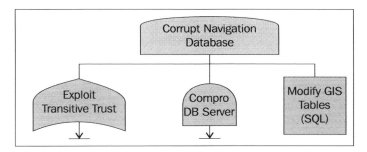

This **Corrupt Navigation Database** node is an AND operator; therefore, each and every one of its children in the tree must be satisfied to achieve it. In this case, each of the following is needed:

- Some attack that exploits a transitive trust relationship needed to get into the supply chain of the navigation database

- A compromise of the navigation database server

- The modification of the **Geographic Information System (GIS)** tables within the navigation database (for example, tell the drone that its destination is 100 m to the North, East, and below its actual destination, and it might just crash into the ground or a building)

Two of the nodes, **Exploit Transitive Trust** and **Compro DB server**, each have subtrees. The third node, modify GIS tables, does not and is therefore called a **leaf node**. Leaf nodes represent the actual attack vector entry points into the model, that is, the attacker's activities, whereas its parents (AND OR nodes) represent either specific device states, system states, or goals that the attacker may achieve through their activities.

Expanding the **Exploit Transitive Trust** subtree gives us the following image:

Without going into detail on every node, it becomes apparent that careful thought and consideration goes into developing an effective, usable attack tree. In summary, trees have subtrees that can be very simple or complex. Typically, the more complex the subtree, the greater the need to analyze it offline of the main tree in what is called subtree analysis. In practice, proper rigor in attack tree modeling requires a number of experts in each of the sub-tree domains. It is strongly suggested that attack tree modeling become a normal part of IoT system (or device) security engineering.

The SecurITree tool goes much further than just creating tree diagrams. Its dialogs assist you in modeling each attack goal by establishing indicators such as the following:

- **Capabilities** of the attacker, such as technical ability, noticeability, cost of the attack, and so on
- **Behaviors and probabilities**
- **Impact of the attack** to the victim (note that by the time the subtree impacts aggregate up to the root node, the final impact can be enormous)
- **Benefits to the attacker** (of given impacts) are motivating impacts for the attack
- **Detriments to the attacker** are demotivators for the attack

Once all of this data is input to the tool, the real fun begins in the analysis and reporting. The tool computes each and every attack vector (attack scenario) based on all of the possible tree traversals and logic operators that define each attack goal. For each attack scenario, the total cost of the attack, its probability and its total impact are computed and then sorted according whatever criteria you select. Note that even a moderately sized tree can generate thousands, tens of thousands, or hundreds of thousands of attack scenarios, though not all are necessarily interesting or likely (the process of whittling down the attack scenarios to the ones that count most is called reduction).

Once the attack scenarios are generated, interesting reports can be generated, for example, a graph of willingness-to-capability ratios (for the analyzed attack scenarios). The slope of the curve can indicate interesting aspects of the psychology of the selected attacker profile, such as to what extent they may continue to pursue attacks in the face of limited capability. This information can be quite useful in selecting and prioritizing the security controls and other mitigations you select. Other reports can be generated as well. For example, cumulative risk can be graphically displayed over a defined period of time as a function of the number of computed attack scenarios (based on each one's characteristics).

The tool has many other interesting and useful features as well. Recommendations for using this tool include the following:

- Prune your trees into separate files (subtrees) and allow experts in each subtree domain (whether internal or external to your organization) to maintain their area. In some cases, certain subtrees remain fairly static and can potentially be shared between companies and industries as long as the attack tree indicators are aligned.

- Add trees and subtrees to your version control system and update any time major system designs are changed, or when anything that might affect the threat profile of your IoT device, system, or deployment changes.

- Create and maintain (again in version management) your attacker profiles. They will most certainly change over time, especially if your deployment begins to collect new and more valuable types of privacy information. Even your company's growth and financial resources can impact your attacker profile.

Real-world attacks may involve numerous feedback loops within the attack tree. Successive attacks and compromises of multiple intermediate devices and systems—each called a pivot—may allow an attacker to reach his final goal. This is something you don't want.

Keep in mind, however, that the cyber-physical aspects of the IoT introduce new attack flavors for the root node, goals that may surpass the severity of data exfiltration, denial of service, and other conventional cyber threats. The new options are the possible physical world interactions and controls ranging from turning off a light bulb to turning off a human heart.

To that end, we must also discuss fault trees.

Fault (failure) trees and CPS

A fault tree discussion may seem to be out of place in a section about attacks and countermeasures. The value of attack trees to IoT implementation and deployment organizations should be clear by now. Obviously, the more accurate the attack model, the better the decisions that can be made from it. Attack trees alone are not sufficient, however, to characterize risks to the many new IoT paradigms. In *Chapter 1, A Brave New World*, we introduced **cyber-physical systems** (**CPS**), a subset of the IoT. CPS represent an uncomfortable domain in which both safety and security engineering disciplines must be combined and reconciled to produce engineering solutions that simultaneously mitigate both safety and security risks.

Safety and reliability engineering's principal modeling tool is called the fault tree (also called the failure tree) as used in **fault tree analysis** (**FTA**). Other than in appearance, fault trees are quite different than attack trees.

Fault trees have their origin in the early 1960s at Bell Labs, who supported the US Air Force to address and help mitigate the frequent reliability failures that befell the Minuteman I ballistic missile program (`https://en.wikipedia.org/wiki/Fault_tree_analysis`). At this time, missile systems—especially their early guidance, navigation, and control subsystem designs—were prone to frequent failures. From that time, FTA began to be adopted into other areas of aerospace (especially commercial aircraft design and certification) and is now used in a variety of industries that need to achieve extremely high levels of safety assurance. For example, typical FAA safety requirements mandate aircraft manufacturers to demonstrate during commercial aircraft certification that their designs meet a 1 x 10-9 (one in a billion) probability of failure. To achieve such low failure rates, significant levels of redundancy (triple and even quadrature levels in some cases) are designed into many aircraft systems. Many regulatory aspects of risk management (for example, as in FAA aircraft certification) lean heavily on FTA.

Author's note *Van Duren*: The author's grandfather, Lt. Col. Arthur Glenn Foster, was based at Vandenberg Air Force Base in California in the early 1960s, and was in charge of the Command and Control of Minuteman and Titan II ICBM missiles worldwide. Many family stories survive to this day of the frequent launches and spectacular failures of many of these rocket launches on California's beautiful central coast.

Fault tree and attack tree differences

The principal difference between an attack tree and a fault tree lies in how one enters and traverses each:

- Fault trees are *not* based on intelligently planned attacks in which multiple leaves of the tree are entered at will at the discretion of an intelligent entity

- Fault trees are traversed based on stochastic processes (failure/fault rates) from each leaf through the dependent, intermediate nodes

- Each fault tree leaf is completely independent (faults occur randomly AND independently of each other) of all other leaves of the tree

In essence, a fault tree can account for the rate at which an aircraft's braking system may fail naturally.

In the tool, SecureITree, we described earlier, one may generate fault trees as well. To do this, one must define a probability indicator at the leaf nodes of the tree. Within the indicator dialog, you may enter a probability (for example, 1/100, 1/10,000, and so on) for the leaf node event/action to transpire.

Merging fault and attack tree analysis

Methods of merging attack tree analysis with FTA exist in the literature, but significant research and work remains to find new, efficient ways of performing combined tree analysis for CPS IoT. Processes are needed that help both safety and security engineers navigate a system's statistical failure modes in a manner cognizant of the different attack modalities that also may be present. One issue to overcome is the potentially enormous state space that may ensue from the analysis and the challenge of making the results useful and actionable for developing optimal mitigations.

With the challenges in mind, high safety and security assurances can still be achieved today with the following recommendations:

- Integrate FTA into safety-critical IoT device and system engineering methodologies (many IoT implementers are probably not doing this today).

- Ensure that the actual, intended IoT use cases are represented in the FTA. For example, if a device's power filter and supply were to fail or produce an under-voltage situation, would its microcontroller shut down automatically, or would it continue to function at high risk of erratic behavior? Maintaining power supply thresholds in processors is fairly standard design, but do you have a redundant battery backup that will allow the device to continue to operate normally as needed, for example, in a safety-critical medical device?

- As fault-tolerant design is performed (for example, built-in redundancies, and so on), ensure the security engineers have a seat at the table. They should perform security threat modeling on the device (or system) in a way that addresses its redundancies, gateways, communications protocols, endpoints and other hosts, environment, and the myriad potential pathways to compromise any one of them.

- As security engineers identify necessary security controls, determine if the controls impact the fault-tolerance design features or the basic functionality and performance needed. This may happen, for example, in time-sensitive safety shutoff/cutoff mechanisms. A security engineer may want to perform some latency-inducing traffic scanning across a data bus or network, but the resultant latencies might cause the safety features to respond too slowly, with disastrous consequences. Workarounds may be possible, for example, by allowing timing information to flow through alternate pathways.

- The scariest combined safety/security threats are those in which an attacker explicitly targets a safety design feature. For example, a microcontroller that handles voltage or temperature cutoffs and prevents a thermodynamic meltdown can possibly be targeted and disabled by an attacker. Redundant devices can also be targeted such that the failure probabilities skyrocket when other targeted attacks take place in parallel or sequence. In these instances, the safety and security experts need to jointly and very carefully come up with:
    - Safety mitigations that don't undermine needed security controls
    - Security mitigations that don't diminish safety controls

- This is not always an easy feat and there may be instances when compromises have to be made that result in residual, accepted risks on both fronts.

Example anatomy of a deadly cyber-physical attack

In the interest of demonstrating an attack tree scenario in the CPS domain of the IoT, this section highlights a devastating example of a hypothetical cyber-physical attack. No doubt, most readers are familiar with the Stuxnet worm that targeted the Iranian CPS responsible for refining Uranium to fissionable levels. Stuxnet, while immensely damaging to Iranian goals, did not result in a safety failure. It resulted in an industrial control process failure that caused uranium refinement rates to come to a standstill. Unfortunately, Stuxnet—while most certainly nation-state in origin—is only a prelude of things to come with regard to CPS attacks. Keep in mind, the hypothetical attack below is not trivial and would typically require the resources of a nation state.

As we mentioned in *Chapter 1, A Brave New World*, CPS comprise a variety of networked sensors, controllers and actuators that collectively make up a standalone or distributed control system. In the world of aviation—a historically safety-driven industry—amazing advances have been made in fault-tolerant engineering approaches; many of the lessons learned came about from root cause analysis investigations of various tragedies. Jet engine reliability, airframe structural integrity, avionics resilience, as well as hydraulics and fly-by-wire system reliability are all elements we take for granted in a modern jet aircraft. Aviation software assurance requirements, as specified in the RTCA standard, DO-178B, are a testament to some of the lessons learned. The safety improvements, whether fault-tolerant features of the software, additional redundancies, mechanical or electrical design features, or software assurance improvements have resulted in failure rate targets reaching 1 in 1x10-9, a miracle in the history of modern safety engineering. Safety engineering, however, needs to be distinguished from security engineering in terms of evolutionary paths; safety engineering by itself may only offer minor protection against the following attack scenario.

This CPS attack example highlights the convergence of engineering disciplines at play in the planning, execution, and defense against such an attack. While this attack is exceedingly improbable today, it is described here to highlight the complexity of system interactions that can be exploited for malicious purposes. The high-level flow of the attack is as follows:

- Prerequisites:
    - The attacker(s) possesses or procures significant aircraft avionics system knowledge (note: there are a number of companies and countries that possess this)

- ° The attacker develops a customized control system exploit for the aircraft in question. The exploit delivery comprises malware designed to automatically execute on the aircraft's system

- The attacker compromises an airline's ground maintenance network. This network hosts the updated avionics software loads that the airline downloads from the aircraft manufacturer. From the network, maintenance crews stage the avionics patches into the airliner's **integrated modular avionics (IMA)** system.

- The attacker physically or logically tampers the aircraft's legitimate software/firmware binary (from the manufacturer) with the chosen exploit delivery mechanism. It is now staged to be loaded into the aircraft avionics hardware by maintenance personnel.

- The software update is uploaded. The malicious code begins to run and delivers the exploit reprogramming the controller. The exploit is a new microcontroller binary that executes logic for the control system's inner loop. Specifically, it contains a re-write of the controller's notch filtering logic.

- The malicious microcontroller binary overwrites the notch filter mechanism, eliminating the system's pitch mode (up/down) dampening of the aircraft's natural and harmonic structural frequencies (imagine bending the wing, letting go and observing the jostling motion for a second—that's the natural frequency you normally want dampened). The normal frequency dampening performed by the notch filter no longer works and is instead replaced with an opposite response, namely an excitation of the structure at its natural frequency.

- The aircraft begins flight and hits mild turbulence shortly after takeoff (note, hitting turbulence would probably not be necessary). The turbulence induces the wing's natural vibration modes that are normally dampened by the control system's notch filter. Instead, the oscillation excites the wing's natural harmonic mode; the controller's excitation response increases in amplitude (the wing tips vibrate wildly up and down) until the wing experiences a catastrophic structural failure and disintegrates.

- The disintegrated wing structure causes the aircraft to crash. The attacker's end goal is achieved.

Now that we have your attention, we must reiterate that this is an exceedingly low probability, highly sophisticated attack, and that there are much easier ways of bringing down an aircraft. However, CPS attacks may become more attractive over time depending on the attacker(s) motivations and the networking of control systems offers new attack vectors to gain initial footholds. The sad news is that such attacks — whether against transportation systems or smart home appliances — will become more feasible over time unless the cross-discipline safety and security collaborations we have already discussed become standard practice and improve.

There are numerous mitigations that could have thwarted the aircraft control system attack, as described. For example, if all avionics binaries were cryptographically signed by the manufacturer, integrity can be protected end-to-end. If the avionics manufacturer only applies a **cyclic redundancy check** (**CRC**), an attacker may be able to find easy ways of thwarting it (CRCs were designed to detect accidental fault-based integrity errors, not intelligently designed integrity attacks). If the binaries are cryptographically integrity-protected, the attacker will find it much more difficult to modify code without failing the integrity check at both installation and system power-up. The redesigned controller logic would be much more difficult to inject. In the safety world, a CRC is generally sufficient, but not in the security world of cyber-physical systems where enhanced, end-to-end security is preferred when possible. Simply transferring an updated avionics binary over a cryptographically protected network connection (for example, TLS) would not meet the goal of protecting the binary end-to-end from the manufacturer into the aircraft. The TLS cryptographic connection would not satisfy the end-to-end need of ensuring the binary has not been tampered in its delivery supply chain. This chain extends from the point of compilation and build (from original sources) all the way to the point of avionics software load, power-on, and self-tests.

In practice, some elements of safety engineering, such as triple or quadruple redundant controllers and independent data buses can help mitigate certain security threats. The unlikely attack we provided above would likely have been thwarted by the redundant controllers, command inputs overriding the rogue one. Redundancies, however, are not sure bets in the security world; therefore, do not let technology companies and government agencies dissuade your skepticism and concern. An intelligent adversary, given time, resources, and motivation, can find a way to maliciously induce what safety engineers call common mode failures. With ingenuity, even the fault-tolerant features of a design — meant to prevent failures — can be weaponized to induce them.

Today's IoT attacks

Many of today's attacks against consumer IoT devices have been largely conducted by researchers with the goal of bettering the state of IoT security. These attacks often gain wide attention, and many times result in changes to the security posture of the device being tested. Conducted responsibly, this type of white hat and gray hat testing is valuable because it helps manufacturers address and fix vulnerabilities before widespread exploitation is achieved by those with less benevolent motives. It is generally bittersweet news for manufacturers, however. Many manufacturers struggle with how to properly respond to reported vulnerabilities by security researchers. Some organizations actively enlist the aid of the research community through organizations such as BuildItSecure.ly where volunteers focus on identifying vulnerabilities in software or hardware implementation at the request of the developer themselves. Some organizations operate their own bug bounty programs, in which security professionals are encouraged to find and report vulnerabilities (and get rewarded for them). Other organizations, however, turn a blind eye to vulnerabilities reported in their products, or worse, attempt to prosecute the researchers.

An attack campaign that received much attention was the hack of a 2014 Jeep Cherokee in 2015 by researchers Charlie Miller and Chris Valasek. The two researchers' discoveries were detailed very well in their report *Remote Exploitation of an Unaltered Passenger Vehicle.*

Miller, Charlie and Valesek, Chris. Remote Exploitation of an Unaltered Passenger Vehicle. 10 August 2015. Downloaded at `http://illmatics.com/Remote%20Car%20 Hacking.pdf`.

Their hack was part of a larger set of research focused on identifying weaknesses in connected vehicles. That research has grown over time by the pair and has been accompanied by continued work at the **University of San Diego, California (UCSD)**. The exploitation of the Jeep relied on a number of factors that, in concert, allowed the researchers to achieve their goal of remotely controlling the vehicle.

Automotive vehicles implement **controller area network (CAN)** buses to allow individual components, known as **electronic control units** (**ECUs**), to communicate. Example ECUs include safety-critical components such as the braking systems, power steering, and so on. The CAN bus typically has no security applied to validate that messages transmitted on the bus originated from an authorized source or that the messages haven't been altered before reaching their destination(s). There is neither authentication nor integrity applied to messages. This may seem counterintuitive to a security practitioner; however, the timing of the messages on the bus is of critical importance to meet real-time control system requirements in which latency is unacceptable.

Data Exchange On The CAN Bus I, Self-Study Programme 238. Available at `http://www.volkspage.net/technik/ssp/ssp/SSP_238.pdf`.

The remote exploitation of the Jeep by Dr. Miller and Mr. Valasek took advantage of a number of flaws in the infrastructure as well as the individual subcomponents of the Jeep. To start, the cellular network that supported telematics for the vehicle allowed direct device-to-device communications from anywhere. This provided the researchers the ability to communicate directly with the vehicle, and even to scan for potential victims over the network.

Once communications were established to the Jeep, the researchers began to take advantage of other security flaws in the system. One example was a feature that was built into the radio unit. The feature was an execute function within the code that could be called to execute arbitrary data. From there, another security flaw provided the ability to move laterally through the system and actually transmit messages remotely onto the CAN buses (IHS and C). In the Jeep architecture, both CAN buses were connected to the radio unit, which communicated through a chip that allowed its firmware to be updated with no cryptographic protections (for example, digital signature). This final flaw and the resulting compromise illustrate that small issues within many systems sometimes add up to big problems.

Attacks

This section outlines a few typical attack categories against enterprise IoT components.

Wireless reconnaissance and mapping

The majority of IoT devices on the market utilize wireless communication protocols such as ZigBee, ZWave, Bluetooth-LE, WiFi802.11, and others. Similar to the war dialing days of old where hackers scanned through telephone switching networks to identify electronic modems, today, researchers are successfully demonstrating scanning attacks against IoT devices. One example is the Texas-based company Praetorian, which in Austin, TX, has used a low-flying drone outfitted with a custom ZigBee protocol scanner to identify thousands of ZigBee-enabled IoT device beacon requests. Just as network scanning using tools such as Nmap is commonly utilized by hackers to gather intelligence about hosts, subnets, ports, and protocols in networks, similar paradigms are being used against IoT devices—things that may open your garage door, lock your front door, turn lights on and off, and so on. Wireless reconnaissance will often precede full-scale device attacks (`http://fortune.com/2015/08/05/researchers-drone-discover-connected-devices-austin/`).

Security protocol attacks

Many security protocols can sustain attacks against vulnerabilities introduced either in the protocol design (specification), implementation and even configuration stages (in which different, viable protocol options are set). As an example, researchers found while testing a ZigBee-based consumer IoT implementation that the protocol was designed for easy setup and usage but lacked configuration possibilities for security and performed vulnerable device pairing procedures. These procedures allow external parties to sniff the exchanged network key during the ZigBee pairing transaction and gain control of the ZigBee device. Understanding the limitations of a chosen protocol is absolutely critical to determining what additional layered security controls must be put in place to keep the system secure (`https://www.blackhat.com/docs/us-15/materials/us-15-Zillner-ZigBee-Exploited-The-Good-The-Bad-And-The-Ugly-wp.pdf`).

Physical security attacks

Physical security is a topic frequently overlooked by IoT vendors that are only familiar with designing equipment, appliances, and other tools historically not subject to exploitation. Physical security attacks include those in which the attacker(s) physically penetrate the enclosure of a host, embedded device, or other type of IoT computing platform to gain access to its processor, memory devices, and other sensitive components. Once accessed over an exposed interface (for example, JTAG), the attacker can readily access memory, sensitive key material, passwords, configuration data, and a variety of other sensitive parameters. Many of today's security appliances now include extensive protections against physical security attacks. Various tamper evidence controls, tamper response mechanisms (for example, automatic wiping of memory), and other techniques exist to protect devices from physical penetration. Smart card chips, hardware security modules (HSM), and many other types of cryptographic module employ such protections to protect cryptographic variables—hence device identity and data—from compromise.

Application security attacks

IoT devices and connections can be exploited through attacks against application endpoints. Application endpoints include web servers as well as mobile device applications (for example, iPhone, Android) that have a role in controlling the device. Application code running on the device itself can also be directly targeted. Application fuzzing can find ways of compromising the application host and taking control of its processes. In addition, reverse engineering and other notable attacks can uncover sad but still common implementation vulnerabilities such as hardcoded keys, passwords, and other strings in the application binary. These parameters can be useful in various exploits.

Lessons learned and systematic approaches

IoT systems can be highly complex implementations that encompass many technology layers. Each layer has the potential to introduce new vulnerabilities into the overall IoT system. Our discussions related to potential airline attacks as well as real-world automobile attacks provide glimpses into understanding how overcoming the vulnerabilities of each component within a system is critical in combating highly motivated attackers from reaching their goals.

This becomes even more concerning as the IoT intersects safety and security engineering in the physical and electronic worlds. Described earlier, collaboration between the security engineering discipline and other engineering disciplines is needed now, to allow system designers to build security into the foundations of their products and guard against attacks that focus specifically on removing, dismantling, or reducing the effectiveness of safety controls in IoT CPS.

An interesting point related to the IoT is the need to be critical of third-party components or interfaces that may be added at a later time to an IoT deployment. Examples of this persist in the automotive industry, such as after-market devices that plug into vehicle ODB-II ports. Research has shown that at least one of these devices can be used to take control of the vehicle under certain circumstances. Security architects must understand that the security of the system as a whole is only as strong as the weakest link in the chain, and understand when the potential is there for a user to introduce new components that make the attack surface much larger than originally intended.

The security community has also collectively learned that many developers are fundamentally not familiar with engineering security into systems. This is primarily true because of the general lack of security training and awareness in the software engineering world. There are also cultural barriers between software developers, security, and other types of engineers. Whether discussing **Supervisory Control and Data Acquisition (SCADA)** systems, connected vehicles, or smart refrigerators, product engineers have historically not had to worry about bad actors gaining remote access to the target. This is no longer true.

The key take-away from this discussion is the need to systematically evaluate the security posture of an IoT implementation and its deployment. This means it is equally important for OEM/ODM vendors developing specific IoT devices as it is for the enterprise architect integrating an IoT system on the fly.

Threat modeling provides us a methodical approach to performing a security evaluation of a system or system design. We next demonstrate the tailored development and use of a threat model. Threat modeling helps develop a thorough understanding of the actors, entry points, and assets within a system. It also provides a detailed view of the threats to which the system is exposed. Note that threat modeling and attack/fault tree modeling go hand in hand. The latter should be performed in the context of an overarching threat modeling approach.

Threat modeling an IoT system

A valuable reference for threat modeling can be found in Adam Shostack's book *Threat Modeling: Designing for Security.*

Source: Shostack, A. (2014), Threat Modeling: Designing for Security. Indianapolis, IN; Wiley

Microsoft also defines a well-thought-out threat modeling approach using multiple steps to determine the severity of threats introduced by a new system. Note that threat modeling is the larger exercise of identifying threats and threat sources; attack modeling, described earlier, is attacker-focused and designed to show the nuances of how vulnerabilities may be exploited. The threat modeling process that we will follow in this example is illustrated in the following diagram:

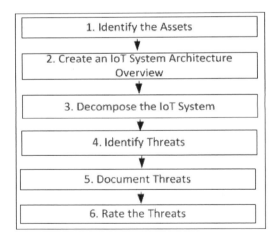

To illustrate the threat modeling process, we will evaluate threats to a *smart parking system*. A smart parking system is a useful IoT reference system because it involves deploying IoT elements into a high-threat environment (some individuals would cheat a parking payment system if they could, and laugh all the way home). The system contains multiple endpoints that capture and feed data to a backend infrastructure for processing. The system provides data analytics to provide trend analysis for decision makers, correlation of sensor data to identify parking violators in real time, and exposes an API to smartphone applications that support customer features such as real-time parking spot status and payments. Many IoT systems are architected with similar components and interfaces.

In this example, our smart parking system is differentiated from a real-life smart parking solution. Our example system provides a richer set of functionalities for illustrative purposes:

- **Consumer-facing service**: This allows customers to determine vacancy status and pricing for nearby parking spots

- **Payment flexibility**: The ability to accept multiple forms of payment, including credit cards, cash/coins, and mobile payment services (for example, Apple Pay, Google Wallet)

- **Entitlement enforcement**: The ability to track the allocated time purchased for a spot, determine when the entitlement has expired, sense when a vehicle has overstayed the purchased period, and communicate the violation to parking enforcement

- **Trend analysis**: The ability to collect and analyze historical parking data and provide trend reports to parking managers

- **Demand-response pricing**: The ability to change pricing depending on the demand for each space

Source: `https://www.cisco.com/web/strategy/docs/parking_aag_final.pdf`

Given that the system is designed to collect payment from consumers, alert enforcement officials when non-payment has occurred, and provide appropriate pricing based on the current demand for parking, the appropriate security goals for the system could be stated as follows:

- Maintain integrity of all data collected within the system

- Maintain confidentiality of sensitive data within the system

- Maintain the availability of the system as a whole and each of its individual components

Within the smart parking system, sensitive data can be defined as payment data as well as data that can leak privacy information. Examples include video recordings that capture license plate information.

Step 1 – identify the assets

Documentation of the assets within the system provides an understanding of what must be protected. Assets are items that are of interest to an attacker. For the smart parking solution, we can see typical assets described in in the following table. Note that for space-saving purposes we have simplified the asset list somewhat:

ID	Asset	Description
1	Sensor data	Sensor data is telemetry that signals whether a parking spot is filled or empty. Sensor data is generated by each sensor, which is placed where convenient within a parking structure. Sensor data is transmitted via ZigBee protocol to the sensor gateway. Data is merged with other sensor data and transmitted via Wi-Fi to a router that is connected to the cloud. Sensor data is then processed by an application and also sent to a database for raw storage.
2	Video streams	Video streams are captured by IP camera and data is transmitted to a wireless router.
3	Payment data	Payment data is transmitted from a smartphone or kiosk to a payment processing system. Payment data is typically tokenized during transmission.
3	Lot sensors	Vehicle sensors are placed in-ground or overhead to determine when a spot is vacant or filled. Sensors communicate via ZigBee with the sensor gateway.
4	Sensor gateway	Aggregate data from all sensors in a geographic area using ZigBee. Gateways communicate using Wi-Fi with backend processing systems.

ID	Asset	Description
5	IP camera	Records video of spots to identify abusers of the system. Data sent over Wi-Fi network to backend processing systems.
6	Parking application	Processes data received from sensors and provides parking and rate information to customers through smartphone app and kiosks.
7	Analytics system	Collects data directly from cameras and sensor gateways.
9	Kiosk	Exposed to the environment and communicates with parking sensors and sensor gateways.
10	Infrastructure communications equipment	Provides communication access across the system and interfaces with all aspects of the system.

Step 2 – create a system/architecture overview

This step provides a solid foundation for understanding not only the expected functionality of the IoT system, but also how an attacker could misuse the system. There are three sub-steps to this part of the threat modeling process:

1. Start with documenting expected functionality.
2. Create an architectural diagram that details the new IoT system. During this process, trust boundaries in the architecture should be established. Trust boundaries should elucidate the trust between actors, and their directionality.
3. Identify technologies used within the IoT system.

Documentation of system functionality is best accomplished by creating a set of use cases such as those that follow:

Use case 1: Customer pays for time in parking spot	
Pre-conditions	Customer has installed parking application onto smartphone. Payment information has been made available for transactions using parking application.
Use case	Customer opens parking application on smartphone. Smartphone communicates with and collects data from parking application, and provides real-time location and pricing for nearby vacant spots. Customer drives to spot. Customer uses smartphone application to pay for spot.
Post-conditions	Customer has paid to park car for a set amount of time.
Use case 2: Parking enforcement officer is alerted to non-payment incident	
Pre-conditions	The time allocated to a parking transaction has expired and the car is still in the parking spot.
Use case	Parking application (backend) records parking session start time. IP video cameras capture video of vehicle in parking spot. Parking application correlates video of car in spot with start time and duration for parking transaction. System flags for video confirmation once transaction duration has expired. IP video cameras provide evidence that vehicle is still parked. Parking application transmits an alert to enforcement application. Enforcement officer receives SMS alert and proceeds in person to ticket the vehicle.
Post-conditions	Parking enforcement officer has ticketed the vehicle.

An architectural diagram of the system details the components of the system, their interactions, and the protocols employed in their interactions. The following figure is an architectural diagram of our example *smart parking solution:*.

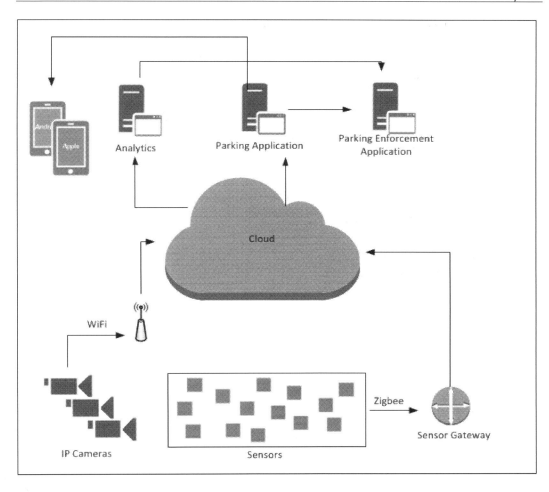

Once the logical architecture view is complete, it is important to identify and examine the specific technologies that will comprise the IoT system. This includes understanding and documenting lower-level details regarding the endpoint devices, such as the processor types and operating systems.

The endpoint details provide the information needed to understand the specific types of potential vulnerabilities that may eventually be exposed and define processes for patch management and firmware updates. Understanding and documenting the protocols that are used by each IoT device will also allow for updates to the architecture, especially if gaps are found in the cryptographic controls applied to the data transmitted throughout the system and the organization:

Technology/Platform	Details
Communication Protocol: ZigBee	Mid-range RF protocol to handle communications between sensors and sensor gateways.
Communication Protocol: 802.11 Wi-Fi	RF protocol supporting communication between IP-enabled cameras and wireless (Wi-Fi) router.
ZigBee smart parking sensor	Supports transmission ranges of 100 m; 2.4 GHz ZigBee transponder; ARM Cortex M0; 3-year battery life; supports magnetic and optical detection sensors.
Wireless sensor gateway	2.4 GHz; 100 m range; physical interfaces include: RS-232, USB, Ethernet; ZigBee communications; capable of supporting up to 500 concurrent sensor nodes.
Wireless (Wi-Fi) router	2.4 GHz Wi-Fi; 100 m+ range outdoor

Step 3 – decompose the IoT system

At this stage, the focus is on understanding the lifecycle of data as it flows through the system. This understanding allows us to identify vulnerable or weak points that must be addressed within the security architecture.

To start, one must identify and document the entry points for data within the system. These points are typically sensors, gateways, or control and management computing resources.

Next, it is important to trace the flow of data from the entry points and document the various components that interact with that data throughout the system. Identify high-profile targets for attackers (these can be intermediate or top-level nodes of an attack tree) — these may be points within the system that aggregate or store data, or they may be high-value sensors that require significant protection to maintain the overall integrity of the system. At the end of this activity, a detailed understanding of the IoT system's attack surface (in terms of data sensitivity and system movements) emerges:

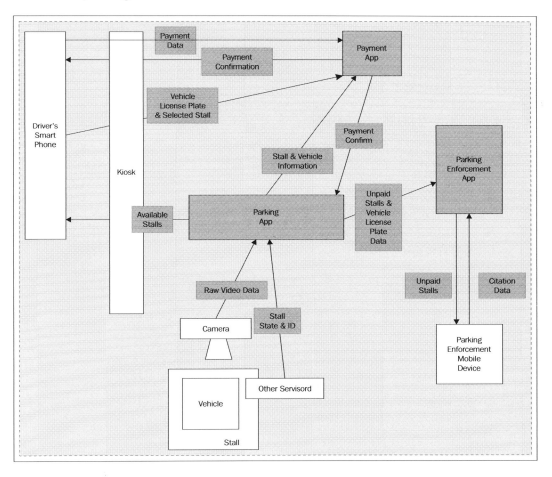

Once data flows have been thoroughly examined, you can begin to catalogue the various physical entry points into the system and the intermediate and internal gateways through which data flows. Also identify trust boundaries. The entry points and trust boundaries have an enormous security bearing as you identify overall threats associated with the system:

Entry points		
ID	Entry point	Description
1	Parking management application	The parking management application provides a web service that accepts incoming REST-based requests over the exposed API. A web application firewall sits in front of this service to filter unauthorized traffic.
2	Smartphone application	Connection is made through an API to the parking management application. Anyone who has downloaded the smartphone application can gain access to the system. The smartphone application is custom-developed and goes through security verification testing. A TLS connection is established between the application and the parking management system.
3	Kiosk	A self-contained kiosk on the lot property. This connects via API to the parking management application. Anyone who physically visits the kiosk gains access to the system.
4	Sensor gateway administrative account	Technicians gain access to the sensor gateway administrative account through remote connectivity over the Wi-Fi network (via SSH). Physical access is also possible via direct serial connection.
5	IP cameras	Technicians gain access to root account on IP cameras remotely over the IP network (via SSH). Ideally, the SSH connection is certificate-based (PEM files); passwords can also be used (though are more susceptible to the common password management deficiencies, dictionary attacks, and so on).
6	Enforcement application	Enforcement officers gain access to enforcement application data through SMS alerts sent from the enforcement application to registered devices. Leverage services such as Google Cloud Messaging (GCM).

Step 4 – identify threats

Within the IoT, there is a clear blending of the physical and electronic worlds. This results in relatively simplistic physical attacks that can be used to thwart a system's functionality. As an example, did the designers of the system include any integrity protections on the position of the cameras that provide data for parking enforcement correlation?

The amount of human involvement in the system also plays a significant factor in the types of attacks that could be used against a system. For example, if human parking enforcement officers aren't involved (that is, the system automatically issues citations for staying over the time limit), then the ability of the system that reads the license plates would have to be thoroughly examined. Could someone spoof a vehicle by simply swapping license plates, or deny the system the ability to read the plate by putting an obscuring layer on top of them?

The popular STRIDE model can be applied to IoT system deployments. Use well-known vulnerability repositories to better understand the environment, such as MITRE's common vulnerabilities and exposures database. Uncovering the unique threats to any particular IoT instantiation will be guided by these threat types (note that is also a good time to utilize attack/fault tree analysis for some implementations and deployments):

Threat type	IoT analysis
Spoofing identity	Examine the system for threats related to the spoofing of machine identity and the ability for an attacker to exploit automated trust relationships between devices.
	Carefully examine the authentication protocols used to set up secure communications between IoT devices as well as other devices and applications.
	Examine the processes for provisioning identities and credentials to each IoT device; ensure that there are proper procedural controls in place to prevent introduction of rogue devices into the system or to leak credentials to attackers.

Threat type	IoT analysis
Tampering with data	Examine data paths across the entire IoT system; identify targetable points in the system where tampering of sensitive data can take place: these will include points of data collection, processing, transport, and storage.
	Carefully examine integrity-protection mechanisms and configurations to ensure that data tampering is effectively dealt with.
	While data is in secure transit (for example, by SSL/TLS), is there a man-in-the-middle attack scenario possible? The use of certificate-pinning techniques can help mitigate these threats.
Repudiation	Examine the IoT system for nodes that provide critical data.
	These nodes are likely sets of sensors that provide various data for analysis. It is important to be able to trace back data to a source and ensure that it was indeed the expected source that provided that data.
	Examine the IoT system for weaknesses that might allow an attacker to inject a rogue node designed to feed bad data. Rogue data injection may be an attempt to confuse upstream processes or take the system out of an operational state.
	Ensure that attackers are not able to abuse the intended functionality of IoT systems (for example, illegal operations are disabled or not allowed).
	State changes and time variations (for example, disrupting message sequencing) should be taken into account.
Information disclosure	Examine data paths across the entire IoT system, including the backend processing systems.
	Ensure that any device that processes sensitive information has been identified and that proper encryption controls have been implemented to guard against disclosure of that information.
	Identify data storage nodes within the IoT system and ensure that data-at-rest encryption controls have been applied.
	Examine the IoT system for instances where IoT devices are vulnerable to being physically stolen and ensure that proper controls, such as key zeroization, have been considered.

Threat type	IoT analysis
Denial of service	Perform an activity that maps each IoT system to business goals, in an effort to ensure that appropriate **Continuity of Operations (COOP)** planning has occurred.
	Examine the throughput provided for each node in the system and ensure that it is sufficient to withstand relevant **denial of service (DoS)** attacks.
	Examine the messaging infrastructure (for example, data buses), data structures, improper use of variables and APIs used within applicable IoT components and determine if there are vulnerabilities that would allow a rogue node to drown out the transmissions of a legitimate node.
Privileged elevation	Examine the administration capabilities provided by the various IoT devices that make up an IoT system. In some cases, there is only one level of authentication, which allows configuration of device details. In other cases, distinct administrator accounts may be available.
	Identify instances where there are weaknesses in the ability to segregate administrative functions from user-level functions within IoT nodes.
	Identify weaknesses in the authentication methods employed by IoT nodes in order to design appropriate authentication controls in the system.
Physical security bypass	Examine the physical protection mechanisms offered by each IoT device; plan mitigations where possible against any identified weaknesses. This is most important for IoT deployments that are in public or remote locations and may be unattended. Physical security controls such as tamper evidence (or signaling) or tamper response (active, automatic destruction of sensitive parameters on the device) may be necessary.
Social engineering	Train staff to guard against social engineering attempts; regularly monitor assets for suspicious behavior.
Supply chain issues	Understand the various technological components that comprise IoT devices and systems; keep track of vulnerabilities related to any of these technology layers.

The application of the STRIDE model with the additional components that support the IoT can be seen in the following table:

Smart parking threat matrix		
Type	**Example**	**Security Control**
Spoofing	Parking thief charges legitimate customer for parking time by accessing that customer's account.	Authentication
Tampering	Parking thief receives free parking through unauthorized access to backend smart parking application.	Authentication Integrity
Repudiation	Parking thief receives free parking by asserting that the system malfunctioned.	Non-repudiation Integrity
Information disclosure	Malicious actor accesses customer financial details through compromise of backend smart parking application.	Authentication Confidentiality
Denial of service	Malicious actor shuts down smart parking system through a DoS attack.	Availability
Elevation of privilege	Malicious actor disrupts smart parking operations by implanting rootkit on backend servers.	Authorization

Step 5 – document the threats

This step focuses on documenting the threats to the parking system:

Threat description #1	**Parking thief charges legitimate customer for parking time by accessing that customer's account.**
Threat target	Legitimate customer account credentials
Attack techniques	Social engineering; phishing; database compromises; MITM attacks (including those against cryptographic protocols)
Countermeasures	Require multi-factor authentication on accounts used to access payment information
Threat description #2	**Parking thief receives free parking through unauthorized access to backend smart parking application.**
Threat target	Parking application
Attack techniques	Application exploit; web server compromise

Countermeasures	Implement web application firewall fronting parking application web server; implement validation of inputs to application over API
Threat description #3	**Parking thief receives free parking by asserting that the system malfunctioned.**
Threat target	Parking attendant or administrator
Attack techniques	Social engineering
Countermeasures	Implement data integrity measures on all sensor and video data captured within the system

Step 6 – rate the threats

Evaluating the likelihood and impact of each threat above allows for selecting appropriate types and levels of control (and their related costs) to mitigate each. Threats with higher risk ratings may require larger amounts of investment to mitigate. Conventional threat-rating methodologies can be used at this step, including Microsoft's DREAD approach.

The DREAD model asks basic questions for each level of risk and then assigns a score (1 – 10) for each type of risk that emerges from a particular threat:

- **Damage**: The amount of damage incurred by a successful attack
- **Reproducibility**: What level of difficulty is involved in reproducing the attack?
- **Exploitability**: Can the attack be easily exploited by others?
- **Affected users**: What percentage of a user/stakeholder population would be affected given a successful attack?
- **Discoverability**: Can the attack be discovered easily by an attacker?

An example of a threat rating for our smart parking system is provided in the following table:

Threat risk ranking: Parking thief charges legitimate customer for parking time by accessing that customer's account		
Item	**Description**	**Item score**
Damage Potential	Damage is limited to a single customer account	3
Reproducibility	Attack is not highly reproducible unless mass compromise of customer database occurs	4
Exploitability	Exploitation of this threat can be done by unskilled persons	8
Affected users	Single user in most scenarios	2
Discoverability	This threat is highly discoverable as it can be accomplished using non-technical activities	9
	Overall score:	**5.2**

Security architects who are responsible for designing in the security controls for an IoT system should continue with this exercise until all threats have been rated. Once complete, the next step is to perform a comparison of each against the others based on each one's threat rating (overall score). This will help prioritize the mitigations within the security architecture.

Summary

This chapter explored IoT vulnerabilities, attacks, and countermeasures by illustrating how an organization can practically define, characterize, and model an IoT system's threat posture. With a thorough understanding of the security (and in some cases, safety) risks, appropriate security architectural development can commence such that appropriate mitigations are developed and deployed to systems and devices throughout the enterprise.

In the next chapter, we will discuss the phases of the IoT security lifecycle.

3
Security Engineering for IoT Development

Security engineering is a complex subject deserving of multiple volumes. *"Security engineering is a specialized field of engineering that focuses on the security aspects in the design of systems that need to be able to deal robustly with possible sources of disruption, ranging from natural disasters to malicious acts"* (`https://en.wikipedia.org/wiki/Security_engineering`).

In today's fast-paced tech industry, security engineering often takes a back seat to the rush to develop competitive market-driven features. That is frequently a costly sacrifice as it provides malicious hackers an opportunity-rich sandbox in which to develop exploits. In an ideal world and project, a methodical approach includes identification and evolution of a series of functional business requirements. These requirements are prototyped, tested, refined, and finalized into an architecture before being developed, tested and deployed. This is how things might happen in a perfect, error-free waterfall model. The world is not ideal, however, and IoT devices and systems will be rolled out by a variety of company types using a multitude of development practices.

Gartner estimates that by 2017, 50% of all IoT solutions will originate from start-up companies less than 3 years old. This imposes challenges as security is frequently an afterthought and minor area of focus for most start-up organizations. The **Cloud Security Alliance (CSA)** IoT WG performed a survey on IoT-based start-ups in 2015 and found that there was a lack of security emphasis and an overall gap in the strong, dedicated workforce of security professionals. Angel investors and venture capital firms may also impose barriers to a start-up's meaningful incorporation of security; security is frequently demoted to a "nice to have" status among an extensive list of features on the road to success. In this environment, start-up companies and even more traditional companies will frequently rely on the supposed security of their suppliers' hardware and software. This occurs regardless of whether the intended deployment target and environment are commensurate with the suppliers' stipulations (http://www.gartner.com/newsroom/id/2869521).

In this chapter, we will address the following topics as they relate to IoT security engineering:

- Selecting a secure development methodology for the IoT
- Designing security in from the start
- Understanding compliance considerations
- Planning for integration of the IoT into existing security systems
- Preparing security processes and agreements
- Selecting security products and services to support the IoT
- Selecting a secure development methodology

Building security in to design and development

In this section, we discuss the need to securely engineer IoT products and systems. This guidance is useful whether you are planning a single IoT product, or the integration and deployment of millions of IoT devices into an enterprise system. Either way, it is important to build security in from the start by focusing on methodically understanding threats, tracing security requirements through to completion, and ensuring that there is a strong focus on securing data.

It is easy to say that a product team or systems engineering team has to build security in from the start, but what does that actually mean? Well, that means that from the very beginning of a project, engineering teams have thought through how to enhance the security rigor of the project all the way through completion. This is something lacking in many of today's fast-paced agile development programs. There is an investment required to achieving this rigor, both in time and money, as teams consider the processes and tools to use to achieve their security goals. However, the upfront costs for these actions pale in comparison to the costs associated with seeing your product or organization on the top of news streams, battered in social media, or fined by a government regulator for gross negligence that resulted in a major compromise.

One of the fundamental tasks as you begin your development or integration effort is to select your development methodology and examine how to enhance that methodology into a more security-conscious one. This chapter outlines some considerations. There are also additional resources available, useful to both product and system teams. One example is the **Building Security In Maturity Model (BSIMM)** that lets you understand the security practices being implemented by peer organizations: `https://www.bsimm.com/`.

Security in agile developments

When selecting a development methodology, consider that security must be built in from the beginning of the process, to ensure that well-thought-out security, safety, and privacy requirements are elicited and made traceable throughout the development and update of an IoT device or system (by system, we mean a collection of IoT devices, applications, and services that are integrated to support a business function). There are templated approaches available that can be applied to any development effort. One example is the Microsoft **Security Development Lifecycle (SDL)**, which incorporates multiple phases, including training, requirements, design, implementation, verification, release, and response. The Microsoft SDL can be found at `https://www.microsoft.com/en-us/sdl/`.

Many IoT products and systems will be developed using agile methodologies, given the ability to quickly design/develop/field feature sets. The agile manifesto defines a number of principles, some of which present difficulties to the integration of security engineering approaches:

- Deliver working software frequently, from a few weeks to a few months, with a preference to the shorter timescale

- Working software is the primary measure of progress

Difficulties that must be addressed in an agile secure development lifecycle revolve around the short development timescales related to agile projects. There are often numerous security requirements that a product must satisfy. It is difficult to address these requirements in a short development cycle. Also, a focus on security decreases the velocity that can be applied to functional user stories in agile development.

Considering how to handle security requirements, it becomes clear that the same thought and attention must be given to it and other nonfunctional requirements such as reliability, performance, scalability, usability, portability, and availability.

Some argue that these nonfunctional requirements should be handled as constraints that are pulled into the definition of *done* and eventually met by each user story. However, the transformation of all security (and nonfunctional) requirements into constraints does not scale well when the development team must deal with dozens or hundreds of security requirements.

A few years back, Microsoft developed an approach to handling security requirements within agile developments (`https://www.microsoft.com/en-us/SDL/discover/sdlagile.aspx`). The process focuses heavily on the handling of security requirements and introduces concepts for categorizing the requirements in a manner that reduces the strain on the development team during each sprint. Microsoft's methodology introduces the concept of One Time, Every Sprint, and Bucket security requirements.

One Time requirements are applicable to the secure setup of a project and other requirements that must be met from the start, for example:

- Establishing secure coding guidelines that must be followed throughout the development
- Establishing an approved software list for third-party components/libraries

Every Sprint requirements are applicable to each sprint and hours are estimated for each requirement during sprint planning, for example:

- To help identify bugs, performing peer reviews on code prior to merging into the baseline
- Ensuring that code is run through static code analysis tools within the **continuous integration (CI)** environment

Bucket requirements are requirements that can be implemented and satisfied over the life of a project. Putting these requirements into buckets allows teams to choose to import them into sprint planning when it makes the most sense.

In addition to these requirement types, there are also functional security requirements that should be added to the backlog. An example of a functional security requirement for an IoT device may be to securely establish a TLS connection to the device's gateway. These requirements can be added to the product backlog and prioritized as needed by the product owner during grooming sessions.

Threat modeling approaches have been well documented and discussed in other publications, including *Chapter 2, Vulnerabilities, Attacks, and Countermeasures*, of this book. Once your initial threat modeling is completed, the resulting mitigations need to be analyzed to understand where they fit within the development or operations of the IoT system. To start, identify functional security requirements that must be integrated into the IoT product or service. You can turn these functional security requirements into user stories and add them to the product backlog. Examples of functional security requirements to be added to the product backlog include the following:

- As a user, I want to ensure that all access passwords on my IoT device or cloud service are strong (for example, complexity, length, composition)

- As a user, I want to be able to track IoT device authorized usage (for example, through entitlement tracking)

- As a user, I want to ensure that any data stored on my IoT device is encrypted

- As a user, I want to ensure that any data transmitted by my IoT device is encrypted

- As a user, I want to ensure that any key material stored on my IoT device is safeguarded from disclosure or other unauthorized access

- As a user, I want to ensure that any unnecessary software and services are disabled and removed from my IoT device

- As a user, I want to ensure that my IoT device only collects data that is meant to be collected

Other examples of security user stories can be found in the SAFECode document *Practical Security Stories and Security Tasks for Agile Development Environments* at `http://safecode.org/publication/SAFECode_Agile_Dev_Security0712.pdf`. An important item to note is that just as the product backlog will include operations-centric user stories, it should also include hardware-centric security user stories:

- As a security and QA engineer, I want to ensure that the UART interface is password protected

- As a security and QA engineer, I want to disable JTAG interfaces prior to product launch

- As a security and QA engineer, I want to implement tamper response into my IoT device casing

Some of these may be user stories or epics in the parlance of agile.

Focusing on the IoT device in operation

An interesting aspect of the IoT is the quick movement towards vendor *products-as-a-service* offerings—where customers pay for a certain set of entitlements on a regular basis (for example, as in the case of expensive medical imaging systems). This model is characterized by the leasing of IoT hardware to customers followed by tracking its use for billing purposes.

Other types of IoT devices are sold to consumers and then linked to the vendor's cloud infrastructure to manage their product for configuration changes as well as account modifications. Sometimes, such products are outsourced to a third-party ODM that manages the IoT infrastructure. The OEM then incorporates such operational expenses in the **master service agreement** (**MSA**) between the two companies. Additionally, many vendors will offer ancillary services that their IoT device offerings can interact with, even when implemented in a customer environment.

Given the reach into customer operational systems as well as the need to support robust and scalable backend infrastructures, leveraging strong development operations (DevOps) processes and technology is vital for operational IoT systems. As a simplistic definition, DevOps blends agile development practices such as Scrum or Kanban with a keen focus on operations.

A fundamental aspect of DevOps is the removal of silos between development and operations. As such, it is important to include operational security requirements (for example, user stories) in the product backlog as well. In order to do this, DevOps teams must do the following:

- Understand the potential deployment environments for the IoT device being developed and design the security capabilities of the IoT device to accommodate these environments.

- Evaluate the security of each component in the IoT ecosystem in addition to the deployment environment (for example, web servers, databases, and so on) to ensure that no security vulnerabilities are introduced at a micro or macro level.

The IoT introduces a shift away from traditional hardware device purchases toward sales of products-as-a-service. As such, vendors of IoT devices that plan to lease their products to customers should strongly consider the operational security aspects of their designs during development. This includes considerations such as the following:

- Compliance landscape for the operational environment(s)

- Methods for safeguarding the device given any physical exposures

- Ancillary systems required to support entitlement management in a secure manner

- Ancillary systems required to support device firmware updates in a secure manner

Secure design

Secure design of IoT devices and systems is only one component in the overarching IoT security lifecycle. The following diagram shows the design aspects of the lifecycle which will be discussed now. Other aspects of the lifecycle will be discussed in *Chapter 4, The IoT Security Lifecycle*.

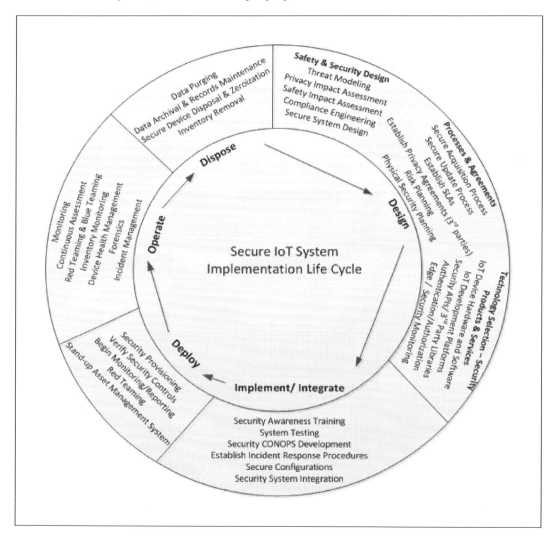

Safety and security design

We've already introduced the need for threat modeling within IoT device and system developments. Now we will expand on additional safety and securing engineering processes to incorporate into your development and integration efforts.

Threat modeling

The IoT security lifecycle is bound to the systems development process. Planning for secure operations of an IoT system should begin while the system is being designed, and as new components of the IoT system are being considered. We therefore consider threat modeling as a key component in any security lifecycle. This is especially true given the iterative nature of the lifecycle, since threat models should always be maintained and updated upon changes to the system design, operation, or exposure. *Chapter 2, Vulnerabilities, Attacks, and Countermeasures*, provided an in-depth review of the threat modeling process and even examined attack trees and other artifacts to accompany it. Always assign someone in the security organization with the responsibility of maintaining the threat model on at least a quarterly basis and through key changes such as architectural modification as well as introduction of new services, configurations, or product and supplier changes and upgrades.

Privacy impact assessment

Each IoT system should undergo a **privacy impact assessment (PIA)** during the design stage. This will provide the information needed to determine mitigations that must be included in the system design, as well as any third-party agreements or **service level agreement (SLA)** details needed with technology providers to protect information. Typically, a PIA will inform the design process in the following ways if it is found that an IoT system collects, processes, or stores **privacy protected information (PPI)**:

- Provisioning of the device may require more administrative approvals
- A review by internal audit or compliance should be conducted to determine if it is viable to have PPI data on IoT devices
- Data stored on the device should be encrypted using sufficiently strong cryptographic algorithms
- Data transmitted from/to the device should be encrypted using sufficiently strong cryptographic algorithms
- Access to the device, both physical and logical, should be restricted to authorized personnel
- End users should be made aware of the use, transfer, and disposal of PPI and provide positive consent

Understanding privacy impacts requires a degree of critical thinking when applied to the IoT. There are IoT privacy concerns that are not always evident. For example, in *Security Analysis of Wearable Fitness Devices* (`https://courses.csail.mit.edu/6.857/2014/files/17-cyrbritt-webbhorn-specter-dmiao-hacking-fitbit.pdf`), researchers found that it is possible to track a Fitbit wearer based on the Bluetooth **Media Access Control (MAC)** address. It is important to understand all of the information that is being collected by an IoT device, and any manner that the device can do the following:

- Be tracked
- Show patterns of activities
- Be linked to an individual identity or even an individual's possession

Note that simply performing a PIA is not sufficient. It is critical to link the outcome from the PIA to your system requirements baseline and track those requirements to closure as the IoT system is developed and fielded. These requirements will also dictate the establishment of SLAs with IoT and infrastructure providers, as well as the creation of privacy agreements with third parties that may handle data generated by the IoT system.

Safety impact assessment

One of the principal differentiators of the IoT with conventional IT security is the need to perform safety impact assessments. Given the cyber-physical characteristics of many IoT devices, some types of device vulnerabilities can be safety-of-life critical. For example, if someone were to compromise a pacemaker via an exposed, low-power wireless interface, obvious malicious acts could be performed. Likewise, if a modern automobile's **electronic control units (ECUs)** are compromised over its CAN Bus OBD2 interface, the new access may allow an attacker to send malicious messages over the CAN bus to safety-critical ECUs such as those that perform the braking function of the car. A safety impact assessment should be performed for any IoT deployment. In the medical space, further health impact assessments should also be performed.

In general, the following items needs to be addressed and answered in a safety impact assessment:

- Given the intended usage of the device, is there anything harmful that could happen if the device stopped working altogether (for example, denial of service)?
- If the device by itself is not safety critical, are there any other devices or services that are safety critical and depend on it?

- How could potential harm (from device failure) be minimized or avoided?

- What issues might others consider safety-related or harmful?

- Are there any other similar or related deployments that have been considered safety relevant or have done harm?

A safety impact assessment not only examines outright stoppage of device or system operation, but also various malfunctions or misbehaviors resulting from a device's vulnerabilities and possible compromises. For example, could an unattended smart thermostat malfunction or be maliciously operated such that upper and lower temperature thresholds are violated? Without an automatic, well-protected, and resilient temperature cutoff feature, serious safety conditions could result.

Another example would be network-connected **roadside equipment** (**RSE**) in the connected vehicle ecosystem. Given the connectivity of a RSE device to traffic signal controllers, backend infrastructure, connected vehicles and other systems, what could various levels of RSE compromise result in from a safety perspective? What type of service could a compromised RSE invoke locally at the roadside? Could it actually cause a safety-of-life event, for example, read out an improper speed warning so that drivers are ill prepared for an upcoming traffic condition? Or, could it invoke a non-safety-related service in the traffic signal controller that merely interrupts and degrades traffic flow around the signalized intersection?

The answers of the previous questions should feed back into the broader risk management discussion when risk mitigations are being developed. Technical and policy mitigations need to simultaneously resolve to acceptable levels the risks to both safety and security.

Compliance

Compliance represents the security and policy requirements that are inherited and applicable to one's IoT deployment. From a security lifecycle perspective, compliance is wholly dependent on the specific industry regulatory environment and whether it is commercial or government. For example, devices and systems playing a role in credit and debit card financial transactions must adhere to the **payment card industry** (**PCI**) series of standards for point-of-sale devices as well as core infrastructure. Military systems typically require DITSCAP and DIACAP types of **certification and accreditation** (**C&A**). Postal devices that perform financial transactions in the form of package and envelope postal metering must adhere to the postal authority's standards for such devices. Postal meters essentially print money in the form of postage to pay for the shipping of an item.

Unfortunately, the IoT can make compliance more difficult since there is a need to understand new and complex data interactions between different parties and identify where all of the data from IoT devices are transmitted (for example, metadata regarding a device that is sent to a manufacturer but may be used to gather information about end users). This is much easier if the IoT data is confined to a single industry or use case; however, given the growing trend of data aggregation and analysis, it is likely that privacy laws and rules will assert some of the most far-reaching compliance requirements on the IoT. The broader the IoT deployment in terms of connectivity and data sharing, the greater the probability of tripping on an unexpected compliance or legal issue.

When determining what compliance standards apply when designing an IoT service offering, it is critical to examine all of the physical and logical points of connection involved in the IoT deployment. Network connections, data flows, data sources, sinks, and organizational boundaries must be fully understood as these may require certain trade-offs to be made in terms of information and connections made versus compliance regimens that may apply. For example, with consumer-wearable technology, it may not be feasible to share heart rate, blood pressure, and other health metrics from such a device with doctors, offices, and hospitals. Why? Because in the US, such data will typically require a variety of HIPAA compliance measures to be in place. In addition, such devices used for actual medicine are typically subject to oversight and compliance from the **Food and Drug Administration** (FDA). If there is sufficient business value in connecting a wearable device to a hospital system, then the device vendor may well want to explore the costs of invoking the new compliance regimen and determine if they pay off in the long run in terms of market penetration, profits, and so on. The following is a non-exhaustive list of various industry-specific compliance regimens:

- **PCI (Payment Card Industry)**: A consortium of Visa, MasterCard, American Express, Discover Financial Services, and JCB International that directs the PCI Security Standards Council to develop and maintain financial transaction security standards such as the PCI **Data Security Standards (DSS)** and **PIN Transaction Services (PTS)**.

- **NERC (North American Electric Reliability Corporation)**: This mandates the **Critical Infrastructure Protection (CIP)** standards for the protection of critical electrical generation and distribution systems. CIP standards address identification of critical assets, security management, perimeter protection, physical security, incident reporting and response, and system recovery.

- **USPS (US Postal Service)**: This standard mandates security requirements and controls for postal security devices. Postal security devices secure the fund transfers associated with printing meter stamps and ensure the integrity of the association between those funds and printed stamps.

- **SAE (Society of Automotive Engineers)**: This imposes a variety of safety and security standards for the automotive industry.

- **NIST (National Institutes for Standards and Technology)**: NIST's standards are far-reaching, and many industries point to them to satisfy specific requirements. NIST's standards consist of a variety of **Special Publications (SP)**, the **Federal Information Protection Standards (FIPS)**, and more recently, the NIST **Risk Management Framework (RMF)**. NIST standards are carefully cross-referenced to ensure scope and dependency is well established. For example, numerous NIST standards (as well as industry-specific ones) reference and mandate the FIPS 140-2 standard to protect cryptographic devices.

- **HIPAA**: The US Department of Health and Human Services oversees HIPAA and defines the HIPAA Security Rule as follows: The HIPAA Security Rule establishes national standards to protect individuals' electronic personal health information that is created, received, used, or maintained by a covered entity. The Security Rule requires appropriate administrative, physical, and technical safeguards to ensure the confidentiality, integrity, and security of electronic protected health information.

Given the multitude of legacy and evolving compliance standards, it is important for one's business use case to explore early what standards may apply, and to which bounded organizational elements and systems. It is vitally important to integrate the compliance needs into the IoT system design and development, product selection, and data selection and sharing processes. In addition, many of the potential standards require regulatory involvement to certify or accredit a system, whereas some allow self-certification. The costs and timelines associated with these activities can be high and impose a significant barrier to entry for an IoT deployment.

Organizations that want to cost-effectively identify necessary security controls for their IoT implementations can also turn to the popular 20 Critical Controls, which map to many compliance standards. The 20 Critical Controls are maintained by the **Center for Internet Security (CIS)**; one of the authors of this book is a member of the CIS 20 Critical Controls editorial panel and helped author a tailored IoT version of the Critical Controls as an appendix to Version 6. Look for the appendix at the CIS website (`www.cisecurity.org`).

Monitoring for compliance

Compliance monitoring is a challenging aspect of the IoT, given the need to maintain the security state of a significant number of devices and device types within an organization. Although there are a limited set of solutions available to address this challenge today, there are some vendors that are building up capabilities that can be used to begin meeting this challenge.

For example, the security vendor Pwnie Express provides compliance monitoring and vulnerability scanning capabilities for the IoT. The Pwnie Express Pwn Pulse system provides the ability to detect and report on unauthorized, vulnerable, and suspicious devices. This software provides security engineers with the ability to validate security policies, configurations, and controls through the use of standard penetration testing tools. Results of scans can be compared against regulatory compliance requirements (`http://www.406ventures.com/news/articles/1677-pwnie_express_unveils_industrys_first_internet_of_everything_threat_detection_system`).

Security system integration

IoT secure system design addresses how implementers ensure that various IoT devices are able to be integrated into a larger security-aware enterprise. This implies that devices can securely provision identities, credentials, undergo testing, monitoring, audit, and be securely upgraded. Obviously, many limited IoT devices will only be provisioned a subset of these capabilities.

Secure Bootstrapping	Accounts and Credentials
Initial Identity Provisioning Default security parameters Initial Enterprise Awareness	PKI Certificates Certificate Status and Lifetime Certificate Monitoring Account and ID Management
Patching and Updates	**Audit and Monitoring**
HW and SW Inventory Secure Downloads Operational Testing Configuration Updates Activation	SIEM integration Behavioral Analysis Compliance Monitoring Audit Maintenance

Artifacts from threat modeling, PIA, SIA, and compliance analysis should be used as inputs into an overarching IoT security system design. For example, during bootstrap (initial provisioning and connection) of an IoT device into a larger enterprise or home network, there may be security-critical processes related to treatment and handling of default passwords, technical controls to enforce the creation of new passwords, one-time symmetric keys, and so on.

The IoT security system should include new technologies that are needed to support the security posture of the IoT system, as well as describe the integration hooks into existing security infrastructure. To achieve this, a recommended approach to achieving IoT security system design is to first segregate security functionality and controls based on directionality of threat. For example, some threats may target the IoT device, in which case the enterprise needs to carefully monitor the device's status and activity (that is, through an SIEM system). In other cases, the device may operate in an insecure physical or network location, imposing a larger attack surface on the enterprise. In this case, it may be necessary to put special network monitoring taps at the IoT's gateway to validate messages, message formats, message authenticity, and so on. Lastly, though it's easy to forget this issue, the enterprise may expose certain threats to IoT devices. For example, a compromised or spoofed command and control server may attempt to reconfigure an IoT device into an insecure or unsafe configuration. The device needs to be self-aware of what constitutes default safety and default security.

Incorporation into the security enterprise, based on the previous figure, incorporates the following topics: secure bootstrap, accounts and credentials, patching and updates, and audit and monitoring.

Secure bootstrap concerns the processes associated with initial provisioning of passwords, credentials, network information, and other parameters to the devices and the enterprise systems (which need to be aware of the devices). When new devices are incorporated into a network, it is vital that they be distinguished as being legitimate versus rogue or hostile devices. Thus, bootstrapping is a security process that is frequently overlooked in importance. Secure bootstrapping consists of the security processes necessary to ensure that a new (or reintroduced) device undergoes the following:

- Receives a secure configuration that has been well vetted according to a security policy
- Receives knowledge of its network, subnet, default gateway, and so on, including ports and acceptable protocols

- Receives knowledge of the network and backend system and server identities—this will frequently be in the form of installing default cryptographic credentials (trust anchors and trust paths)

- Registers—either directly or indirectly—its identity to the network and/or the backend systems to which it connects

Serious security issues can ensue from an insecure bootstrap process that does not conform to well-engineered security patterns. For example, many devices will be, by default, in a highly insecure state after manufacture and even during shipping. In these cases, secure bootstrap processes must frequently be performed in secure facilities or rooms by personnel who have been well vetted. In the case of home and other consumer IoT devices, the secure bootstrap processes may be performed by the homeowner, for example, but should be well described and difficult to bypass or perform incorrectly.

Accounts and credentials

Accounts and credentials consider the IoT device's identity and identity management in the larger enterprise. Part of the bootstrap process frequently addresses the initial provisioning of certificates or updated passwords; however, once provisioned, the device and backend systems must maintain the identity and update credentials on a periodic basis. For example, if the device hosts a TLS server or performs TLS client certificate authentication to other systems, it will likely have X.509 credentials with which it cryptographically signs TLS negotiation handshake messages. These X.509 certificates should have an expiration date, and this date should be closely tracked so that it does not expire and the device loses its identity. Broader identity management must also be performed as part of maintaining accounts and credentials, and these processes should be integrated with hardware and software inventory management systems (frequently maintained in an SIEM database).

Patching and updates

Patching and updates concern how software and firmware binaries are provisioned to IoT devices. Most legacy and even some new systems require direct connections (for example, USB, console, JTAG, Ethernet, or others) to locally and manually update a device to new versions. Given the migration to cloud-based monitoring and management, many newer devices have the capability to update or patch software over the network from the manufacturer or dedicated device/system manager. Severe vulnerabilities are possible in software update and patching workflows; therefore, in the device engineering process, it is crucial that the following be supported in any *over the air* patching capability:

- End-to-end software/firmware integrity and authentication from the build system through any staged transit to the device (in many cases, confidentiality may also be needed)

- The software/update process should only be performed via a special access function that is only available to a highly privileged role or identity (that is, administrator), or it should be performed by the device (pull) based on its authenticated queries to a secure backend software update system

Additional information on secure software provisioning is provided in the *Processes and agreements* section, later in this chapter.

Audit and monitoring

Audit and monitoring concerns the enterprise security systems and their ability to capture and analyze for anomalies. This includes both host and network anomalies pertinent to a given IoT device. It is critical that IoT devices be allocated based on the threat environment to specifically established security zones and that these zones be monitored at their gateways by integrated firewall and SIEM systems. Many IoT devices should be auditable if they are managed by an enterprise responsible for their operation. If they are home-based appliances/devices, they should be given the ability to provide audit and event data to a manufacturer web service to which the device owner is given access. It is imperative, however, that privacy data is not divulged over the audit interface without explicit permission and agreement by the device owner or user. This type of information should be discovered and evaluated during a privacy impact assessment.

Processes and agreements

Security is not simply about finding technology solutions. Putting the right processes and procedures in place is required to establish a strong security foundation.

Secure acquisition process

For an organization that is procuring many IoT devices on a regular basis, it is important that the acquisition process itself is not used as an attack vector into the enterprise. Lay out rules for acquiring new IoT devices from trusted vendors to ensure that rogue devices with malicious software aren't procured and installed within the network.

Secure update process

Design a secure update process that can be used to maintain approved patches, software, and firmware versions for an IoT system. This requires an understanding of the update processes of each vendor supporting your IoT device inventory. IoT devices typically require the loading of an image onto the device, which includes the underlying operating system (if present), and any application code. Other devices may segregate these update functions. It is important to establish a process that keeps all layers of the IoT device technology stack up to date.

Although keeping IoT devices updated is a critical aspect of guarding against the exploit of software vulnerabilities, it is also important to guard against the insertion of malicious software/firmware images during the update process. This typically requires that a staging solution be created, where cryptographic signatures can be validated prior to passing updates to the devices themselves.

Operational testing should also be considered as part of the update strategy. Creating an IoT test network will aid in making sure that the introduction of updated software does not result in negative functional behavior. Include the operational testing of updates and patches in the approval process prior to allowing code to be updated on an IoT device.

Establish SLAs

Mentioned earlier, IoT vendors will often lease smart hardware to organizations, a feature that allows the setting up of entitlements. Some entitlements may comprise thresholds, for example, a set number of transactions that can occur during a pre-defined time period. As the IoT continues to gain traction in various industries, enterprises will be faced with deciding whether to lease or buy smart products. It is important that these enterprises include security objectives in the lease SLAs to help keep the network secure.

SLAs with IoT device vendors should be written to ensure that the devices introduce minimal additional risk into the enterprise. Examples of IoT lease SLAs can include the following:

- The time to patch an IoT device after a new critical update is available
- The time to respond to an incident involving the device
- IoT device availability
- How the vendor handles privacy of data collected by the IoT device
- Compliance targets—ensuring that the device maintains compliance with applicable regulations
- Incident response functions and collaboration agreements
- How the vendor handles confidentiality of the data collected by the device

Additional SLAs that should be considered involve the cloud-based infrastructures that will support the IoT deployments. Good guides for cloud SLAs can be found by visiting the **Cloud Security Alliance (CSA)** website: `www.cloudsecurityalliance.org`.

Establish privacy agreements

Privacy agreements should be established between organizations that share IoT data. This is especially important for the IoT as data is often expected to be shared across organizational boundaries. Artifacts from the threat modeling exercise performed for the IoT system should be used to understand the flow of data across all organizations, and agreements should be drawn up by all organizations involved in those data flows.

The CSA authored a *Privacy Level Agreement Outline for the Sale of Cloud Services in the European Union* which can be found at `https://downloads.cloudsecurityalliance.org/initiatives/pla/Privacy_Level_Agreement_Outline.pdf`. This is a good starting point to understand the content that should be considered within a privacy agreement. Examples include the following:

- How the data will be processed
- What regulations the data transfers fall under
- The security measures applied to the data
- How systems processing the data will be monitoring for intrusion
- How breach notifications will occur
- Whether data will be provided to other parties and if so, what permissions or reporting must be put in place first

- How long data will be retained
- How and when data will be deleted
- Who is accountable for the safeguarding of data

Consider new liabilities and guard against risk exposure

The IoT introduces concerns that haven't traditionally been relevant to enterprise IT practitioners. Because the IoT is focused on network-enabled physical objects, organizations must begin to consider what liability these new connected devices introduce.

Take an extreme example of a **self-driving vehicle (SDV)**. At the time of writing, SDVs are just beginning to be available. Tesla provides a mode of operation that allows a vehicle to be driven autonomously, and Freightliner was even able to get one of its trucks a license in the state of Nevada. As SDVs become more commonplace, organizations will begin to consider using them in their fleets. It is important to discuss the implications of this shift from a liability perspective.

Another example is unmanned aircraft (drones). Thus far, the regulatory aspects of commercial, unmanned aircraft in the US National Airspace System have been dictated by Section 333 of the FAA Modernization and Reform Act of 2012. Liability risks from drones are new, however. Thus far, drone liability risks have been offset by private insurance companies, many of which support underwriting for today's general aviation aircraft. Given the remarkable variety of drone operational use cases emerging, however, new pay-per-use insurance paradigms for managing liability are emerging in the drone industry. An example of this is Dromatics, a **pay-per-use (PPU)** drone insurance solution from Transport Risk Management, Inc. (`http://www.transportrisk.com/unmaticspayperuse.html`). Using this model, the operator pays to insure each flight according to the usage model in question. Such usage-based liability management models may gain traction in other IoT domains, especially if their usage needs to quickly and dynamically scale. Specific monitoring features can be integrated into IoT devices to help satisfy compliance checks needed in such PPU schemes.

A more dominant IoT liability risk is related to the potential for misuse or disclosure of sensitive information, however. While it is critical that privacy agreements be drafted between all parties involved in data sharing, it is also important to consider whether any new liability is taken on should one of these third-party partners be breached.

The networking of legacy systems such as **Supervisory Acquisition and Data Control (SCADA)** systems into cyber-physical systems should also be examined from a liability perspective. Is the risk of a breach of one of these systems greater given the enhanced connectivity? If yes, how does that increase the risk of injury or worse to workers or citizens?

Establish an IoT physical security plan

Spend time understanding the physical security needs of an IoT implementation to safeguard information from disclosure as well as guard against the introduction of malicious software. Physical security safeguards impact architectural design, policies, and procedures and even technology acquisition approaches. The output from the threat model should guide the physical security plan creation and should take into account whether IoT assets are placed in exposed locations. When this is so, attempt to drive IoT device procurements that include physical tamper protections.

Also, ensure that the security team has a good understanding of the low-level security risks associated with any particular IoT device. For example, spend time reverse engineering a proposed IoT device to understand the safeguards that are applied should one of your devices fall in the wrong hands. Look to understand whether debug ports such as JTAG are password protected, and verify that no account passwords are hardcoded into the device. As this information is found, make updates to your threat models accordingly, or modify your technology acquisition approach.

In addition, many IoT devices provide physical ports, including **universal serial bus (USB)** ports, that support the connection of another device or computer to the asset, or even support connecting the asset to a higher-level component. Carefully consider whether these ports should be enabled when deployed and operational.

Finally, physical security can also mean deployment of monitoring solutions such as cameras, which may themselves be IoT components. This introduces a significant concept. Cisco systems has advocated making cybersecurity and physical security systems work together to support a more holistic security view of the environment and also allow for security systems to coordinate directly with limited human intervention.

Technology selection – security products and services

This section is focused on security considerations for IoT technology selection as well as security products and services that will aid in meeting security and privacy requirements identified during the secure design of the IoT system.

IoT device hardware

IoT device developers have many options to choose from when selecting the technology components that will enable their device. These options typically come with one or more security features that can be used to protect customer information and safeguard from threats. Products that are being connected often make use of **microcontrollers** (MCUs) that are paired with transceivers and optionally sensors, and embedded within the IoT product. Each of these MCUs offers options for security that developers should consider.

Selecting an MCU

Selection of an MCU for an IoT implementation is a typical starting point for hardware design. The selection of an MCU is heavily based on the functional requirements of the IoT device, as MCUs that offer support for low-power applications, performance applications, and even wireless applications are all available. These **system on chip** (**SoC**) solutions provide many of the core capabilities that some IoT devices require. As an example, an SoC solution may provide an MCU with a **Near Field Communication** (**NFC**) transponder that is tightly integrated onto a single platform.

Although some IoT devices are more complex, many sensors are significantly limited, requiring only minimal additional technology components on top of the chosen SoC solution. Either way, the selection of the SoC foundation for your IoT device development is a crucial security consideration. The following should be considered when choosing an SoC. Does the SoC offer the following?

- A cryptographic bootloader that can be leveraged to support secure firmware updates
- Cryptographic hardware acceleration to support efficient cryptographic processing, and what algorithms are supported by the accelerator?
- Secure memory protection
- Built-in tamper protection (for example, JTAG security fuses or a tamper-responsive envelope)
- Protection against reverse engineering
- Secure mechanisms for cryptographic key storage in nonvolatile memory

There is additional hardware security engineering work to perform after the selection of the SoC as well. Developers must be sure to identify any test/debug ports and lock them down. The approach depends heavily on the functionality offered by the SoC itself. For example, some SoC solutions may offer JTAG security fuses, while others allow for the placement of password protection to keep the debug interface locked down.

Selecting a real-time operating system (RTOS)

In addition to micro-hardware security protections, where possible, the use of secured operating systems is warranted. Many IoT device profiles are shrinking to small but powerful SoC units capable of running a variety of secured-boot operating systems featuring strict access controls, trusted execution environments, high-security microkernels, kernel separation, and other security features. Also note that different categories of IoT devices may require different RTOS solutions, as outlined in the following figure:

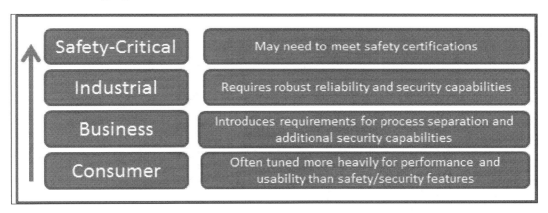

At the top end of the spectrum (safety-critical IoT devices), RTOS selection should be based heavily on whether there is a need to meet industry-specific standards. Examples of these include the following:

- **DO-178B**: Software considerations in airborne systems and equipment certification for avionics systems
- **IEC 61508**: Functional safety for industrial control systems
- **ISO 62304**: Medical device software—software lifecycle processes, for medical devices
- **SIL3/SIL4**: Safety integrity level for transportation and nuclear systems

There are highly robust RTOSes available, for example, from LynxOS and Green Hills Software, that should be considered when dealing with safety-critical IoT systems. These are commonly referred to as cyber-physical systems.

IoT relationship platforms

One of the most important IoT technology considerations is whether to leverage an IoT product relationship platform for an enterprise's IoT systems. These platforms are becoming more prevalent; the market leaders at this time seem to be Xively and ThingWorx. These vendors offer solutions that support security features in addition to functional capabilities. Typically, development teams can use these platforms to build in the following:

- Asset management functions
- Authentication and authorization functions
- Monitoring functions

Xively

At its core, Xively and ThingWorx are both connected product management platforms. They allow developers to build in relationships to an organization's IoT devices through **software development kits (SDKs)**, APIs, and adapters. Leveraging such platforms for in-house IoT developments removes much of the integration burden downstream. Xively offers additional services on top of their standard features. These include Xively Identity Manager and Xively Blueprint. Blueprint allows devices, people, and applications to be connected through Xively's cloud services, supporting the provisioning of identities and the mapping of those identities to privileges in the cloud. Xively's Identity Manager supports management of these identities.

Xively supports multiple protocols for communication, including HTTP, WebSockets, and MQTT, and mandates the use of TLS over each of these channels to achieve end-to-end security. The security of TLS relies heavily on the ability to generate true random numbers, which is the basis of unique and non-guessable secrets—a task that can be challenging for embedded devices.

ThingWorx

ThingWorx provides starter kits for popular IoT platforms such as Raspberry Pi. ThingWorx even provides a marketplace for pre-built IoT applications. Enterprises that are making use of third-party vendors for this type of functionality should verify that the applications have gone through sufficient security testing; they should also perform in-house security testing to ensure a proper security baseline.

Organizations that have adopted ThingWorx for enterprise IoT development should also leverage the platform for asset management and secure remote management capabilities. ThingWorx recently added **Federal Information Processing Standards (FIPS)** 140-2-compliant software cryptographic libraries for end devices, and offers management utilities that support device remote management and asset management. This includes secure remote delivery of software updates to IoT devices.

Cryptographic security APIs

Security **application programming interfaces** (**APIs**) are typically implemented as cryptographic libraries underlying a variety of management, networking, or data application binaries. They may be statically linked or dynamically linked at runtime depending on the needs of the caller and its own place in the software stack. They may also come embedded in secure chips. Security APIs (and binaries) are called in the following instances:

- Application data (at rest and in transit):
  - Encryption
  - Authentication
  - Integrity protection

- Network data/packet:
  - Encryption
  - Authentication
  - Integrity protection

Given the variety of locations in which security can be implemented, the security designer must take into account issues such as whether secure communications are needed to protect all application data (that is, mask the application protocols) end-to-end, whether intermediate systems need access to data (that is, point-to-point protection), and whether the security protections are only for data located on the device (internal storage), among others. In addition, it is possible to protect the integrity and authenticity of data without encrypting it end-to-end; this may benefit certain use cases where intermediate systems and applications need to inspect or retrieve non-confidential data but not break an end-to-end security relationship (protecting end-to-end data origin authentication and integrity). Application-level cryptographic processing can accomplish this, or the use of existing secure networking libraries that implement TLS and IPSec, among other protocols.

The size and footprint of the library is a frequent consideration in the selection of a security library for the IoT. Many devices are low cost and severely constrained in memory or processing power, limiting the available resources for cryptographic security processing. In addition, some cryptographic libraries are designed to take advantage of lower-layer hardware acceleration, using technologies such as AES-NI (for example, as used by Intel processors). Hardware acceleration, if available, has the ability to reduce processor cycles, reduce memory consumption, and accelerate cryptographic cycles on application or network data.

Security engineering and the selection of cryptographic libraries should also take into account potential vulnerabilities in certain libraries and how sensitive IoT application data could be impacted by those vulnerabilities. For example, the OpenSSL Heartbleed vulnerability that was discovered in 2014 resulted in a worldwide, catastrophic security hole exposing the majority of the Internet's web servers: `https://en.wikipedia.org/wiki/Heartbleed`.

Many companies did not even know about their exposure to this vulnerability because they did not adequately track and follow the software supply chain into the end systems on which they depend. The role of IoT security engineering organizations, therefore, needs to include tracking of open source and other security library vulnerability information and ensure the vulnerabilities are mapped to the specific devices and systems deployed in their organizations.

A variety of cryptographic security libraries are on the market today, implemented in a variety of languages. Some are free, and some come with various commercial licensing costs. Examples include the following:

- mbedTLS (formerly PolarSSL)
- BouncyCastle
- OpenSSL
- WolfCrypt (wolfSSL)
- Libgcrypt
- Crypto++

A deeper background into the cryptographic functionality typically offered by libraries such as the preceding ones will be performed later in *Chapter 5, Cryptographic Fundamentals for IoT Security Engineering*.

Authentication/authorization

As you begin to define your IoT security architecture, understanding the optimal methods for deploying authentication and authorization capabilities is one of the most important areas for security technology selection. The actual solution choices will depend heavily on the deployment designs for your IoT infrastructure. As an example, if you are making use of the **Amazon Web Services (AWS)** IoT cloud offering, you should examine the built-in authentication and authorization solutions. Amazon provides two options at the time of writing: X.509 certificates and Amazon's own SigV4 authentication. Amazon only offers two protocol choices for IoT deployments: MQTT and HTTP. With MQTT, security engineers must choose X.509 certificates for authentication of devices. Also note that you can map certificates to policies, which provides fine-grained authorization support. Security engineers can make use of AWS's **Identity and Access Management (IAM)** service to manage (issue, revoke, and so on) certificates and authorizations: `https://aws.amazon.com/iot/how-it-works/`.

Organizations that are not making use of a cloud-based IoT service such as AWS IoT may also want to leverage **public key infrastructure (PKI)** certificates for authentication functionality. Given the large quantities of IoT devices expected to be deployed within a typical organization, the traditional price-points that the industry has seen using **secure sockets layer (SSL)** certificates are not practical. Instead, organizations that are deploying IoT devices should evaluate vendors advertising IoT-specific certificate offerings that can drive the price per certificate down to pennies per certificate. Examples of vendors that have begun to tailor IoT-specific certificate offerings include GlobalSign and DigiCert.

X.509 certificates only provide a starting point for building an IoT authentication and authorization capability. Consider vendors that have begun to support **Identity Relationship Management (IRM)** as outlined by the Kantara Initiative. IRM is built on pillars that focus in part on consumers and things over employees; Internet-scale over enterprise-scale; and borderless over perimeter. Organizations such as GlobalSign have begun to build these concepts into their IAM solutions and support delivery of high volumes of certificates via RESTful JSON APIs.

An alternative to procuring X.509 certificates is building your own infrastructure. This build-your-own approach is only recommended if your organization has considerable experience designing and securely deploying these infrastructures. Secure PKI design is a highly specialized field. There are many opportunities to get something wrong, from failing to safeguard the root certificates properly, to inadvertently allowing a **registration authority (RA)** account to be compromised.

Another consideration regarding PKI certificates is that X.509 may not continue to be the de facto standard for the IoT. In the Connected Vehicle market, for example, the infrastructure being stood up to support authentication certificates for cars is based on the IEEE 1609.2 standard. These certificates are more efficient than their X.509 cousins, when used in high-volume environments and in resource-constrained endpoints.

Other vendors that offer IoT-specific authentication and authorization solutions include Brivo Labs, which focuses on authenticated social interactions between people and devices (`http://www.brivolabs.com/`), ForgeRock (`https://www.forgerock.com/solutions/devices-things/`), and Nexus (`https://www.nexusgroup.com/en/solutions/internet-of-things/`).

Edge

Fog Computing and protocol translation—Cisco systems has been very vocal about the need to extend data processing infrastructure to the network edge within an IoT architecture. Cisco refers to this concept as **Fog Computing**. The concept is that data from IoT devices does not need to make the trip all the way back to cloud processing and analytics centers, in order to be useful. Initial analytics processing can occur in these new edge data centers, allowing useful information to be gleaned quickly and at lower cost and even allowing positive action to be taken on that data in short order. Security architects faced with these edge-heavy designs need to examine more traditional security architectures, such as boundary-defense, in order to secure the edge infrastructure equipment. Security architects must also focus on protection of the data itself, often in many forms (pre-processed/processed) in order to safeguard customer-, employee-, and partner-sensitive information.

More traditional IoT gateways that act as go-betweens and protocol translators are also offered by various vendors. Products such as Lantronix's IoT gateway line have built-in SSL encryption and SSH for management functions. AWS's IoT Gateway also has built-in TLS encryption (`http://www.lantronix.com/products-class/iot-gateways/`).

Software defined networks and IoT security—pushing a variety of IoT services and processing to the network edge brings about other interesting considerations with respect to IoT devices and routing. The continued growth and promulgation of **software defined networking (SDN)** as a means of dynamically managing physical and virtual network devices gives rise to a number of security issues with IoT devices. These issues need to be considered in the security lifecycle. Implementing SDN protocols, for example, OpenFLow, into IoT devices can provide network and device managers with a means of conveniently configuring device routing switching, tables, and associated policies. Such control plane manipulation of an IoT device exposes a variety of sensitive data elements and device communication behaviors; as a result, it is critical to adopt authenticated, integrity- and confidentiality-protected protocols to secure 1) the SDN southbound interface (SDN protocols between IoT devices and SDN controllers) and 2) the SDN northbound interface (SDN networking applications providing the upstream networking business logic). In addition, the SDN protocol business logic (that is, an SDN agent running on IoT devices) should run as a protected process and control data structures (for example, routing tables and policies) should be integrity protected within the IoT device. Disregarding these types of security controls could allow attackers a means of reconfiguring and re-routing (or multi-homing) private data to illegitimate parties.

Security monitoring

An interesting aspect of the IoT is that security monitoring now means something different than with traditional enterprise security solutions. Traditionally, enterprises would acquire a **security information and event management (SIEM)** tool that collects data from hosts, servers, and applications. An ideal IoT monitoring solution can collect data from each device in your inventory, which is often a challenge in and of itself. Designing an overarching security monitoring solution for the IoT requires an integrated mix of security products.

It is often difficult to extract appropriate security log files from the full range of IoT devices, as constraints exist that limit the ability to do so in a timely manner. As an example, instantiating an RF connection simply to pass security log data to an aggregator is costly from a battery-preservation perspective. Additionally, some devices do not even collect security-relevant data. Organizations that are looking to build up an effective IoT security monitoring solution should begin with tools that offer a flexible foundation for interfacing to diverse devices. Splunk is a great example of this—and given the flexibility in protocol coverage offered by their platforms, it is a good candidate for evaluation.

Splunk can ingest data in many formats (for example, JSON, XML, TXT) and then normalize it into a format that is required for further evaluation. Organizations have already built modules for accessing data directly from IoT protocols such as MQTT, CoAP, AMQP, and, of course, REST. Splunk also provides additional capabilities for the IoT. As an example, Splunk offers a module that allows for indexing data from Amazon's Kinesis, the component within AWS that collects data from IoT devices (`http://blogs.splunk.com/2015/10/08/splunk-aws-iot/`).

AWS also offers a level of logging that can be used for rudimentary security analysis in AWS IoT implementations. The AWS CloudWatch service enables event logging from IoT devices (AWS requires IoT devices to speak either MQTT or REST). Logging can be set to `DEBUG`, `INFO`, `ERROR`, and `DISABLED`. The AWS CloudWatch API describes the following log entries for AWS IoT devices (`http://docs.aws.amazon.com/iot/latest/developerguide/cloud-watch-logs.html`):

- **Event**: Description of the action
- **Timestamp**: Log generation time
- **TraceId**: Random identifier
- **PrincipalId**: Either a certificate fingerprint (HTTP) or a thing name (MQTT)
- **LogLevel**: The level of logging
- **Topic Name**: The MQTT topic name
- **ClientId**: The ID of the MQTT client
- **ThingId**: The ID of the thing
- **RuleId**: The ID of the rule that was triggered

Being able to identify anomalies within IoT devices, either individual devices or populations of devices, will be an important security capability. Although more research is needed to support new product development in this area, we are already seeing some point solutions that offer behavioral-based monitoring for smaller-scale IoT deployments. As an example, Dojo labs is about to begin sales of their Dojo home IoT monitoring solution, which provides user-friendly security monitoring to detect and resolve security issues in home-based IoT devices. The Dojo labs product provides color-coded signaling to communicate to homeowners whether there is a security issue within the home's IoT ecosystem. The product can tell whether there is an event of concern based on an understanding of the standard behavioral characteristics of a particular device type. As an example, according to Dojo:

"if an Internet-connected thermostat normally only sends small data points like temperatures, and it suddenly starts sending a high-bandwidth stream of packets that looks like a video transmission, that's a clue that the device may have been compromised."

Source: `http://www.networkworld.com/article/3006560/home-iot-security-could-come-from-a-glowing-rock-next-year.html`

Expect more security capabilities such as this as time moves forward. The challenge related to behavioral analysis, however, is the need to understand the operating patterns of the specific devices the system is monitoring for anomalies. Unlike human behavioral analysis, where security patterns such as equipment use at certain times of the day are monitored, IoT-based behavioral analysis is highly diverse. Depending on the type of device—for example a **self-driving vehicle (SDV)** versus a smart meter—the normal operating parameters will be completely different. This requires an in-depth understanding of those normal operating parameters per device, and significant analysis to determine what operations outside of those normal parameters could signal.

The **Defense Advanced Research Projects Agency (DARPA)** is even looking into ways that network defenders can identify malicious behavior based on the analog operating characteristics of a device (for example, the sound it makes, or the power that it draws). While these techniques are still a long way from the market, it should be noted that security researchers such as Ang Cui have begun to show that IoT devices can be compromised using novel techniques such as vibrating MCU pins to establish data exfiltration channels over AM radio—a hack known as **Funtenna**.

Another security engineering facet relates to the use of wireless communications. Wireless introduces new issues that affect the monitoring capabilities of an enterprise. For example, being able to detect rogue devices within a geographic area or building is important and requires a new approach to monitoring since there is a need to listen in for RF communications such as Bluetooth, ZigBee, and ZWave. One company that is leading the way towards new IoT monitoring techniques required to solve this problem is Bastille. Bastille offers a product (C-Suite radio security solution) that monitors the airspace and provides alerts whenever new devices attach to an enterprise network (`https://www.bastille.io/`).

The complex nature of the IoT means that organizations will need to spend resources designing a holistic security monitoring solution from multiple vendor offerings. In the meantime, **managed security service providers (MSSPs)** are starting to spin up IoT monitoring offerings as well. One example is the managed IoT security service from Trustwave (`http://betanews.com/2015/07/20/new-security-service-helps-protect-the-internet-of-things/`).

Summary

This chapter provided information on the many issues and techniques related to securely engineering IoT systems. It also included safety, privacy, and security designs; establishment of processes and agreements; and the selection of relevant security products and services.

In our next chapter, we will explore in detail the operational aspects of the IoT security lifecycle.

4
The IoT Security Lifecycle

Large or federated organizations will face the challenge of deploying not only thousands of devices within a single IoT system, but potentially hundreds or thousands of individual IoT endpoints. Increasing the complexity, each IoT implementation can differ significantly in form and function. For example, an organization that operates retail stores may have warehouse-based RFID systems used in inventory management, beacons in retail establishments that support tailored customer experiences, and may also begin to incorporate technologies such as connected vehicles, drones, and robotics throughout various aspects of their operations.

The security engineer's job is to be able to examine and characterize each of these disparate systems and define an appropriate lifecycle focused on maintaining a secure state across the enterprise. This chapter discusses the IoT system security lifecycle, which is tightly integrated into a secure development, integration, and deployment process. The lifecycle is designed to be iterative, allowing for the secure addition of new IoT capabilities throughout an enterprise. Technical, policy, and procedural lifecycle topics are addressed to enable a robust enterprise IoT security capability that is continuously updated and tailored to the unique operating needs of the system. An IoT security lifecycle should support an enterprise IoT ecosystem with the following:

- Privacy considerations due to the potential to leak sensitive information or metadata through third-party relationships, requiring comprehensive confidentiality controls.

- Large quantities of new devices and device types that must be configured securely to guard against new attack vectors into the enterprise.

- Autonomous operations and device-to-device transactions that worsen the impact of an intrusion.

- Safety-related risks to which IT staff have not traditionally been exposed. These risks can result in harm to employees and customers if an adversary compromises an IoT system with the potential to do physical harm.

- Potential for leased (non-owned) products. This introduces confusion into the need for lifecycle support as vendors now must be provided with the ability to maintain their systems.

- Preprocessing and initial data analytics (application as well as security) at the edge of the network, with transmission of log and event data to the cloud for additional analytics.

The secure IoT system implementation lifecycle

In *Chapter 3, Security Engineering for IoT Development*, we addressed security design within the overarching IoT system implementation lifecycle. This chapter focuses on the other critical aspects of the IoT security lifecycle, to include implementation and integration, operation and maintenance, and disposal. The following figure provides a graphical depiction of the IoT security lifecycle that begins with the introduction of safety, privacy, and security engineering in the system design stage, and concludes with the secure disposal of IoT assets as their effective lifetime is reached.

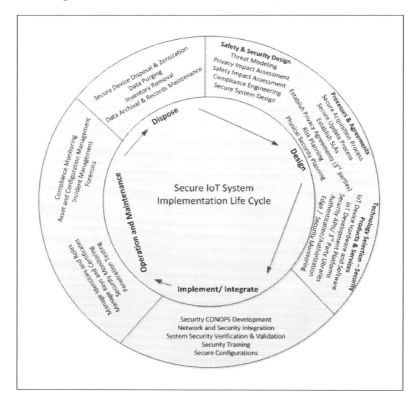

Implementation and integration

End-user organizations will have many options for deploying functional IoT capabilities. Some organizations will develop IoT systems themselves; however, many options will exist for the procurement of pre-packaged IoT systems that include IoT devices with pre-established connectivity to edge infrastructures, cloud interfaces, backend analytics processing systems, or some combination thereof.

For example, as forthcoming regulations for **Beyond Line of Sight (BLOS) Unmanned Aircraft Systems (UAS)** operations in the United States emerge, system integrators will package drone management and control systems that can be procured by an enterprise for surveillance, security, and a variety of other features. These systems will be designed to capture many types of data from UAS endpoints and transmit that data over preconfigured channels to gateway systems. Gateways will then feed the data to backend or ground station systems that provide automated route planning and potentially swarm coordination for certain mission types.

While such systems should ideally come pre-configured with the proper amount of security engineering rigor during design and development, an organization planning to integrate one must still perform a slew of activities to securely incorporate the features into its existing enterprise.

The first step in the security lifecycle is to create a security **concept of operations (CONOPS)** document reflecting the given system, its security needs, and how to satisfy them.

IoT security CONOPS document

A security CONOPS document provides organizations with a tool for methodically detailing the security operations of the IoT system. The document should be written and maintained by IoT system operators to provide a roadmap for system implementers during implementation and integration. No facet of security should be left to the imagination in the CONOPS; otherwise, implementers may encounter confusion and take liberties they should not take. Examples of security CONOPS templates can be found from a number of organizations. One example is NIST SP-800-64 at `http://csrc.nist.gov/publications/nistpubs/800-64-Rev2/SP800-64-Revision2.pdf`.

An IoT security CONOPS document should contain material covering, at a minimum, the following:

Security service	CONOPS coverage
Confidentiality and integrity	How IoT devices will be provisioned with cryptographic keys, certificates, and ciphersuites, and how those cryptographic materials will be managed. Are existing privacy policies sufficient to safeguard against inadvertent leakage of sensitive information?
Authentication and access control	Whether existing central directory service authentication systems such as Active Directory or Kerberos will be integrated to support the system. The roles required for system operation and whether attribute-based access controls, role-based controls, or both will be implemented (for example, time of day access restrictions). The security roles within the system and how those roles will be provisioned. What access controls need to be considered on a per-topic basis (for example, to support publish/subscribe protocols).
Monitoring, compliance, and reporting	How security monitoring will be performed and how data will be mined from IoT device logs. Will gateways serve as log aggregators? What rules will need to be written for SIEM event alerts? Systems to which log files must be forwarded to for security event log analysis. What compliance regulations must be adhered to during the lifecycle of the IoT system. The role of big data analytics being used for enhanced security monitoring of the IoT system.
Incident response and forensics	Who is responsible for defining and executing incident response activities. Mapping of business functions to new IoT systems. Impact analysis of failed/compromised IoT systems.

Security service	CONOPS coverage
Operations and maintenance and disposal	What additional security documentation will be required to support secure IoT system operation, including configuration management plans, continuous monitoring plans, and contingency plans.
	How the system will be maintained regularly to keep a sound security posture.
	What security training will be made available to stakeholders and the frequency for completing that training.
	How the disposal of IoT system assets will be securely conducted and verified.

Network and security integration

It is difficult to characterize a typical IoT network implementation, given that there are potentially so many different and diverse types of IoT functions. Here we take a quick look at network and security integration considerations for **wireless sensor networks (WSNs)** and connected cars.

Examining network and security integration for WSNs

Examining a typical **WSN**, one will find many thousands or more low-powered, battery-operated sensors that probably communicate using a RF-based protocol such as ZigBee. These devices may communicate at the application layer using tailored IoT protocols such as MQTT-SN, which can be run directly over ZigBee and similar protocols (eliminating the need for IP-based communications at the edge). In this scenario, the implementation of MQTT-SN within each sensor would then mandate a gateway that translates between the MQTT-SN and the MQTT protocol.

Gateways provide the ability to deploy IoT devices without IP connectivity back to the cloud. Instead, the gateway serves as the protocol intermediary between a network of IoT devices and the analytics systems that consume data from them. Given that gateways aggregate data from multiple devices (and often store data at least temporarily), it is important to make sure that each is deployed with secure communications configurations to both the end IoT devices as well as the backend cloud services.

Looking at the security services required to protect these communications, one would typically leverage the security capabilities of the underlying RF protocol between the sensors and the gateway. One would also expect to leverage the capabilities of a protocol such as TLS between the MQTT gateway and backend services.

Organizations do not always need to implement the tailored MQTT-SN protocol, however. Some IoT devices may support the ability to communicate directly using MQTT with the gateway. Examining Amazon Web Services' recent support of MQTT, the solution utilizes a cloud-based MQTT gateway supporting direct connections such as this – the connection is protected using a TLS channel.

Examining network and security integration for connected cars

Other implementations have significantly different characteristics. Imagine a fleet of connected vehicles that each communicate using the DSRC protocol. These vehicles send messages to each other and to **roadside equipment (RSE)** many times per second, and depend on proximity to another component for consumption of these messages. These messages are secured using the inherent capabilities of the DSRC protocol, which include the ability to provide data origin authentication. Organizations will often be required to configure infrastructure components that securely communicate with connected vehicles in their fleets, using these protocols.

No matter the type of IoT deployment, these systems need to be configured to communicate with an organization's existing technology infrastructure. From a security lifecycle perspective, engineers should spend considerable time planning these integration activities. Improper planning of IoT system integration within the enterprise can introduce new weaknesses ripe for exploitation.

Planning for updates to existing network and security infrastructures

This lifecycle activity involves the integration planning needed to incorporate new IoT services into existing infrastructures, an activity that can sometimes lead to significant overhauls of legacy architectures. Consider that some IoT implementations require near-real-time feedback in support of automated decision making. Although the initial incarnations of the IoT will focus heavily on collecting data through sensors, the focus will shift toward making that data useful in our daily lives. Provisioning of analytics, control systems, and other functionality across an organization will encourage this.

In situations where IoT systems must process and act upon data in near real time, it is necessary to re-evaluate the move toward centralized data processing (http://www.forbes.com/sites/moorinsights/2015/08/04/how-the-internet-of-things-will-shape-the-datacenter-of-the-future/).

Cisco Systems has coined the term Fog Computing to address the need to shift to a more decentralized model focused on enhancing reliability, scalability, and fault-tolerance of IoT systems. The Fog Computing model places compute, storage, and application services at the network edge or within gateways that service IoT devices (http://blogs.cisco.com/perspectives/iot-from-cloud-to-fog-computing). This concept of edge computing allows near-real-time initial analytics support and improvements in performance versus maintaining a continuous need to depend on the most centralized systems. Data can be more locally processed and analyzed with less need to send gargantuan amounts of it inefficiently to highly centralized applications. Once edge-processed, the resultant data can be sent directly to the cloud for long-term storage or ingested into additional analytics services.

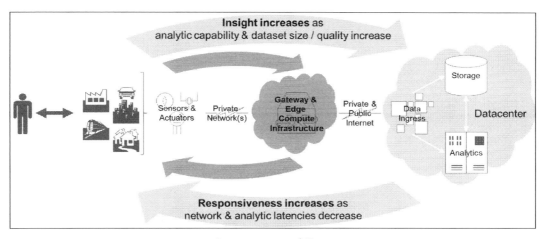

Image courtesy of Cisco

Designing an IoT deployment that can scale and at the same time defend against attacks such as **denial of service (DoS)** is important. Re-thinking the network infrastructure and analytics architecture is an important aspect to this. Decentralization of IoT services during the planning and upgrade of existing infrastructure is an opportunity to both add new services also improve resilience.

Planning for provisioning mechanisms

Engineers must also plan to provision network information required for the IoT devices and gateways to operate properly. In some cases, this includes planning for IP address allocation. The choice of supported IoT protocols will frequently dictate IP addressing requirements. WSNs that use communication protocols such as Bluetooth, ZigBee, and ZWave do not require the provisioning of an IP address; however, protocols such as 6LoWPAN require the provisioning of an IPv6 address for each device. Some devices simultaneously support various wireless protocols and IP connectivity.

Organizations choosing to provision devices with IPv6 addresses face additional security engineering tasks as they must ensure that the IPv6 routing infrastructure is enabled securely.

Organizations must also plan for any required **domain name system (DNS)** integration. This is required for any endpoint or gateway that needs to communicate using URLs. Consider protocols such as **DNS-based Authentication of Named Entities (DANE)** for gateway to infrastructure communication and backhaul service communication. DANE allows much tighter association of certificates to named entities (URL) by leveraging DNSSEC, and can significantly help deter various web-based MITM attack scenarios.

Integrating with security systems

IoT systems will also need to be integrated with existing enterprise security systems, requiring the integration and testing of the interfaces to those systems. Ideally, interfaces to these systems would have been created during development of the IoT system, but in some cases, glue-code must be developed to complete the integration. In other instances, simple configurations are required to interface with or consume the security products of those enterprise systems. Examples of enterprise security systems that an IoT deployment will likely integrate with include the following:

- Directory systems
- **Identity and access management (IAM)** systems
- **Security information and event management (SIEM)** systems
- Asset management and configuration management systems
- Boundary defense systems (for example, firewalls and intrusion detection systems)
- Cryptographic key management systems
- Wireless access control systems
- Existing analytics systems

IoT and data buses

Beyond IP-and wireless-based IoT systems, there are also IoT-based systems that rely upon data buses for communication to neighboring devices. For example, within today's automobiles, the **controller area network** (**CAN**) bus is typically used for real-time messaging between vehicle components (electronic control units). In the recent past, automobile manufacturers began implementing enhanced entertainment-based functionality into vehicle platforms. In many instances, there are connections between these new systems (for example, infotainment systems) and the safety-critical CAN bus. Good security practice dictates that these systems be segregated; however, even when segregation occurs, it is possible to leave the safety-critical CAN bus open to attack.

Examining the research conducted by Charlie Miller and Chris Valasek in 2015, you can understand some of the challenges faced in vehicles. Through improper configuration of a carrier network, poor security design within a software component, and reverse engineering of one of the MCUs (responsible for segmenting the vehicle's infotainment system from the safety-critical CAN buses), the researchers were able to effectively take control of a connected vehicle remotely (`http://illmatics.com/Remote%20Car%20Hacking.pdf`).

In situations where IoT systems are integrated into safety-critical systems, security domain separation is vital. This implies that segmentation techniques are used to isolate sensitive functions from non-sensitive ones. In addition, providing support for integrity protection, authentication, guarding against message replay, and confidentiality is appropriate in many cases. In traditional networks, SIEM integration is critical to inspecting traffic and ensuring adherence to rules when data crosses established security zones. Analogous systems are needed in future, real-time data buses as well.

System security verification and validation (V&V)

Sufficient testing needs to be conducted, both positive and negative, to verify that functional security requirements have been satisfied. This testing should be performed in an operational environment, after the system has been integrated with other enterprise infrastructure components. Ideally, this testing will occur throughout the development lifecycle as well as the implementation/integration, deployment, and operations ones.

Verification provides the assurances that the system operates according to a set of requirements that appropriately meet stakeholder needs. Validation is the assurance that an IoT system product, service, or system meets the needs of the customer and other identified stakeholders—in an IoT system, this means that the system definition and design is sufficient to safeguard against threats. Verification is the evaluation of whether or not a product, service, or system complies with a regulation, requirement, specification, or market-imposed constraint. For IoT systems, this means that the security services and capabilities were implemented according to the design (`https://en.wikipedia.org/wiki/Verification_and_validation`).

One approach to verifying functional security requirements is to create test drivers or emulators that exercise functionality. For example, creating an emulator that emulates the instantiation of a secure connection (for example, TLS) and the authentication between devices would provide implementers with confidence that each device is operating according to defined security requirements.

System testing is required to verify that the functional security requirements of the IoT implementation have been met during development and integration. IoT system testing should be automated as much as possible, and should address both the expected and unexpected behavior of the system.

Discrepancy reports (DRs) should be created whenever issues are identified; those DRs should be tracked to closure by development teams as the system is updated and new releases are made available. Tracking of DRs can be performed in a variety of tracking tools from formal configuration management tools such as DOORS to agile-based tools such as Jira in the Atlassian suite.

Security training

The 2015 OpenDNS in the Enterprise report provided an early glimpse into challenges that security practitioners will soon face. The report identified that employees are already bringing their own IoT devices into the enterprise, and found that devices such as smart televisions were reaching out through enterprise firewalls to various Internet services. This research shows one aspect of the need to re-train employees and security administrators in what is appropriate to attach to the network as well as how to identify inappropriately attached consumer IoT devices.

The creation of security training requires periodic review and the possible creation of new security policies needed to support different IoT paradigms. These policies should be used as source material for both end-user security awareness training as well as security administration training (`https://www.opendns.com/enterprise-security/resources/research-reports/2015-internet-of-things-in-the-enterprise-report/`).

Security awareness training for users

IoT systems often have unique characteristics that are not found in traditional IT systems. Topics to consider addressing in updated user security awareness training include the following:

- The data, network and physical risks associated with IoT devices
- Policies related to bringing personal IoT devices into the organization
- Privacy protection requirements related to data collected by IoT devices
- Procedures for interfacing (if allowable) with corporate IoT devices

Security administration training for the IoT

Security administrators must be provided with the technical and procedural information needed to keep the IoT systems operating securely. Topics to consider addressing in updated security administration training include the following:

- Policies for allowable IoT use within an organization
- Detailed technology overview of the new IoT assets and sensitive data supported by the new IoT systems
- Procedures for bringing a new IoT device online
- Procedures to monitor the security posture of IoT devices
- Procedures for updating IoT device and gateway firmware/software
- Approved methods for administering IoT assets
- How to detect unauthorized personal IoT devices within an organization
- Procedures for responding to incidents involving IoT devices
- Procedures for properly disposing of IoT assets

Anyone interacting with IoT systems or IoT-originated data within an organization should be required to take the appropriate training.

Secure configurations

IoT systems involve many diverse components and each must be configured in a secure manner. Each component must also be configured to interface with other components securely. It is often easy to overlook the need to change default settings and choose the right security modes for operation. Always try to leverage existing security configuration guidance to understand how to lock down IoT system and communication services.

IoT device configurations

Some of the more powerful IoT devices make use of a **real-time operating system (RTOS)** that requires a review of configuration files and default settings. For example, operating system bootloading features should be reviewed and updated so that only authenticated and integrity-protected firmware updates are allowed. One should review open ports and protocols and lock down any that are not required for approved operation. In addition, default port settings should be managed when possible to implement application whitelisting controls. In short, create a secure by default baseline for each device type.

The security of the hardware configurations is equally important. As discussed in previous chapters, lock down any open test interfaces (for example, JTAG) to combat the ability of an attacker to gain access to devices that are stolen or left exposed. In conjunction with designers, also make use of any physical security features that may be included in the hardware. Such features may include active tamper detection and response (for example, automated wiping of sensitive data upon tamper), coverage and blocking of critical interfaces, and others.

Secure protocol configuration is crucial as well. Any protocol-related literature providing best practices for an IoT protocol or protocol stack should be reviewed, understood, and followed prior to the IoT system being deployed. Examples of secure Bluetooth IoT configuration guidance include the following:

- **National Security Agency (NSA) Information Assurance Directorate (IAD)** guide to Bluetooth security (`https://www.nsa.gov/ia/_files/factsheets/i732-016r-07.pdf`)
- NIST SP 800-121 NIST *Guide to Bluetooth Security* (`http://csrc.nist.gov/publications/nistpubs/800-121-rev1/sp800-121_rev1.pdf`)

Often, the proverbial usability over security argument is argued by manufacturers resulting in IoT components being shipped with insecure default configurations. For example, the ZigBee protocol uses application profiles that support interoperability between ZigBee implementations. These application profiles include default keys that must be changed prior to system operation.

Tobias Zillner and Sebastian Strobl provided a useful briefing on the need to change these default keys. The researchers noted that the default Trust Center Link keys for both the **ZigBee Light Link Profile (ZLL)** and the **ZigBee Home Automation Public Application Profile (HAPAP)** are both based on the passphrase **ZigBeeAlliance09**. Implementing any IoT system that doesn't enforce modification of default keys can render many of communication security controls useless within an enterprise. These keys should always be updated prior to bringing a ZigBee-based IoT network online (`https://www.blackhat.com/docs/us-15/materials/us-15-Zillner-ZigBee-Exploited-The-Good-The-Bad-And-The-Ugly.pdf`).

Secure gateway and network configurations

After making secure configuration updates to IoT devices, examine the configuration of gateway devices that interact with the IoT endpoints. Gateways are aggregation points for numerous IoT devices and special attention must be paid to their secure configuration. In some cases, these gateways are located on-premises with the IoT devices, but in other cases, the IoT devices may communicate directly with a gateway located in the cloud (as is the case with the AWS IoT service).

One critical aspect of gateway configuration is how they implement secure communication with both upstream and downstream assets. Gateway communication to backend infrastructure should always be configured to run over a TLS or other VPN connection (for example, IPSec) and ideally require two-way (mutual) certificate-based authentication. This requires that the communication infrastructure that the gateway interacts with be configured with proper access controls based on the provisioned gateway certificate. A frequently overlooked aspect of these configurations is the strength of allowable ciphersuites supported. Ensure that both endpoints are configured to only support the strongest ciphersuites each mutually supports. Further, it is recommended that organizations and developers use the latest versions of TLS. For example, at the time of writing, TLS 1.2 should be used instead of TLS 1.1 or 1.0, since the previous versions both have published vulnerabilities. TLS 1.3 is currently in IETF draft status. As soon as it is finalized and its implementations become widely available, they should be adopted.

In addition to ciphersuites, gateways communicating with other application servers should ensure that the service is associated with the PKI certificate. One manner of achieving this, mentioned earlier, was the use of the DANE, a protocol in which DNSSEC is leveraged along with DANE records to verify correlation of a digital certificate to a server. DANE was created to mitigate a number of real-world PKI deployment threats related to rogue certificates in conjunction with the DNS.

Gateway communications to downstream devices should also provide secure communications. It is important to configure the IoT devices to communicate using secure modes of their respective protocols. For example, IoT devices that communicate using Bluetooth-LE to a gateway have a variety of available options (`http://www.ncbi.nlm.nih.gov/pmc/articles/PMC3478807/`).

		Pairing	Encryption	Data Integrity	Layer
LE Security Mode 1	Level 1	No	No	No	Link Layer
	Level 2	Unauthenticated	Yes	Yes	
	Level 3	Authenticated	Yes	Yes	
LE Security Mode 2	Level 1	Unauthenticated	No	Yes	ATT layer
	Level 2	Authenticated	No	Yes	

Upstream databases must also be configured securely. One should consider security lockdown procedures such as disabling anonymous access, encrypting data between nodes (to include **remote procedure calls (RPCs)**), configuring daemons to not run as root, and changing default ports.

Operations and maintenance

The secure operations and maintenance of IoT systems supports activities such as managing credentials, roles and keys, as well as both passively and actively monitoring the security posture of the system.

Managing identities, roles, and attributes

One of the first and most challenging issues to address within an enterprise is the creation of a common namespace for IoT devices. In addition to naming, establish clear registration processes. Registration processes should be broken into tiers based on the sensitivity of the data handled by the devices and the impact of compromise. For example, registration of security-critical devices should require an in-person registration process that associates the device with an administrator/group of administrators. Less critical devices may be provisioned with organizational identities online based on some pre-configured trust anchor.

Some existing IoT implementations have suffered from improper management of identities and role-based permissions used in device administration. For example, there have been early connected vehicle RSE implementations that have been deployed using default username/passwords or shared username/password combinations. Given the geographic dispersion of these devices, it is easy to understand why these less than secure configurations were chosen; however, to properly lock down an IoT infrastructure, care must be taken to require appropriate credentials and privileges for performing administrative functions.

There are a variety of security-related functions that must be allowable within an IoT system. It is useful to examine these functions prior to mapping them to roles within an IoT environment. Although not all IoT devices have this entire set of capabilities, some security functions required for proper IoT administration include the following:

- View audit logs
- Delete (rotate off) audit logs
- Add/delete/modify device user accounts
- Add/delete/modify device privileged accounts
- Start/stop and view current device services
- Load new firmware to a device
- Access physical device interfaces/ports
- Modify device configurations (network, and so on)
- Modify device access controls
- Manage device keys
- Manage device certificates
- Pair device or update pairing configurations

Identity relationship management and context

Given the unique nature of the IoT, consider adopting **identity relationship management (IRM)**. The Kantara Initiative is leading efforts to define and evangelize this new paradigm, which heavily relies on the concept of context within authentication procedures. The Kantara Initiative has defined a set of IRM pillars that focus in part on the following:

- Consumers and things over employees
- Internet-scale over enterprise-scale
- Borderless over perimeter

Attribute-based access control

Context is important to understand as it relates to the IoT and in particular how it relates to **attribute-based access control** (**ABAC**). Context provides an authentication and authorization system with additional input into the decision-making process on top of the identity of the device:

- An IoT device that is outside of a geo-fenced boundary might be restricted from establishing a connection with the infrastructure

- A connected car that is at an approved repair facility might be allowed to upload new firmware

NIST has provided a useful resource for understanding ABAC at `http://nvlpubs.nist.gov/nistpubs/specialpublications/NIST.sp.800-162.pdf`.

Role-based access control

Part of secure identity management includes first identifying the pertinent identities and privileged roles they play. These roles can of course be tailored to meet the unique needs of any particular IoT system deployment, and in some cases, consideration should be given to separation of duties using **role-based access control** (**RBAC**). For example, providing a separate and distinct role for managing audit logs decreases the threat of insider administrators manipulating those logs. Lacking any existing, defined roles, the following table identifies an example of security-relevant roles/services mappings that can be leveraged in an administration and identity and access control system:

Role	Responsibility
IoT Enterprise Security Administrator	Add/delete/modify device privileged accounts
IoT Device Security Administrator	View audit logs Add/delete/modify device user accounts Start/stop device services Load new firmware to a device Access physical device interfaces/ports Modify device access controls Manage device keys
IoT Network Administrator	Modify device configurations (network, and so on) Manage device certificates Pair device or update pairing configurations
IoT Audit Administrator	Delete (rotate off) audit logs

There are additional service roles that may be required as well for an IoT device to communicate either directly or indirectly with other components in the infrastructure. It is crucial that these services be sufficiently locked down by restricting privileges whenever possible.

Consider third-party data requirements

Device manufacturers will often require device data access for monitoring device health, and tracking statistics and/or entitlements. Consider design updates to your AAA systems to support secure transmission of this data to the manufacturers when needed.

Consider also updating your AAA systems to support consumer definition of privacy preferences consent for access to consumer profile data. This requires management of external identities such as consumers and patients, who are allowed to give their consent preferences for which attributes of their profile can be shared and to whom. In many cases, this requires the integration of AAA services with third-party services that manage consumer and business partner preferences for handling of data.

Manage keys and certificates

In the transportation sector, the department of transportation and auto industry are working on the creation of a new, highly robust and scalable PKI system that is capable of issuing over 17 million certificates per year to start, and scaling up to eventually support 350 million devices (billions of certificates), including light vehicles, heavy vehicles, motorcycles, pedestrians, and even bicycles. The system, called the **security credential management system (SCMS)**, provides an interesting reference point for understanding the complexities and scales that cryptographic support of the IoT will require.

Keys and certificates enable secure data in transit between devices and gateways, between multiple devices, as well as between gateways and services. Although most organizations have existing agreements with PKI providers for **secure sockets layer (SSL)** certificates, the provisioning of certificates to IoT devices frequently do not fit the typical SSL model. There are a number of considerations when deciding which third-party PKI provider to leverage for IoT certificates and there are also trade-off considerations when deciding whether to use existing in-house PKI systems.

More in-depth guidance on PKI certificates can be found in *Chapter 6, Identity and Access Management Solutions for the IoT*. Considerations related to operations and maintenance of keys and certificates for IoT devices include answering the following:

- How will secure bootstrapping of keys/certificates be handled with the IoT devices?
- How IoT device identity verification will be achieved?
- How will revocation checking be handled by IoT devices and services? Will **Online Certificate Status Protocol (OCSP)** responders be used and if so, how will the devices be configured to connect with them?
- How many certificates will be required per device and what validity period per certificate should be set? Some IoT use cases show a strong rationale for very short validity periods.
- Are there privacy considerations that preclude binding a certificate to a device (for example, if a device can be tied directly to a person as in the case of a Connected Vehicle)?
- Is the price-per-certificate offered by third-party providers going to meet the scaling needs within a deployment's cost constraints?
- Are X.509 certificates the optimal approach given any constraints of the system (for example, communication requirements and storage requirements)?

There are new certificate formats being introduced in support of the IoT. One example is the IEEE 1609.2 specification format that is being used within the SCMS for secure **vehicle-to-vehicle (V2V)** communications. These certificates were designed for environments that require minimal latency and reduced bandwidth overhead for limited devices and spectrum. They employ the same elliptic curve cryptographic algorithms used in a variety of X.509 certificates but are significantly smaller in overall size and are well suited for machine-to-machine communication. The authors hope to see this certificate format adopted in other IoT realms and eventually integrated into existing protocols such as TLS (especially given their explicit application and permissions attributes).

Security monitoring

Operation of IoT systems requires that assets be sufficiently monitored for abnormal behavior to mitigate potential security incidents. The IoT presents a number of challenges that make monitoring using traditional SIEM systems alone insufficient. This is due to the following reasons:

- Some IoT devices may not generate any security audit logs

- IoT devices don't typically support formats such as syslog and may require custom connectors

- Gaining timely access to audit logs from IoT devices may prove difficult in various scenarios

- Confidence in the integrity of IoT device audit logs may be somewhat limited

Preparation for IoT device security monitoring should begin with an inventory of what data is available from each IoT device, gateway, service, and how event data can and should be correlated across the IoT system to identify suspicious events. This ideally will include correlation with surrounding infrastructure components and even other IoT devices/sensors. Understanding the available inputs will provide a solid foundation for defining the rules that will be implemented within the enterprise SIEM system.

In addition to defining traditional SIEM-based rules, consider the opportunity to begin applying data analytics to IoT-based messaging. This can be useful for identifying anomalies within operation of an IoT system quickly, even when device audit logs are not readily available. For example, understanding that the normal behavior of networked temperature sensors is that each is within a certain percentage range of the closest neighbors allows for the creation of an alert when a single sensor deviates from that range (based on a defined variance). This is an example of where CPS control system monitoring needs to be integrated with security monitoring systems. Integration of physical, logical, network, and IoT devices (sensors, actuators, and so on) is possible using tools such as ArcSite and developing or acquiring custom Flex Connectors.

Typical anomalies to look for within an IoT system may include the following:

- Device not reachable

- Time-based anomalies

- Spikes in activity, especially at odd times of day

- New protocols emanating or targeting an IoT device

- Variances in data collected past a threshold

- Authentication anomalies

- Attempted elevation of privilege

- Drops in velocity or activity

- Rapid changes in device physical state (for example, rapid temperature increase, vibration, and so on)

- Communications with unexpected destinations (even within IoT network) that may indicate attempted lateral movements

- Receipt of corrupted data
- Unexpected audit results
- Unexpected audit volume and purged audit trails (devices or gateways)
- Sweeping for topics (in case of publish/subscribe protocols)
- Repeated connection attempts
- Abnormal disconnections

Although these might be interesting anomalies, each IoT system should be individually examined to understand the proper operational baseline operations and what constitutes anomalous behavior. In a CPS, integrating and baselining the security rules with the safety rules is crucial. Where possible, integrate security and safety self-checks into IoT devices and systems. These can be used to verify detection of anomalies during operation by confirming security and safety services are operating correctly.

One platform that can provide good support for IoT monitoring is Splunk. Splunk was created as a product designed to process machine data and as such began with a solid foundation for supporting the IoT. Splunk supports data collection, indexing, and search/analysis.

Splunk already supports a number of IoT protocols through add-on apps. Some of the IoT support provided by Splunk includes message handling for MQTT, AMQP, and REST, as well as support for indexing data from Amazon Kinesis.

Penetration testing

Assessing the organization's IoT implementations requires testing of hardware and software, and should include regularly scheduled penetration test activities as well as autonomous tests that occur throughout the cycle of operation.

Aside from being a good security practice, many regulations require third-party penetration tests that in the future will include IoT devices/systems. Penetration tests can also validate the existing security controls and identify gaps within the implemented security controls.

Blue teams should also be used to continuously evaluate the security posture of the enterprise as red teams are conducting their exercises. Also, it is vital to assess the security posture of new IoT infrastructure software and hardware components prior to introducing them into the architecture.

Red and blue teams

Conducting a penetration test of an IoT system is not significantly different from pen testing more traditional IT systems, although there are additional aspects to consider. The end goal is to routinely find and report vulnerabilities that may eventually be exploited. In the case of an IoT system, pen testers must have tools available to identify security weaknesses in software, firmware, hardware, and even in the protocol configurations that make use of the RF spectrum.

Conducting effective penetration tests requires that testers limit their efforts to the most important aspects of an implementation. Consider what is of most business value to the organization (for example, protection of user data privacy, continuity of operations, and so on) and then lay out a plan to test the security of the information assets most likely to impact those goals.

Penetration testing can be conducted as either whitebox or blackbox testing. Both types are recommended, and while blackbox testing is used to simulate an outside attacker, whitebox testing provides a more thorough evaluation that allows the test team to fully engage the technology to find weaknesses.

It also helps to create attacker profiles that mimic the types of attackers that would be interested in attempting to compromise a particular system. This is of benefit for both cost-savings as well as providing a more realistic attack pattern based upon the likely approaches used by adversaries with different financial resources.

Given that the goal of a penetration test is to identify weaknesses in the security posture of a system, IoT system testers should always look for low-hanging items that are often left open. These include things such as the following:

- Default passwords used in IoT devices or the gateways, servers, and other hosts and networking equipment that support them
- Default cryptographic keys used in IoT devices or the gateways or services that support them
- Default configurations that are well known that would open a system up to enumeration if not modified (for example, default ports)
- Insecure pairing processes implemented on IoT devices
- Insecure firmware update processes on devices and within the infrastructure
- Unencrypted data streams from IoT devices to gateways
- Non-secure RF (Bluetooth, ZigBee, ZWave, and so on) configurations

Evaluating hardware security

Hardware security must also be evaluated. This may be a challenge given the relative lack of test tools available for this activity; however, there are security platforms that are beginning to emerge. One example, created by researchers Julien Moinard and Gwenole Audic, is known as Hardsploit.

Hardsploit is designed as a flexible and modular tool that can be used to interface with various data bus types, including UART, Parallel, SPI, CAN Modbus and others. More information about Hardsploit is available at `https://hardsploit.io/`.

The process for evaluating hardware security in an enterprise IoT implementation is straightforward. Testers need to understand whether hardware devices introduce new weaknesses in a system that detracts from the ability to protect system assets and data. A typical IoT hardware evaluation flow during a penetration test would go as follows:

1. Identify whether the device is in a protected or unprotected location. Can the device be taken without someone noticing? If it is taken, is there any reporting that it is no longer online? Can it be swapped out?

2. Evaluate tamper protections and break open the device.

3. Attempt to dump memory and try to steal sensitive information.

4. Attempt to download the firmware for analysis.

5. Attempt to upload new firmware and make that firmware operational.

The airwaves

Another aspect of the IoT that differs from traditional IT implementations is the increasing reliance on wireless communications. Wireless introduces a variety of potential back doors into an enterprise that must be guarded. It is important to take time during penetration tests to determine if it is possible to leave rogue RF devices behind that may be able to covertly monitor or exfiltrate data from the environment.

IoT penetration test tools

Many traditional pen test tools are applicable to the IoT, although there are also IoT-specific tools now coming online. Examples of tools that may be useful during IoT penetration testing are provided in the following table:

IoT test tools		
Tool	**Description**	**Available at**
BlueMaho	Suite of Bluetooth security tools. Can scan/track BT devices; supports simultaneous scanning and attacking.	`http://git.kali.org/gitweb/?p=packages/bluemaho.git;a=summary`
Bluelog	Good for long-term scanning at a location to identify discoverable BT devices.	`http://www.digifail.com/software/bluelog.shtml`
crackle	A tool designed to crack BLE encryption.	`https://github.com/mikeryan/crackle`
SecBee	A ZigBee vulnerability scanner. Based on KillerBee and scapy-radio.	`https://github.com/Cognosec/SecBee`
KillerBee	A tool for evaluating the security posture of ZigBee networks. Supports emulation and attack of end devices and infrastructure equipment.	`http://tools.kali.org/wireless-attacks/killerbee`
scapy-radio	A modification to the scapy tool for RF-based testing. Includes support for Bluetooth-LE, 802.15.4-based protocols and ZWave.	`https://bitbucket.org/cybertools/scapy-radio/src`
Wireshark	An old favorite.	`https://www.wireshark.org/`
Aircrack-ng	A wireless security tool for exploiting Wi-Fi networks – supports 802.11a, 802.11b and 802.11g.	`www.aircrack-ng.org/`
Chibi	An MCU with integrated with an open sourced ZigBee stack.	`https://github.com/freaklabs/chibiArduino`
Hardsploit	A new tool aimed at providing Metasploit-like flexibility to IoT hardware testing.	`https://hardsploit.io/`
HackRF	Flexible and turnkey platform for RX and TX 1 MHZ to 6 GHZ.	`https://greatscottgadgets.com/hackrf/`
Shikra	The Shikra is a device that allows the user to interface (via USB) to a number of different low-level data interfaces such as JTAG, SPI, I2C, UART, and GPIO.	`http://int3.cc/products/the-shikra`

Test teams should of course also keep track of the latest vulnerabilities that can impact IoT implementations. For example, is always useful to track the **National Vulnerability Database (NVD)** at `https://nvd.nist.gov/`. In some cases, vulnerabilities may not be directly in the IoT devices, but in the software and systems to which they connect. IoT system owners should maintain a comprehensive version tracking system for all devices and software in their enterprise. This information should be regularly checked against vulnerability databases, and of course shared with the whitebox penetration testing teams.

Compliance monitoring

Continuous monitoring for IoT security compliance is a challenge and will continue to be a challenge as regulators attempt to catch up with mapping and extending existing guidance to the IoT.

As discussed in *Chapter 2, Vulnerabilities, Attacks, and Countermeasures*, the **Center for Internet Security (CIS)** released an addendum to the 20 Critical Controls that details coverage of each control within the IoT. This provides a starting point as continuous monitoring and compliance software often incorporate the 20 Critical Controls as a component of the online monitoring capability.

Asset and configuration management

There is more to discuss related to IoT asset management than simply keeping track of the physical location of each component. Some IoT devices can benefit from predictive analytics to help identify when an asset requires maintenance and also detect in real time when an asset has gone offline. By incorporating new data analytics techniques into an IoT ecosystem, organizations can benefit from these new capabilities and apply them to the IoT assets themselves.

Imaging a device such as an autonomous connected vehicle working on a construction site, or perhaps a robot on a manufacturing floor, the ability to predict failure becomes significant. Prediction is only the first step, however, as the IoT matures with new capabilities to automatically respond to failures and even autonomously swap out broken components for new replacements.

Consider a set of drones used in security and surveillance applications. Each drone is essentially an IoT endpoint that must be managed by the organization like any other asset. This means that within an asset database there is an entry for each drone that includes various attributes such as the following:

- Registration number
- Tail number

- Sensor payloads
- Manufacturer
- Firmware versions
- Maintenance logs
- Flight performance characteristics, including flight envelope limitations

Ideally, these drone platforms can also be self-monitoring. That is, the drones can be outfitted with a multitude of sensors that monitor aircraft health and can feed the data back to a system capable of performing predictive analytics. For example, the drone may measure data such as temperature, strain, and torque, which can be used to predict part failures within individual components of the platform. From a security perspective, ensuring that the data is integrity protected end-to-end is important, as is building in checks within the predictive algorithms to look for variances that should not be included in calculations. This is just one more example of where safety and security intersect in the same ecosystem.

Proper asset management requires having the ability to maintain a database of the attributes related to a particular IoT device in order to properly perform routine maintenance on each asset. IoT system deployers should consider two configuration management models:

- IoT asset components (for example, firmware) are fully integrated and updated by the IoT device vendor in a single update
- IoT asset is developed modularly with many different technologies that must each be maintained and separately updated

In the first instance, updating the IoT asset is straightforward, although there are still, of course, opportunities for vulnerability exploitation. Always ensure that the new firmware is digitally signed at a minimum (and that the public key trust anchor verifying the firmware signature is securely stored). Care must also be taken to secure the firmware distribution infrastructure, including the systems that provision the signing certificates in the first place. When new firmware is loaded into an IoT platform, the platform should verify the digital signature using a protected trust anchor (public key) before allowing the firmware to boot and load into executable memory.

In addition to digitally signing firmware packages, verify that the devices are configured to only allow signed updates. Enable encrypted channels between the firmware update server and the device, and establish policies, procedures, and appropriate access controls for those performing the updates.

Look to vendors such as Xively and Axeda for robust IoT asset and configuration management solutions.

Incident management

Just as the IoT blends together the physical and electronic world, the IoT also blends together traditional IT capabilities with business processes—business processes that have the ability to impact the bottom line of an organization when interrupted. Impacts can include financial loss, reputation damage, and even personnel safety and loss of life. Managing IoT-related incidents requires that security staff have better insights into how the compromise or disruption of a particular IoT system impacts the business. Responders should be familiar with Business Continuity Plans (which need to be developed established with the IoT system in mind) to determine what the appropriate remediation steps to take are during the incident response.

Microgrids provide a valuable example for incident management. Microgrids are self-contained energy generation, distribution, and management systems that may or may not be connected to a larger power distribution infrastructure. Identifying an incident involving one of the **programmable logic controllers** (PLCs) may require that responders first understand the impact of taking a certain PLC offline. At a minimum, they must work very closely with the impacted business operations during the response. This requires that for each IoT system across an organization, the security staff maintain an up-to-date database of the emergency PLCs, as well as a general description of critical assets and business functions.

Forensics

The IoT opens up new data-rich opportunities to facilitate forensics processes. From a forensics perspective, keeping as much data as possible from each IoT endpoint can aid in an investigation. Unlike traditional IT security, the assets themselves may not be available (for example, they may be stolen), may not be capable of storing any useful data, or may have been tampered with. Gaining access to the data that was generated by compromised IoT devices, as well as related devices in the environment, gives a good starting point in instances such as this.

Just as IoT data can be useful in enabling and benefiting from predictive analytics, research into the use of historical IoT data for establishing security incident root causes should be explored.

Dispose

The disposal phase of a system can apply to the system as a whole or to individual components of the system. IoT systems can generate significant data; however, minimal data is typically kept on the devices themselves. This does not, however, mean that the controls associated with IoT devices can be overlooked. Proper disposal procedures can aid against adversaries intent on using any means to gain physical access to IoT devices (for example, dumpster diving for old electronics).

Secure device disposal and zeroization

Many IoT devices are configured with cryptographic material that allows them to join local networks or authenticate and communicate securely with other remote devices and systems. This cryptographic material should be deleted and wiped from the devices prior to their disposal. Ensure that policies and procedures address how authorized security staff should perform secure removal of keys, certificates, and other sensitive device data when devices need to be disposed of. Accounts that have been provisioned to IoT devices must also be scrubbed to ensure that any account credentials used for automated transactions are not discovered and hijacked.

Data purging

Gateway devices should also be thoroughly inspected when being decommissioned from a system. These devices may have latent data stored on them, including critical authentication material that must be erased and rendered irretrievable.

Inventory control

Asset management is a crucial enabler of enterprise information security. Keeping track of assets and their states is essential to maintaining a healthy security posture. The relatively low cost of many IoT devices does not mean that they can be swapped out and replaced without adhering to stringent processes. If possible, keep track of all IoT assets in your inventory through an automated inventory management system and ensure that processes are followed to remove these devices from inventory following secure disposal. Many SIEM systems maintain device inventory databases; keeping the communication pathways open between system operators and SIEM operators can help ensure consistent inventory management.

Data archiving and records management

The amount of time that data must be kept depends heavily on the specific requirements and regulations in a given industry. Satisfying such regulations within an IoT system may be manual or may frequently require a data warehousing capability that collects and stores data for extended periods of time. Apache and Amazon data warehouses (S3) offer capabilities that one may want to consider for IoT records management.

Summary

In this chapter, we discussed the IoT security lifecycle management processes associated with IoT device implementation, integration, operation, and disposal. Each has vital subprocesses that must be created or adopted for use in any IoT deployment and in just about any industry. While much attention is given in the literature to secure device design (or lack thereof), firm attention must also be given to secure integration and operational deployment.

In the next chapter, we will provide a background in applied cryptography as it relates to the IoT. We provide this background because many legacy industries new to security may struggle to correctly adopt and integrate cryptography into their products.

5
Cryptographic Fundamentals for IoT Security Engineering

This chapter is directed squarely at IoT implementers, those developing IoT devices (consumer or industrial) or integrating IoT communications into their enterprises. It provides readers a background on establishing cryptographic security for their IoT implementations and deployments. While most of this book is devoted to practical application and guidance, this section diverges a bit to delve into deeper background topics associated with applied cryptography and cryptographic implementations. Some security practitioners may find this information common sense, but given the myriad cryptographic implementation errors and deployment insecurities even security-aware tech companies still deploy today, we decided this background was needed. The risks are growing worse, evidenced by the fact that many industries historically unfamiliar with security (for example, home appliance vendors) continue to network-connect and IoT-enable their products. In the process, they're making many avoidable errors that can harm their customers.

A detailed review of the use of cryptography to protect IoT communication and messaging protocols is provided, along with guidance on how the use of certain protocols drives the need for additional cryptographic protections at different layers of the technology stack.

This chapter is a critical prerequisite to the following chapter on **public key infrastructures** (**PKIs**) and their use in IoT identity and trust management. It explains the underlying security facets and cryptographic primitives on which PKI depends.

This chapter is broken up into the following topical sections:

- Cryptography and its role in securing the IoT
- Types and uses of the cryptographic primitives in the IoT
- Cryptographic module principles
- Cryptographic key management fundamentals
- Future-proofing your organization's rollout of cryptography

Cryptography and its role in securing the IoT

Our world is witnessing unprecedented growth in machine connectivity over the Internet and private networks. Unfortunately, on any given day, the benefits of that connectivity are soured by yet more news reports of personal, government, and corporate cybersecurity breaches. Hacktivists, nation-states, and organized crime syndicates play a never-ending game of cat and mouse with the security industry. We are all victims, either as a direct result of a cyber breach or through the costs we incur to improve security technology services, insurance, and other risk mitigations. The demand for more security and privacy is being recognized in corporate boardrooms and high-level government circles alike. A significant part of that demand is for wider adoption of cryptography to protect user and machine data. Cryptography will play an ever growing role in securing the IoT. It is and will continue to be used for encrypting wireless edge networks (network and point-to-point), gateway traffic, backend cloud databases, software/firmware images, and many other uses.

Cryptography provides an indispensable tool set for securing data, transactions, and personal privacy in our so-called information age. Fundamentally, when properly implemented, cryptography can provide the following security features to any data whether in transit or at rest:

Security feature	Cryptographic service(s)
Confidentiality	Encryption
Authentication	Digital signature or **Message authentication code (MAC)**
Integrity	Digital signature or MAC
Non-repudiation	Digital signature

Revisiting definitions from *Chapter 1, A Brave New World*, the previously mentioned controls represent four out of five pillars of **information assurance (IA)**. While the remaining one, availability, is not provided by cryptography, poorly implemented cryptographic instances can certainly deny availability (for example, communication stacks with crypto-synchronization problems).

The security benefits provided by cryptography — confidentiality, authentication, integrity, and non-repudiation — provide direct, one-to-one mitigations against many host, data, and communications security risks. In the not-too-distant past, the author (Van Duren) spent considerable time supporting the FAA in addressing the security needed in pilot-to-drone communications (a prerequisite to safe and secure integration of unmanned aircraft into the national airspace system). Before we could recommend the controls needed, we first needed to understand the different communication risks that could impact unmanned aircraft.

The point is, it is vital to understand the tenets of applied cryptography because many security practitioners — while they may not end up designing protocol level controls — will at least end up making high-level cryptographic selections in the development of security embedded devices and system level security architectures. These selections should always be based on risks.

Types and uses of cryptographic primitives in the IoT

When most people think about cryptography, it is encryption that most comes to mind. They understand that data is "scrambled", so to speak, so that unauthorized parties cannot decrypt and interpret it. Real-world cryptography is comprised of a number of other primitives, however, each partially or fully satisfying one of the previous IA objectives. Securely implementing and combining cryptographic primitives together to achieve a larger, more complex security objective should only be performed or overseen by security professionals well versed in applied cryptography and protocol design. Even the most minor error can prevent the security objective(s) from being fulfilled and result in costly vulnerabilities. There are far more ways to mess up a cryptographic implementation than to get it right.

Cryptographic primitive types fall into the following categories:

- Encryption (and decryption):
  - ○ Symmetric
  - ○ Asymmetric

- Hashing
- Digital signatures
  - ○ **Symmetric**: MAC used for integrity and data-origin authentication
  - ○ **Asymmetric**: **Elliptic curve (EC)** and **integer factorization cryptography (IFC)**. These provide integrity, identity, and data-origin authentication as well as non-repudiation

- **Random number generation**: The basis of most cryptography requires very large numbers originating from high entropy sources

Cryptography is seldom used in isolation, however. Instead, it provides the underlying security functions used in upper layer communication and other protocols. For example, Bluetooth, ZigBee, SSL/TLS, and a variety of other protocols specify their own underlying cryptographic primitives and methods of integrating them into messages, message encodings, and protocol behavior (for example, how to handle a failed message integrity check).

Encryption and decryption

Encryption is the cryptographic service most people are familiar with as it is used to so-called scramble or mask information so that unintended parties cannot read or interpret it. In other words, it is used to protect the confidentiality of the information from eavesdroppers and only allow it to be deciphered by intended parties. Encryption algorithms can be symmetric or asymmetric (explained shortly). In both cases, a cryptographic key and the unprotected data are given to the encryption algorithm, which ciphers—encrypts—it. Once in this state, it is protected from eavesdroppers. The receiving party uses a key to decrypt the data when it is needed. The unprotected data is called plaintext and the protected data is called **ciphertext**. The basic encryption process is depicted in the following diagram:

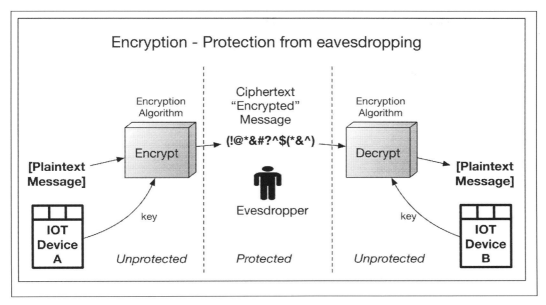

Encrypt-decrypt.graffle

It should be clear from the preceding diagram that, if the data is ever decrypted prior to reaching IOT Device B, it is vulnerable to the Eavesdropper. This brings into question where in a communication stack and in what protocol the encryption is performed, that is, what the capabilities of the endpoints are. When encrypting for communication purposes, system security engineers need to decide between point-to-point encryption and end-to-end encryption as evidenced in their threat modeling. This is an area ripe for error, as many encrypted protocols operate only on a point-to-point basis and must traverse a variety of gateways and other intermediate devices, the paths to which may be highly insecure.

In today's Internet threat environment, end-to-end encryption at the session and application layers is most prominent due to severe data losses that can occur when decrypting within an intermediary. The electrical industry and the insecure SCADA protocols commonly employed in it provide a case in point. The security fixes often include building secure communication gateways (where newly added encryption is performed). In others, it is to tunnel the insecure protocols through end-to-end protected ones. System security architectures should clearly account for every encryption security protocol in use and highlight where plaintext data is located (in storage or transit) and where it needs to be converted (encrypted) into ciphertext. In general, whenever possible, end-to-end data encryption should be promoted. In other words, a secure-by-default posture should always be promoted.

Symmetric encryption

Symmetric encryption simply means the sender (encryptor) and the receiver (decryptor) use an identical cryptographic key. The algorithm, which is able to both encrypt and decrypt—depending on the mode—is a reversible operation, as shown in the following diagram:

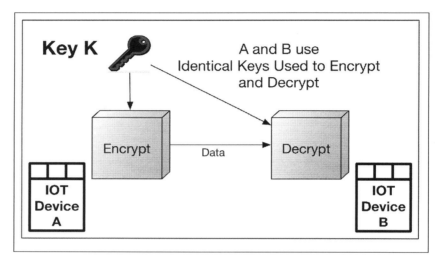

Symmetric-encryption.graffle

In many protocols, a different symmetric key is used for each direction of travel. So, for example, Device A may encrypt to Device B using key X. Both parties have key X. The opposite direction (B to A) may use key Y which is also in the possession of both parties.

Symmetric algorithms consist of a ciphering operation using the plaintext or ciphertext input, combined with the *shared* cryptographic key. Common ciphers include the following:

- **AES—advanced encryption standard** (based on Rijndael and specified in FIPS PUB 197)
- Blowfish
- DES and triple-DES
- Twofish
- CAST-128
- Camellia
- IDEA

The source of the cryptographic keys is a subject that spans applied cryptography as well as the topic of cryptographic key management, addressed later in this chapter.

In addition to the cryptographic key and data that is fed to the cipher, an **initialization vector** (**IV**) is frequently needed to support certain cipher modes (explained in a moment). Cipher modes beyond the basic cipher are simply different methods of bootstrapping the cipher to operate on successive chunks (blocks) of plaintext and ciphertext data. **Electronic code book** (**ECB**) is the basic cipher and operates on one block of plaintext or ciphertext at a time. The ECB mode cipher by itself is very rarely used because repeated blocks of identical plaintext will have an identical ciphertext form, thus rendering encrypted data vulnerable to catastrophic traffic analysis. No IV is necessary in ECB mode, just the symmetric key and data on which to operate. Beyond ECB, block ciphers may operate in block chaining modes and stream/counter modes, discussed next.

Block chaining modes

In **cipher block chaining** (**CBC**) mode, the encryption is bootstrapped by inputting an IV that is XOR'd with the first block of plaintext. The result of the XOR operation goes through the cipher to produce the first block of encrypted ciphertext. This block of ciphertext is then XOR'd with the next block of plaintext, the result of which goes through the cipher again. The process continues until all of the blocks of plaintext have been processed. Because of the XOR operation between iterating blocks of plaintext and ciphertext, two identical blocks of plaintext will not have the same ciphertext representation. Thus, traffic analysis (the ability to discern what the plaintext was from its ciphertext) is far more difficult.

Other block chaining modes include **cipher-feedback chaining** (**CFB**) and output feedback modes (OFB), each a variation on where the IV is initially used, what plaintext and ciphertext blocks are XOR'd, and so on.

Advantages of block chaining modes include the fact, stated previously, that repeated blocks of identical plaintext do not have an identical ciphertext form. This prevents the simplest traffic analysis methods such as using dictionary word frequency to interpret encrypted data. Disadvantages of block chaining techniques include the fact that any data errors such as bit flipping in RF communications propagate downstream. For example, if the first block of a large message M encrypted by AES in CBC mode were corrupted, all subsequent blocks of M would be corrupted as well. Stream ciphers, discussed next, do not have this problem.

CBC is a common mode and is currently available as an option (among others), for example, in the ZigBee protocol (based on IEEE 802.15.4).

Counter modes

Encryption does not have to be performed on complete blocks, however; some modes make use of a counter such as **counter mode (CTR)** and **Galois counter mode (GCM)**. In these, the plaintext data is not actually encrypted with the cipher and key, not directly anyway. Rather, each bit of plaintext is XOR'd with a stream of continuously produced ciphertext comprising encrypted counter values that continuously increment. In this mode, the initial counter value is the IV. It is encrypted by the cipher (using a key), providing a block of ciphertext. This block of ciphertext is XOR'd with the block (or partial block) of plaintext requiring the protection. CTR mode is frequently used in wireless communications because bit errors that happen during transmission do not propagate beyond a single bit (versus block chaining modes). It is also available within IEEE 802.15.4, which supports a number of IoT protocols.

Asymmetric encryption

Asymmetric encryption simply means there are two different, pairwise keys, one public and the other private, used to encrypt and decrypt, respectively. In the following diagram, IoT device A uses IoT device B's public key to encrypt to device B. Conversely, device B uses device A's public key to encrypt information to device A. Each device's private keys are kept secret, otherwise anyone or anything possessing them will be able to decrypt and view the information.

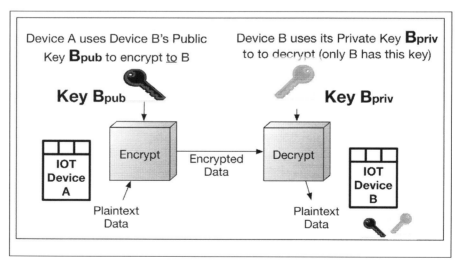

Asymmetric-Encryption.graffle

The only asymmetric encryption algorithm in use today is that of **RSA (Rivest, Shamir, Adelman)**, an **integer factorization cryptography (IFC)** algorithm that is practical for encrypting and decrypting small amounts of data (up to the modulus size in use).

The advantage of this encryption technique is that only one party possessing the pairwise RSA private key can decrypt the traffic. Typically, private key material is not shared with more than one entity.

The disadvantage of asymmetric encryption (RSA), as stated earlier, is the fact that it is limited to encrypting up to the modulus size in question (1024 bits, 2048 bits, and so on). Given this disadvantage, the most common use of RSA public key encryption is to encrypt and transport other small keys—frequently symmetric—or random values used as precursors to cryptographic keys. For example, in the TLS client-server protocol, RSA is leveraged by a client to encrypt a **pre-master secret (PMS)** with the server's public RSA key. After sending the encrypted PMS to the server, each side has an exact copy from which to derive the session's symmetric key material (needed for session encryption and so on).

Integer factorization cryptography using RSA, however, is becoming less popular due to advances in large number factorization techniques and computing power. Larger RSA modulus sizes (for improved computational resistance to attack) are now recommended by NIST.

Hashes

Cryptographic hashes are used in a variety of security functions for their ability to represent an arbitrarily large message with a small sized, unique thumbprint (the hash). They have the following properties:

- They are designed not to disclose any information about the original data that was hashed (this is called resistance to first pre-image attacks)

- They are designed to not allow two different messages to have the same hash (this is called resistance to second pre-image attacks and collisions)

- They produce a very random-looking value (the hash)

The following image denotes an arbitrary chunk of data D being hashed into H(D). H(D) is a small, fixed size (depending on the algorithm in use); from it, one can not (or should not be able to) discern what the original data D was.

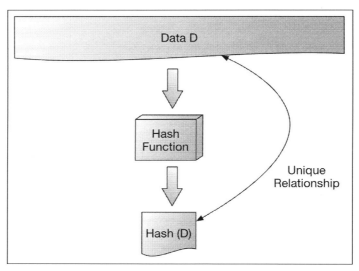

Hash-functions.graffle

Given these properties, hash functions are frequently used for the following purposes:

- Protecting passwords and other authenticators by hashing them (the original password is then not revealed unless by a *dictionary attack*) into a random looking digest

- Checking the integrity of a large data set or file by storing the proper hash of the data and re-computing that hash at a later time (often by another party). Any modification of the data or its hash is detectable.

- Performing asymmetric digital signatures

- Providing the foundation for certain message authentication codes

- Performing key derivation

- Generating pseudo-random numbers

Digital signatures

A **digital signature** is a cryptographic function that provides integrity, authentication, data origin, and in some cases, non-repudiation protections. Just like a hand-written signature, they are designed to be unique to the *signer*, the individual or device responsible for signing the message and who possesses the signing key. Digital signatures come in two flavors, representing the type of cryptography in use: symmetric (secret, shared key) or asymmetric (private key is unshared).

The originator in the following diagram takes his message and signs it to produce the signature. The signature can now accompany the message (now called the signed message) so that anyone with the appropriate key can perform the inverse of signature operation, called **signature verification**.

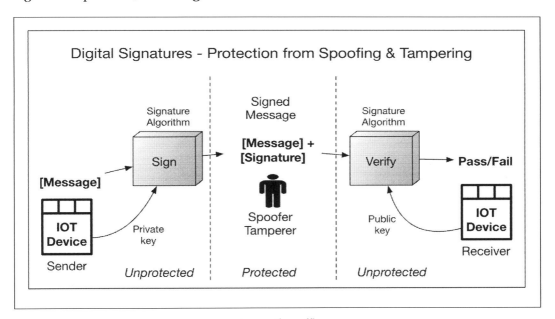

sign-verify.graffle

If the signature verification is successful, the following can be claimed:

- The data was, indeed, signed by a known or declared key
- The data has not been corrupted or tampered with

If the signature verification process fails, then the verifier should not trust the data's integrity or whether it has originated from the right source. This is true of both asymmetric and symmetric signatures, but each has unique properties, described next.

Asymmetric signature algorithms generate signatures (that is, sign) using a private key associated with a shared public key. Being asymmetric and the fact that private keys are generally not (nor should they typically ever be) shared, asymmetric signatures provide a valuable means of performing both entity and data authentication as well as protecting the integrity of the data and providing non-repudiation capabilities.

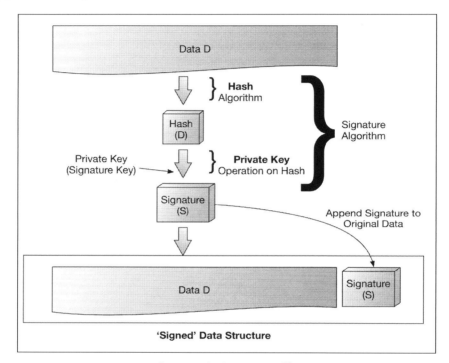

Asymmetric-signature.graffle

Common asymmetric digital signature algorithms include the following:

- RSA (with PKCS1 or PSS padding schemes)
- **DSA (digital signature algorithm)** (FIPS 180-4)
- **Elliptic curve DSA (ECDSA)** (FIPS 180-4)

Asymmetric signatures are used to authenticate from one machine to another, sign software/firmware (hence, verify source and integrity), sign arbitrary protocol messages, sign PKI public key certificates (discussed in *Chapter 6, Identity and Access Management Solutions for the IoT*) and verify each of the preceding ones. Given that digital signatures are generated using a single private (unshared) key, no entity can claim that it did not sign a message. The signature can only have originated from that entity's private key, hence the property of non-repudiation.

Asymmetric digital signatures are used in a variety of cryptographic-enabled protocols such as SSL, TLS, IPSec, S/MIME, ZigBee networks, Connected Vehicle Systems (IEEE 1609.2), and many others.

Symmetric (MACs)

Signatures can also be generated using symmetric cryptography. Symmetric signatures are also called MAC and, like asymmetric digital signatures, produce a MAC of a known piece of data, D. The principal difference is that MACs (signatures) are generated using a symmetric algorithm, hence the same key used to generate the MAC is also used to verify it. Keep in mind that the term MAC is frequently used to refer to the algorithm as well as the signature that it generates.

Symmetric MAC algorithms frequently rely on a hash function or symmetric cipher to generate the message authentication code. In both cases (as shown in the following diagram), a MAC key is used as the shared secret for both the sender (signer) and receiver (verifier).

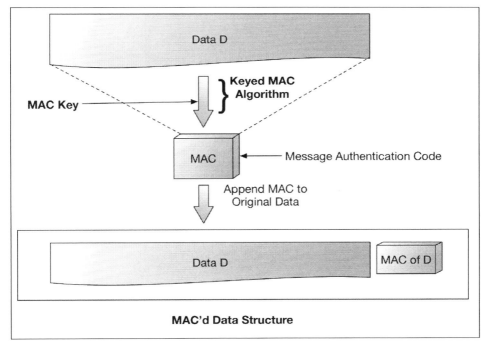

Symmetric-signature.graffle

Given that MAC-generating symmetric keys may be shared, MACs generally do not claim to provide identity-based entity authentication (therefore, non-repudiation cannot be claimed), but do provide sufficient verification of origin (especially in short term transactions) that they are said to provide data origin authentication.

MACs are used in a variety of protocols, such as SSL, TLS, IPSec, and many others. Examples of MACs include the following:

- HMAC-SHA1
- HMAC-SHA256
- CMAC (using a block cipher like AES)
- GMAC (**Galois message authentication code** is the message authentication element of the GCM mode)

MAC algorithms are frequently integrated with encryption ciphers to perform what is known as authenticated encryption (providing both confidentiality as well as authentication in one fell swoop). Examples of authenticated encryption are as follows:

- **Galois counter mode (GCM)**: This mode combines AES-CTR counter mode with a GMAC to produce ciphertext and a message authentication code.
- **Counter mode with CBC-MAC (CCM)**: This mode combines a 128-bit block cipher such as AES in CTR mode with the MAC algorithm CBC-MAC. The CBC-MAC value is included with the associated CTR-encrypted data.

Authenticated encryption is available in a variety of protocols such as TLS.

Random number generation

Randomness of numbers is a keystone of cryptography given their use in generating a number of different cryptographic variables such as keys. Large, random numbers are difficult to guess or iterate through (brute force), whereas highly deterministic numbers are not. Random number generators—RNGs—come in two basic flavors, deterministic and nondeterministic. Deterministic simply means they are algorithm-based and for a single set of inputs they will always produce the same output. Non-deterministic means the RNG is generating random data in some other fashion, typically from very random physical events such as circuit noise and other low bias sources (even semi-random interrupts occurring in operating systems). RNGs are frequently among the most sensitive components of a cryptographic device given the enormous impact they have on the security and source of cryptographic keys.

Any method of undermining a device's RNG and discerning the cryptographic keys it generated renders the protections of that cryptographic device completely useless.

RNGs (the newer generation are called **deterministic random bit generators**, or **DRBGs**) are designed to produce random data for use as cryptographic keys, initialization vectors, nonces, padding, and other purposes. RNGs require inputs called **seeds** that must also be highly random, emanating from high entropy sources. A compromise of seed or its entropy source — through poor design, bias, or malfunction — will lead to a compromise of the RNG outputs and therefore a compromise of the cryptographic implementation. The result: someone decrypts your data, spoofs your messages, or worse. A generalized depiction of the RNG entropy seeding process is shown in the following diagram:

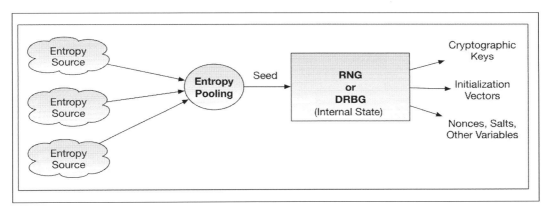

RandomNumberGeneration.graffle

In this depiction, several arbitrary entropy sources are pooled together and, when needed, the RNG extracts a seed value from this pool. Collectively, the entropy sources and entropy pooling processes to the left of the RNG are often called a **non-deterministic random number generator (NDRNG)**. NDRNG's almost always accompany RNGs as the seeding source.

Pertinent to the IoT, it is absolutely critical for those IoT devices generating cryptographic material that IoT RNGs be seeded with high entropy sources and that the entropy sources are well protected from disclosure, tampering, or any other type of manipulation. For example, it is well known that random noise characteristics of electrical circuits change with temperature; therefore, it is prudent in some cases to establish temperature thresholds and logically stop entropy gathering functions that depend on circuit noise when temperature thresholds are exceeded. This is a well-known feature used in smart cards (for example, chip cards for credit/debit transactions, and so on) to mitigate attacks on RNG input bias by changing the temperature of the chip.

Entropy quality should be checked during device design. Specifically, the min-entropy characteristics should be evaluated and the IoT design should be resilient to the NDRNG becoming 'stuck' and always feeding the same inputs to the RNG. While less a deployment consideration, IoT device vendors should take extraordinary care to incorporate high quality random number generation capabilities during the design of a device's cryptographic architecture. This includes production of high quality entropy, protection of the entropy state, detection of stuck RNGs, minimization of RNG input bias, entropy pooling logic, RNG state, RNG inputs, and RNG outputs. Note that if entropy sources are poor, engineering tradeoffs can be made to simply collect (pool) more of the entropy within the device to feed the RNG.

NIST Special Publication 800-90B (`http://csrc.nist.gov/publications/drafts/800-90/sp800-90b_second_draft.pdf`) provides an excellent resource for understanding entropy, entropy sources, and entropy testing. Vendors can have RNG/DRBG conformance and entropy quality tested by independent cryptographic test laboratories or by following guidance in SP800-90B (`http://csrc.nist.gov/publications/drafts/800-90/draft-sp800-90b.pdf`).

Ciphersuites

The fun part of applied cryptography is combining one or more of the above algorithm types to achieve specifically desired security properties. In many communication protocols, these algorithm groupings are often called **ciphersuites**. Depending on the protocol at hand, a cipher-suite specifies the particular set of algorithms, possible key lengths, and uses of each.

Ciphersuites can be specified and enumerated in different ways. For example, **transport layer security (TLS)** offers a wide array of ciphersuites to protect network sessions for web services, general HTTP traffic, **real-time protocols (RTP)**, and many others. An example TLS cipher-suite enumeration and their interpretation is as follows:

`TLS_RSA_WITH_AES_128_GCM_SHA256`, which interprets to using:

- RSA algorithm for the server's public key certificate authentication (digital signature). RSA is also the public key-based key transport (for passing the client-generated pre-master secret to the server).

- AES algorithm (using 128-bit length keys) for encrypting all data through the TLS tunnel.

- AES encryption is to be performed using the **Galois counter mode (GCM)**; this provides the tunnel's ciphertext as well as the MACs for each TLS datagram.

- SHA256 to be used as the hashing algorithm.

Using each of the cryptographic algorithms indicated in the cipher-suite, the specific security properties needed of the TLS connection and its setup are realized:

1. The client authenticates the server by validating an RSA-based signature on its public key certificate (the RSA signature was performed over a SHA256 hash of the public key certificate, actually).

2. Now a session key is needed for tunnel encryption. The client encrypts its large, randomly generated number (called **pre-master secret**) using the server's public RSA key and sends it to the server (that is, only the server, and no man-in-the-middle, can decrypt it).

3. Both the client and server use the pre-master secret to compute a master secret. Key derivation is performed for both parties to generate an identical key blob containing the AES key that will encrypt the traffic.

4. The AES-GCM algorithm is used for AES encryption/decryption—this particular mode of AES also computes the MAC appended to teach TLS datagram (note that some TLS ciphersuites use the HMAC algorithm for this).

Other cryptographic protocols employ similar types of ciphersuites (for example, IPSec), but the point is that no matter the protocol—IoT or otherwise—cryptographic algorithms are put together in different ways to counter specific threats (for example, MITM) in the protocol's intended usage environment.

Cryptographic module principles

So far, we have discussed cryptographic algorithms, algorithm inputs, uses, and other important aspects of applied cryptography. Familiarity with cryptographic algorithms is not enough, however. The proper implementation of cryptography in what are called cryptographic modules, though a topic not for the faint of heart, is needed for IoT security. Earlier in my (Van Duren) career, I had the opportunity not only to test many cryptographic devices, but also manage, as laboratory director, two of the largest NIST-accredited FIPS 140-2 cryptographic test laboratories. In this capacity, I had the opportunity to oversee and help validate literally hundreds of different device hardware and software implementations, smart cards, hard drives, operating systems, **hardware security modules (HSM)**, and many other cryptographic devices. In this section, I will share with you some of the wisdom gained from these experiences. But first, we must define a cryptographic module.

A cryptographic implementation can come from device OEMs, ODMs, BSP providers, security software establishments, just about anyone. A cryptographic implementation can be realized in hardware, software, firmware, or some combination thereof, and is responsible for processing the cryptographic algorithms and securely storing cryptographic keys (remember, compromise of your keys means compromise of your communications or other data). Borrowing NIST's term from the US Government's cryptographic module standard, FIPS 140-2, a cryptographic module is "the set of hardware, software, and/or firmware that implements approved security functions (including cryptographic algorithms and key generation) and is contained within the cryptographic boundary" (http://csrc.nist.gov/publications/fips/fips140-2/fips1402.pdf). The cryptographic boundary, also defined in FIPS 140-2, is *an explicitly defined continuous perimeter that establishes the physical bounds of a cryptographic module and contains all the hardware, software, and/or firmware components of a cryptographic module.* A generalized representation of a cryptographic module is shown in the following image:

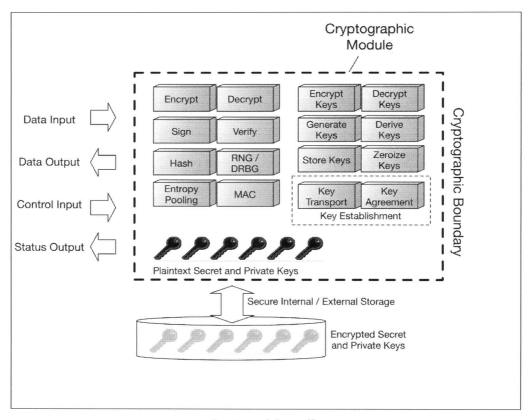

Crypto-modules.graffle

Without creating a treatise on cryptographic modules, the security topics that pertain to them include the following:

- Definition of the cryptographic boundary

- Protecting a module's ports and other interfaces (physical and logical)

- Identifying who or what connects (local or remote users) to the cryptographic module, how they authenticate to it and what services—security-relevant or not – the module provides them

- Proper management and indication of state during self tests and error conditions (needed by the host IoT device)

- Physical security—protection against tampering and/or response to tamper conditions

- Operating system integration, if applicable

- Cryptographic key management relevant to the module (key management is discussed in much more detail from a system perspective later), including how keys are generated, managed, accessed, and used

- Cryptographic self tests (health of the implementation) and responses to failures

- Design assurance

Each of the preceding areas roughly maps to each of the 11 topic areas of security in the FIPS 140-2 standard (note that, at this time, the standard is poised to be updated and superseded).

One of the principal functions of the cryptographic module is to protect cryptographic keys from compromise. Why? Simple. If keys are compromised, there's no point encrypting, signing, or otherwise protecting the integrity of the data using cryptography. Yes, if one doesn't properly engineer or integrate the cryptographic module for the threat environment at hand, there may little point in using cryptography at all.

One of the most important aspects of augmenting IoT devices with cryptography is the definition, selection, or incorporation of another device's cryptographic boundary. Generally speaking, a device can have an internal, embedded cryptographic module, or the device can itself be the cryptographic module (that is, the IoT device's enclosure is the crypto boundary).

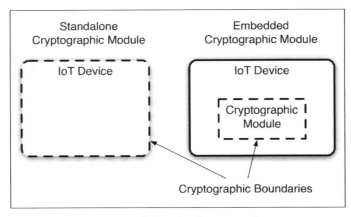

crypto-module-embodiments.graffle

From an IoT perspective, the cryptographic boundary defines the cryptographic island on which all cryptographic functions are to be performed within a given device. Using an embedded crypto module, IoT buyers and integrators should verify with IoT device vendors that, indeed, no cryptography whatsoever is being performed outside of the embedded cryptographic module's boundary.

There are advantages and disadvantages to different cryptographic module embodiments. In general, the smaller and tighter the module, 1) the less attack surface and 2) the less software, firmware, and hardware logic there is to maintain. The larger the boundary (as in some standalone crypto modules), the less flexibility to alter non-cryptographic logic, something much more important to vendors and system owners who may be required to use, for example, US Government validated FIPS 140-2 crypto modules (discussed next).

Both product security designers and system security integrators need to be fully aware of the implications of how devices implement cryptography. In many cases, product vendors will procure and integrate internal cryptographic modules that have been validated by independent FIPS testing laboratories.

This is strongly advisable for the following reasons:

- **Algorithm selection**: While algorithm selection can be a contentious issue with regard to national sovereignty, in general, most organizations such as the US government do not desire weak or otherwise unproven cryptographic algorithms to be used to protect sensitive data. Yes, there are excellent algorithms that are not approved for US government use, but in addition to ensuring the selection and specification of good algorithms, NIST also goes to great lengths to ensure old algorithms and key lengths are discontinued when they become outdated from advances in cryptanalytic and computational attacks. In other words, sticking to well established and well-specified algorithms trusted by a large government is not a bad idea. A number of NIST-accepted algorithms are also trusted by the **National Security Agency (NSA)** for use in protecting up to top secret data — with the caveat that the cryptographic module meets NSA type standards relevant to assurance levels needed for classified information. Algorithms such as AES (256-bit key lengths), ECDSA and ECDH are both allowed by NIST (for unclassified) and the NSA (for classified) under certain conditions.

- **Algorithm validation**: Test laboratories validate — as part of a crypto module test suite — the correctness (using a variety of known answer and other tests) of cryptographic algorithm implementations as they operate on the module. This is beneficial because the slightest algorithmic or implementation error can render the cryptography useless and lead to severe information integrity, confidentiality, and authentication losses. Algorithm validation is NOT cryptographic module validation; it is a subset of it.

- **Cryptographic module validation**: Test laboratories also validate that each and every applicable FIPS 140-2 security requirement is satisfied at or within the defined cryptographic boundary according to its security policy. This is performed using a variety of conformance tests, ranging from device specification and other documentation, source code, and very importantly, operational testing (as well as algorithm validation, mentioned previously).

This brings us to identifying some of hazards of FIPS 140-2 or any other security conformance test regimen, especially as they relate to the IoT. As a US government standard, FIPS 140-2 is applied incredibly broadly to any number of device types, and as such, can lose a degree of interpretive specificity (depending on the properties of the device to which one attempts to apply the standard). In addition, the validation only applies to a vendor-selected cryptographic boundary—and this boundary may or may not be truly suitable for certain environments and related risks. This is where NIST washes its hands. There were a number of instances when consulting with device vendors where I advised vendors against defining a cryptographic boundary that I knew was disingenuous at best, insecure at worst. However, if the vendor was able to meet all of the FIPS 140-2 requirements at their selected boundary, there was nothing I could do as an independent test laboratory to deny them the strategy. Conformance requirements versus actual security obtained by satisfying them is a never-ending struggle in standards bodies and conformance test regimes.

Given the previous benefits (and also hazards), the following advice is given with regard to utilization and deployment of FIPS 140-2 cryptographic modules in your IoT implementations:

- No device should use interfaces to a cryptographic algorithm aside from those provided by its parent crypto module (meaning outside of the cryptographic boundary). In fact, a device should not perform any cryptographic functions outside of a secured perimeter.

- No device should ever store a plaintext cryptographic key outside of its crypto module's boundary (even if it is still within the device but outside its embedded crypto module). Better yet, store all keys in encrypted form and then apply the strictest protections to the key-encrypting key.

- System integrators, when integrating cryptographic devices, should consult the device vendors and check the publicly available database on how the crypto module was defined prior to integration into the device. The definition of its cryptographic boundary, by US regulation, is identified in the module's non-proprietary security policy (posted online). Validated FIPS 140-2 modules can be checked at the following location: `http://csrc.nist.gov/groups/STM/cmvp/documents/140-1/140val-all.htm`. It is necessary to understand the degree to which an embedded module secures itself versus relying on its host (for example, with regard to physical security and tampering).

- Select cryptographic modules whose FIPS 140-2 validation assurance levels (1-4) are commensurate with the threat environment into which you plan to deploy them. For example, physical security at FIPS 140-2, level 2 does not require a tamper response mechanism (to wipe sensitive key material upon tamper); levels 3 and 4 do, however. If deploying modules into very high threat environments, select higher levels of assurance OR embed lower-level assurance modules into additionally secured hosts or facilities.

- When integrating a cryptographic module, ensure that the intended operators, host devices, or interfacing endpoints identified in the module's Security Policy map to actual users and non-human devices in the system. Applicable roles, services and authentication to a cryptographic module may be external or internal to a device; integrators need to know this and ensure the mapping is complete and secure.

- When implementing more complicated integrations, consult individuals and organizations that have expertise not only in applied cryptography, but also in cryptographic modules, device implementation, and integration. There are far more ways to get the cryptography wrong than to get it right.

Using validated cryptographic implementations is an excellent practice overall, but do it smartly and don't assume that certain cryptographic modules that would seem to meet all of the functional and performance requirements are a good idea for all environments.

Cryptographic key management fundamentals

Now that we have addressed basic cryptography and cryptographic modules, it is necessary to delve into the topic of cryptographic key management. Cryptographic modules can be considered cryptographically secured islands in larger systems, each module containing cryptographic algorithms, keys, and other assets needed to protect sensitive data. Deploying cryptographic modules securely, however, frequently requires cryptographic key management. Planning key management for an embedded device and/or full scale IoT enterprise is essential to securing and rolling out IoT systems. This requires organizations to normalize the types of cryptographic material within their IoT devices and ensure they work across systems and organizations. Key management is the art and science of protecting cryptographic keys within devices (crypto modules) and across the enterprise. It is an arcane technical discipline that was initially developed and evolved by the US Department of Defense long before most commercial companies had an inkling of what it was or had any need for cryptography in the first place. Now, more than ever, it is a subject that organizations must get right in order to secure connected things in our world.

The fallout from the Walker spy ring led to the creation of many of the key management systems and techniques widely used today by the Department of Defense and NSA today. Starting in 1968, US Navy officer John Walker began selling classified cryptographic key material to the Soviet intelligence services. Because this internal compromise was not discovered for many years (he was not caught until 1985), the total damage to US national security was enormous. To prevent crypto key material compromise and maintain a highly accountable system of tracking keys, various DoD services (the Navy and the Air Force) began creating their own key management systems that were eventually folded into what is today known as the NSA's **Electronic Key Management System (EKMS)**. The EKMS is now being modernized into the **key management infrastructure (KMI)** (https://en.wikipedia.org/wiki/John_Anthony_Walker).

The topic of cryptographic key management is frequently misunderstood, often more so than cryptography itself. Indeed, there are few practitioners in the discipline. Cryptography and key management are siblings; the security provided by each depends enormously on the other. Key management is often not implemented at all or is implemented insecurely. Either way, unauthorized disclosure and compromise of cryptographic keys through poor key management renders the use of cryptography moot. Necessary privacy and assurance of information integrity and origin is lost.

It is also important to note that the standards that specify and describe PKIs are based on secure key management principles. PKIs, by definition, *are* key management systems. Regarding the IoT, it is important for organizations to understand the basic principles of key management because not all IoT devices will interact with and consume PKI certificates (that is, be able to benefit from third party key management services). A variety of other cryptographic key types—symmetric and asymmetric—will be utilized in the IoT whether it's administering devices (SSH), providing cryptographic gateways (TLS/IPSec), or just performing simple integrity checks on IoT messages (using MACs).

Why is key management important? Disclosure of many types of cryptographic variables can lead to catastrophic data loss even years or decades after the cryptographic transaction has taken place. Today's Internet is replete with people, systems, and software performing a variety of man-in-the-middle attacks, ranging from simple network monitoring to full-scale nation state attacks and compromises of hosts and networks. One can collect or re-route otherwise encrypted, protected traffic and store it for months, years, or decades. In the meantime, the collectors can clandestinely work for long periods of time to exploit people (human intelligence, as in John Walker) and technology (this usually requires a cryptanalyst) to acquire the keys that were used to encrypt the collected transactions. Within IoT devices, centralized key generation and distribution sources or storage systems, key management systems and processes perform the dirty work of ensuring cryptographic keys are not compromised during machine or human handling.

Key management addresses a number of cryptographic key handling topics pertinent to the devices and the systems in which they operate. These topics are indicated in the following relational diagram:

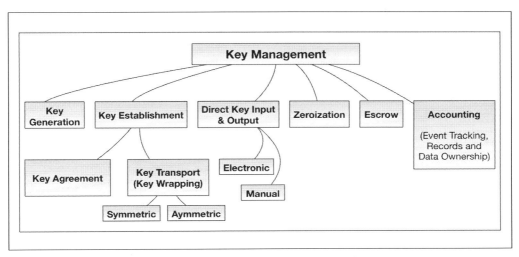

KeyMgmt-hierarchy.graffle

Key generation

Key generation refers to how, when, and on what devices cryptographic keys are generated and using what algorithms. Keys should be generated using a well vetted RNG or DRBG seeded with sufficient min-entropy (discussed earlier). Key generation can be performed directly on the device or in a more centralized system (the latter requiring subsequent distribution to the device).

Key establishment

Much confusion exists in terms of what constitutes cryptographic *key establishment*. Key establishment is simply the act of two parties either 1) agreeing on a specific cryptographic key or 2) acting as sender and receiver roles in the transport of a key from one to the other. More specifically, it is as follows:

- **Key agreement** is the act of two parties contributing algorithmically to the creation of a shared key. In other words, generated or stored public values from one party are sent to the other (frequently in plaintext) and input into complementary algorithm processes to arrive at a shared secret. This shared secret (in conventional, cryptographic best practices) is then input to a key derivation function (frequently hash-based) to arrive at a cryptographic key or set of keys (key blob).

- **Key transport** is the act of one party transmitting a cryptographic key or its precursor to another party by first encrypting it with a **key encryption key (KEK)**. The KEK may be symmetric (for example, an AES key) or asymmetric (for example, a RSA public key). In the former case, the KEK must be securely pre-shared with the recipient or also established using some type of cryptographic scheme. In the latter case, the encrypting key is the recipient's public key and only the recipient may decrypt the transported key using their private key (not shared).

Key derivation

Key derivation refers to how a device or piece of software constructs cryptographic keys from other keys and variables, including passwords (so called password-based key derivation). NIST SP800-108 asserts "....*a key derivation function (KDF) is a function with which an input key and other input data are used to generate (that is, derive) keying material that can be employed by cryptographic algorithms.*" Source: `http://csrc.nist.gov/publications/nistpubs/800-108/sp800-108.pdf`.

A generalized depiction of key derivation is shown in the following image:

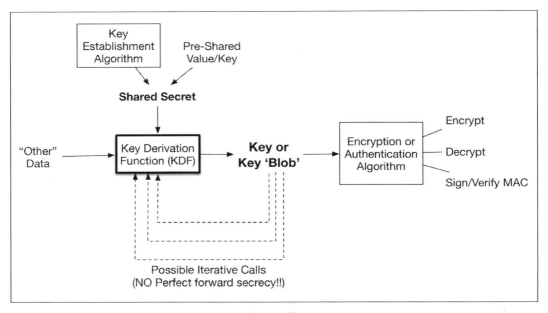

KDF.graffle

Poor practices in key derivation led to the US government disallowing their use with certain exceptions until best practices could be incorporated into the NIST special publications. Key derivation is frequently performed in many secure communication protocols such as TLS and IPSec by deriving the actual session keys from an established shared secret, transported random number (for example, pre-master secret in SSL/TLS), or current key.

Password-based key derivation (**PBKDF**) is the process of deriving, in part, a cryptographic key from a unique password and is specified in NIST SP 800-132. A generalized depiction of this process is shown in the following image:

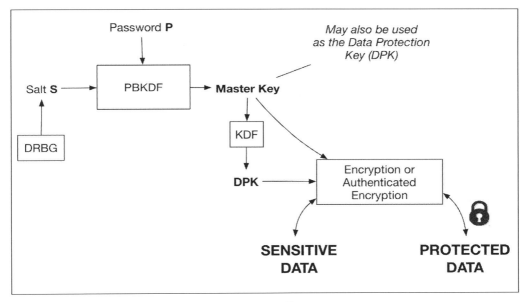

PBKDF.graffle

Source: http://csrc.nist.gov/publications/nistpubs/800-132/nist-sp800-132.pdf

Key storage

Key storage refers to how secure storage of keys (frequently encrypted using KEKs) is performed and in what type of device(s). Secure storage may be achieved by encrypting a database (with excellent protection of the database encryption key) or other types of key stores. In enterprise key escrow/storage systems, cryptographic keys should be encrypted using a **hardware security module** (**HSM**) prior to long-term storage. HSMs, themselves cryptographic modules, are specifically designed to be very difficult to hack by providing extensive physical and logical security protections. For example, most HSMs possess a tamper-responsive enclosure. If tampered with, the HSM will automatically wipe all sensitive security parameters, cryptographic keys, and so on. Regardless, always ensure that HSMs are stored in secure facilities. In terms of secure HSM access, HSMs are often designed to work with cryptographic tokens for access control and invoking sensitive services. For example, the SafeNet token—called a PED key—allows users to securely access sensitive HSM services (locally and even remotely).

Example HSM vendors include Thales e-Security and SafeNet.

Key escrow

Key escrow is frequently a necessary evil. Given that encrypted data cannot be decrypted if the key is lost, many entities opt to store and backup cryptographic keys, frequently offsite, to use at a later time. Risks associated with key escrow are simple; making copies of keys and storing them in other locations increases the attack surface of the data protection. A compromised, escrowed key is just as impactful as compromise of the original copy.

Key lifetime

Key lifetime refers to how long a key should be used (actually encrypting, decrypting, signing, MACing, and so on.) before being destroyed (zeroized). In general, asymmetric keys (for example, PKI certificates) can be used for much longer periods of time given their ability to be used for establishing fresh, unique session keys (achieving perfect forward secrecy). Symmetric keys, in general, should have much shorter key lifetimes. Upon expiration, new keys can be provisioned in myriad ways:

- Transported by a central key management server or other host (key transport, using algorithms such as AES-WRAP—the AES-WRAP algorithm encrypts the key being transported and as such the AES-WRAP key makes use of a KEK)

- Securely embedded in new software or firmware
- Generated by the device (for example, by a NIST SP800-90 DRBG)
- Mutually established by the device with another entity (for example, Elliptic Curve Diffie Hellman, Diffie Hellman, MQV)
- Manually entered into a device (for example, by typing it in or electronically squirting it in from a secure key loading device)

Key zeroization

Unauthorized disclosure of a secret or private cryptographic key or algorithm state effectively renders the application of cryptography useless. Encrypted sessions can be captured, stored, then decrypted days, months, or years later if the cryptographic key used to protect the session is acquired by a malicious entity.

Securely eradicating cryptographic keys from memory is the topic of zeroization. Many cryptographic libraries offer both conditional and explicit zeroization routines designed to securely wipe keys from runtime memory as well as long term static storage. If your IoT device(s) implement cryptography, they should have well-vetted key zeroization strategies. Depending on the memory location, different types of zeroization need to be employed. Secure wiping, in general, does not just dereference the cryptographic key (that is, setting a pointer or reference variable to null) in memory; zeroization must actively overwrite the memory location either with zeroes (hence the term zeroization) or randomly generated data. Multiple overwrites may be necessary to sufficiently render the crypto variables irretrievable from certain types of memory attacks (for example, freezing memory). If an IoT vendor is making use of cryptographic libraries, it is imperative that proper use of its APIs is followed, including zeroization of all key material after use (many libraries do this automatically for session-based protocols such as TLS).

Disposal of IoT devices containing highly sensitive PII data may also need to consider active destruction of memory devices. For example, hard drives containing classified data have been degaussed in strong electromagnetic fields for years to remove secret and top secret data and prevent it from falling into the wrong hands. Mechanical destruction sufficient to ensure physical obliteration of memory logic gates may also be necessary, though degaussing and mechanical destruction are generally necessary only for devices containing the most sensitive data, or devices simply containing massive amounts of sensitive data (for example, hard drives and SSD memory containing thousands or millions of health records or financial data).

Zeroization is a topic some readers may know more about than they think. The recent (2016) conflict between the US Federal Bureau of Investigation and Apple brought to light the FBI's limitation in accessing a terrorist's iPhone without its contents (securely encrypted) being made irretrievable. Too many failed password attempts would trigger the zeroization mechanism, rendering the data irretrievable.

Accounting and management

Identifying, tracking, and accounting for the generation, distribution, and destruction of key material between entities is where accounting and management functions are needed.

It is also important to balance security and performance. This is realized when establishing cryptographic key lifetimes, for example. In general, the shorter the key lifetime, the smaller the impact of a compromise, that is, the less data surface dependent on the key. Shorter lifetimes, however, increase the relative overhead of generating, establishing, distributing, and accounting for the key material. This is where public key cryptography — that enables forward secrecy — has been invaluable. Asymmetric keys don't need to be changed as frequently as symmetric ones. They have the ability to establish a new, fresh set of symmetric keys on their own. Not all systems can execute public key algorithms, however.

Secure key management also requires vendors to be very cognizant of the cryptographic key hierarchy, especially in the device manufacturing and distribution process. Built-in key material may emanate from the manufacturer (in which case, the manufacturer must be diligent about protecting these keys), overwritten, and used or possibly discarded by an end user. Each key may be a prerequisite for transitioning a device to a new state or deploying it in the field (as in a bootstrapping or enrollment process). Cryptographic-enabled IoT device manufacturers should carefully design and document the key management processes, procedures, and systems used to securely deploy products. In addition, manufacturer keys should be securely stored in HSMs within secure facilities and access-controlled rooms.

Access controls to key management systems (for example, HSMs and HSM-connected servers) must be severely restricted given the large ramifications of the loss or tampering of even one single cryptographic key. One will often find key management systems — even in the most secure facility or data center — housed within a cage under lock and key and continuous camera surveillance.

Summary of key management recommendations

Given the above definitions and descriptions, IoT vendors and system integrators should also consider the following recommendations with regard to key management:

- Ensure that validated cryptographic modules securely store provisioned keys within IoT devices—physical and logical protection of keys in a secure trust store will pay security dividends.

- Ensure that cryptographic keys are sufficiently long. An excellent guide is to refer to NIST SP 800-131A (`http://nvlpubs.nist.gov/nistpubs/ SpecialPublications/NIST.SP.800-131Ar1.pdff`), which provides guidance on appropriate key lengths to use for FIPS-approved cryptographic algorithms. If interested in equivalent strengths (computational resistance to brute forcing attacks), one can reference NIST SP800-57. It is important to sunset both algorithms and key lengths when they are no longer sufficiently strong relative to state-of-the-art attacks.

- Ensure that there are technical and procedural controls in place to securely wipe (zeroize) cryptographic keys after use or expiration. Don't keep any key around any longer than is necessary. Plaintext cryptographic variables are known to exist in memory for long periods after use unless actively wiped. A well-engineered cryptographic library may zeroize keys under certain circumstances, but some libraries leave it to the using application to invoke the zeroization API when needed. Session based keys, for example, the ciphering and HMAC keys used in a TLS session, should be immediately zeroized following termination of the session.

- Use cryptographic algorithms and protocol options in a manner that **perfect forward secrecy (PFS)** is provided. PFS is an option in many communication protocols that utilize key establishment algorithms such as Diffie Hellman and Elliptic Curve Diffie Hellman. PFS has the beneficial property that a compromise of one set of session keys doesn't compromise follow-on generated session keys. For example, utilizing PFS in DH/ECDH will ensure that ephemeral (one time use) private/public keys are generated for each use. This means that there will be no backward relationship between adjacent shared secret values (and therefore the keys derived from them) from session to session. Compromise of today's key will not allow forward, adversarial computation of tomorrow's key, thus tomorrow's key is better protected.

- Severely restrict key management system roles, services, and accesses. Access to cryptographic key management systems must be restricted both physically and logically. Protected buildings and access-controlled rooms (or cages) are important for controlling physical access. User or administrator access must also be carefully managed using principles such as separation of duties (not giving one single role or identity full access to all services) and multi-person integrity (requiring more than one individual to invoke sensitive services)

- Use well vetted key management protocols to perform primitive key management functions such as key transport, key establishment, and more. Being an arcane topic, and the fact that many vendors utilize proprietary solutions, there are few key management protocols commonly deployed today. The OASIS group, however, maintains a relatively recently designed industry solution called the **key management interoperability protocol (KMIP)**. KMIP is now in use by a number of vendors as a simple backbone protocol for performing sender-receiver key management exchanges. It supports a number of cryptographic key management algorithms and was designed keeping multi-vendor interoperability in mind. KMIP is programming language agnostic and useful in everything from large enterprise key management software to embedded device management.

Examining cryptographic controls for IoT protocols

This section examines cryptographic controls as integrated into various IoT protocols. Lacking these controls, IoT point-to-point and end-to-end communications would be impossible to secure.

Cryptographic controls built into IoT communication protocols

One of the primary challenges for IoT device developers is understanding the interactions between different types of IoT protocols and the optimal approach for layering security across these protocols.

There are many options for establishing communication capabilities for IoT devices and often these communication protocols provide a layer of authentication and encryption that should be applied at the link layer. IoT communication protocols such as ZigBee, ZWave, and Bluetooth-LE all have configuration options for applying authentication, data integrity, and confidentiality protections. Each of these protocols supports the ability to create wireless networks of IoT devices. Wi-Fi is also an option for supporting the wireless link required for many IoT devices and also includes inherent cryptographic controls for maintaining confidentiality, integrity and authentication.

Riding above the IoT communication protocols are data-centric protocols. Many of these protocols require the services of lower layer security capabilities, such as those provided by the IoT communication protocols or security-specific protocols such as DTLS or SASL. IoT data centric protocols can be divided into two categories that include REST-type protocols such as CoAP and publish/subscribe protocols such as DDS and MQTT. These often require an underlying IP layer; however, some protocols, such as MQTT-SN, have been tailored to operate on RF links such as ZigBee.

An interesting aspect of publish/subscribe IoT protocols is the need to provide access controls to the topics that are published by IoT resources, as well as the need to ensure that attackers cannot publish unauthorized information to any particular topic. This can be handled by applying unique keys to each topic that is published.

ZigBee

ZigBee leverages the underlying security services of the IEEE 802.15.4 MAC layer. The 802.15.4 MAC layer supports the AES algorithm with a 128-bit key for both encryption/decryption as well as data integrity by appending a MAC to the data frame (`http://www.libelium.com/security-802-15-4-zigbee/`). These security services are optional, however, and ZigBee devices can be configured to not use either the encryption or MAC capabilities built into the protocol. In fact, there are multiple security options available as described in the following table:

ZigBee security configuration	Description
No security	No encryption and no data authentication
AES-CBC-MAC-32	Data authentication using a 32-bit MAC; no encryption
AES-CBC-MAC-64	Data authentication using a 64-bit MAC; no encryption
AES-CBC-MAC-128	Data authentication using a 128-bit MAC; no encryption
AES-CTR	Data is encrypted using AES-CTR with 128-bit key; no authentication

ZigBee security configuration	Description
AES-CCM-32	Data is encrypted and data authentication using 32-bit MAC
AES-CCM-64	Data is encrypted and data authentication using 64-bit MAC
AES-CCM-128	Data is encrypted and data authentication using 128-bit MAC

The 802.15.4 MAC layer in the preceding table, ZigBee supports additional security features that are integrated directly with the layer below. ZigBee consists of both a network layer and an application layer and relies upon three types of keys for security features:

- Master keys, which are pre-installed by the vendor and used to protect a key exchange transaction between two ZigBee nodes

- Link keys, which are unique keys per node, allowing secure node-to-node communications

- Network keys, which are shared across all ZigBee nodes in a network and provisioned by the ZigBee trust center; these support secure broadcast communications

Setting up the key management strategy for a ZigBee network can be a difficult challenge. Implementers must weigh options that run the spectrum from pre-installing all keys or provisioning all keys from the trust center. Note that the trust center default network key must always be changed and that any provisioning of keys must occur using secure processes. Key rotation must also be considered since ZigBee keys should be refreshed on a pre-defined basis.

There are three options for ZigBee nodes to obtain keys. First, nodes can be pre-installed with keys. Second, nodes can have keys (except for the master key) transported to them from the ZigBee Trust Center. Finally, nodes can establish their keys using options that include **symmetric key establishment (SKKE)** and **certificate-based key establishment (CBKE)** (`https://www.mwrinfosecurity.com/system/assets/849/original/mwri-zigbee-overview-finalv2.pdf`).

Master keys support the generation of link keys on ZigBee devices using the SKKE process. Link keys shared between a ZigBee node and the trust center are known as **trust center link keys** (**TCLK**). These keys allow the transport of a new network key to nodes in the network. Link and network keys can be pre-installed; however, the more secure option is to provide for key establishment for link keys that support node-to-node communications.

Network keys are transmitted in an encrypted APS transport command from the trust center.

Although link keys are optimal for node-to-node secure communication, research has shown that they are not always optimal. They require more memory resources per device, something often not available for IoT devices (`http://www.libelium.com/security-802-15-4-zigbee/`).

The CBKE process provides another mechanism for ZigBee link key establishment. It is based on an **Elliptic Curve Qu-Vanstone** (**ECQV**) implicit certificate that is tailored towards IoT device needs; it is much smaller than a traditional X.509 certificate. These certificates are called implicit certificates and their structure provides a significant size reduction as compared to traditional explicit certificates such as X.509 (this is a nice feature in constrained wireless networking) (`http://arxiv.org/ftp/arxiv/papers/1206/1206.3880.pdf`).

Bluetooth-LE

Bluetooth-LE is based on the Bluetooth Core Specification Version (4.2) and specifies a number of modes that provide options for authenticated or unauthenticated pairing, data integrity protections, and link encryption. Specifically, Bluetooth-LE supports the following security concepts (reference: Bluetooth Specification, Version 4.2):

- **Pairing**: Devices create one or more shared secret keys
- **Bonding**: The act of storing the keys created during pairing for use in subsequent connections; this forms a trusted device pair
- **Device authentication**: Verification that the paired devices have trusted keys
- **Encryption**: Scrambling of plaintext message data into ciphertext data
- **Message integrity**: Protects against tampering with data

Bluetooth-LE provides four options for device association:

Model	Details
Numeric comparison	The user is shown a six-digit number and enters *YES* if the numbers are the same on both devices. Note that with Bluetooth 4.2 the six-digit number is not associated with the encryption operations between the two devices.
Just works	Designed for devices that do not include a display. Uses the same model as numeric comparison however the user is not shown a number.
Out of band	Allows use of another protocol for secure pairing. Often combined with **near-field communications** (**NFC**) to allow for secure pairing. In this case, the NFC protocol would be used to exchange the device Bluetooth addresses and cryptographic information.
Passkey entry	Allows a six-character passkey to be entered on one device and displayed on another for confirmation.

Bluetooth-LE makes use of a number of keys that are used together to provide the requested security services. The following table provides a view into the cryptographic keys that play a role in Bluetooth-LE security.

Key type	Description
Temporary key (TK)	Determined by the type of Bluetooth pairing used, the TK can be different lengths. It is used as an input to the cipher-based derivation of the **short-term key** (**STK**).
Short-term key (STK)	STK is used for secure distribution of key material and is based on the TK and a set of random values provided by each device participating in the pairing process.
Long-term key (LTK)	The LTK is used to generate a 128-bit key employed for link-layer encryption.
Connection signature resolving key (CSRK)	The CSRK is used for signing data at the ATT layer.
Identity resolving key (IRK)	The IRK is used to generate a private address based on a device public address. This provides a mechanism for device identity and privacy protection.

Bluetooth-LE supports cryptographically signed data through the use of the CSRK. The CSRK is used to apply a signature to a Bluetooth-LE **protocol data unit** (**PDU**). The signature is a MAC that is generated by the signing algorithm and a counter that increments for each PDU sent. The addition of the counter provides additional replay protections.

Bluetooth-LE also supports the ability to provide privacy protections for devices. This requires the use of the IRK which is used to generate a special private address for the device. There are two options available for privacy support, one where the device generates the private address and one where the Bluetooth controller generates the address.

Near field communication (NFC)

NFC does not implement native cryptographic protection; however, it is possible to apply endpoint authentication across an NFC negotiation. NFC supports short-range communication and is often used as a first-step protocol to establish out-of-band pairings for use in other protocols, such as Bluetooth.

Cryptographic controls built into IoT messaging protocols

We will discuss here the various controls that are built into the messaging protocols.

MQTT

MQTT allows sending a username and password. Until recently, the specification recommended that passwords be no longer than 12 characters. The username and password are sent in the clear as part of the CONNECT message. As such it is critical that TLS be employed when using MQTT to prevent MITM attacks on the password. Ideally, end-to-end TLS connectivity between the two endpoints (vice gateway-to-gateway) should be used along with certificates to mutually authenticate the TLS connection.

CoAP

CoAP supports multiple authentication options for device-to-device communication. This can be paired with Datagram TLS (D-TLS) for higher-level confidentiality and authentication services.

CoAP defines multiple security modes based on the types of cryptographic material used: `https://tools.ietf.org/html/rfc7252#section-9`.

Mode	Description
NoSec	There is no protocol-level security as DTLS is disabled. This mode *may* be sufficient if used in cases where alternate forms of security can be enabled, for example, when IPsec is being used over a TCP connection or when a secure link layer is enabled; however, the authors do not recommend this configuration.
PreSharedKey	DTLS is enabled and there are pre-shared keys that can be used for nodal communication. These keys may also serve as group keys.
RawPublicKey	DTLS is enabled and the device has an asymmetric key pair without a certificate (a raw public key) that is validated using an out-of-band mechanism. The device also has an identity calculated from the public key and a list of identities of the nodes it can communicate with.
Certificate	DTLS is enabled and the device has an asymmetric key pair with an X.509 certificate (RFC5280) that binds it to its subject and is signed by some common trust root. The device also has a list of root trust anchors that can be used for validating a certificate.

DDS

The Object Management Group's **Data Distribution Standard (DDS)** security specification provides endpoint authentication and key establishment to enable message data origin authentication (using HMAC). Both digital certificates and various identity/authorization token types are supported.

REST

HTTP/REST typically requires the support of the TLS protocol for authentication and confidentiality services. Although basic authentication (where credentials are passed in the clear) can be used under the cover of TLS, this is not a recommended practice. Instead, attempt to stand up a token-based authentication (and authorization, if needed) approach such as OpenID identity layer on top of OAuth2. Additional security controls should be in place when using OAuth2, however. References for these controls can be found at the following websites:

* `http://www.oauthsecurity.com`
* `https://www.sans.org/reading-room/whitepapers/application/attacks-oauth-secure-oauth-implementation-33644`

Future directions of the IoT and cryptography

The cryptography used in the IoT today comprises the same cryptographic trust mechanisms used in the broader Internet. Like the Internet, however, the IoT is scaling to unprecedented levels that require far more distributed and decentralized trust mechanisms. Indeed, many of the large-scale, secure IoT transactions of the future will not be made of just simple client-server or point-to-multipoint cryptographic transactions. New or adapted cryptographic protocols must be developed and added to provide scalable, distributed trust. While it is difficult to predict what types of new protocols will ultimately be adopted, the distributed trust protocols developed for today's Internet applications may provide a glimpse into where things may be going with the IoT.

One such protocol is that of blockchain, a decentralized cryptographic trust mechanism that underlies the Bitcoin digital currency and provides a decentralized ledger of all legitimate transactions occurring across a system. Each node in a blockchain system participates in the process of maintaining this ledger. This is accomplished automatically through trusted consensus across all participants, the results of which are all inherently auditable. A blockchain is built up over time using cryptographic hashes from each of the previous blocks in the chain. As we discussed earlier in this chapter, hash functions allow one to generate a one-way fingerprint hash of an arbitrary chunk of data. A Merkle tree represents an interesting application of hash functions, as it represents a series of parallel-computed hashes that feed into a cryptographically strong resultant hash of the entire tree.

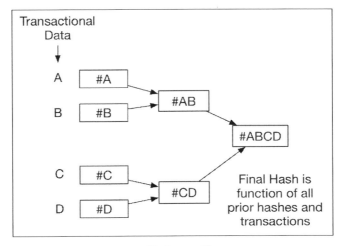

merkle-tree.graffle

Corruption or integrity loss of any one of the hashes (or data elements that were hashed) provides an indication that integrity was lost at a given point in the Merkle tree. In the case of blockchain, this Merkle tree pattern grows over time as new transactions (nodes representing hashable transactions) are added to the ledger; the ledger is available to all and is replicated across all nodes in the system.

Blockchains include a consensus mechanism that is used by nodes in the chain to agree upon how to update the chain. Considering a distributed control system, for example, a controller on a network may want to command an actuator to perform some action. Nodes on the network could potentially work together to agree that the controller is authorized to command the action and that the actuator is authorized to perform the action.

An interesting twist on this, however, is that the blockchain can be used for more than this base functionality. For example, if the controller typically receives data from a set of sensors and one of the sensors begins to provide data that is not within norms or acceptable tolerances (using variance analysis for instance), the controller can update the blockchain to remove authorizations from the wayward sensor. The update to the blockchain can then be hashed and combined with other updated (for example, transactions) hashes through a Merkle tree. The resultant would then be placed in the proposed new block's header, along with a timestamp and the hash of the previous block.

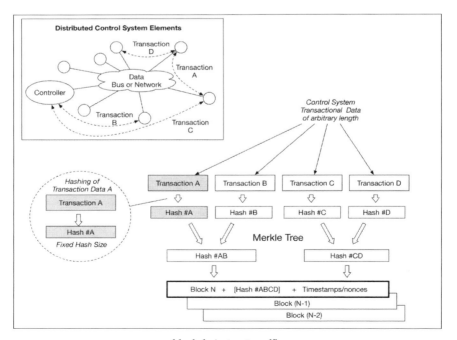

blockchain-trust.graffle

This type of solution may begin to lay the groundwork for resilient and fault-tolerant peer-to-peer networks within distributed, trusted CPS. Such functionality can be achieved in real time and near-real time use cases with appropriate performance requirements and engineering. Legacy systems can be augmented by layering the transactional protocols in front of the system's control, status, and data messages. While we don't ultimately know how such techniques may or may not be realized in future IoT systems, they offer us ideas on how to employ powerful cryptographic algorithms to solve the enormous challenges of ensuring distributed trust at a large scale.

Summary

In this chapter, we touched on the enormously large and complex world of applied cryptography, cryptographic modules, key management, cryptographic application in IoT protocols, and possible future looks into cryptographic enablement of distributed IoT trust in the form of blockchain technology.

Perhaps the most important message of this chapter is to take cryptography and its methods of implementation seriously. Many IoT devices and service companies simply do not come from a heritage of building secure cryptographic systems and it is unwise to consider a vendor's hyper-marketed claims that their "256 bit AES" is secure. There are just too many ways to thwart cryptography if not properly implemented.

In the next chapter, we will dive into **identity and access management (IAM)** for the IoT.

6
Identity and Access Management Solutions for the IoT

While society begins to adopt smart home and IoT wearables, IoT devices and applications are diversifying toward broader application in professional, government, and other environments as well. The network connectivity needed to support them is becoming ubiquitous and to that end devices will need to be identified and access provisioned in new and different environments and organizations. This chapter provides an introduction to identity and access management for IoT devices. The identity lifecycle is reviewed and a discussion on infrastructure components required for provisioning authentication credentials is provided, with a heavy focus on PKI. We also examine different types of authentication credentials and discuss new approaches to providing authorization and access control for IoT devices. We address these subjects in the following topic areas:

- Introductory discussion on **identity and access management (IAM)**
- Discussion of the identity lifecycle
- A primer on authentication credentials
- Background on IoT IAM infrastructure
- A discussion of IoT authorization and access control

An introduction to identity and access management for the IoT

Security administrators have traditionally been concerned with managing the identities of and controlling access for the people that are part of or interact with their technology infrastructure. Relatively recently, the concept of **bring your own device (BYOD)** was introduced, which allowed authorized individuals to associate mobile phones or laptops with their corporate account to receive network services on their personal devices. The allowed network services were typically provided once certain minimal security assurances were deemed to have been satisfied on the device. This could include using strong passwords for account access, application of virus scanners, or even mandating partial or full disk encryption to help with data loss prevention.

The IoT introduces a much richer connectivity environment than BYOD. Many more IoT devices are expected to be deployed throughout an organization than the usual one or two mobile phones or laptops for each employee. IAM infrastructures must be designed to scale to the number of devices that an organization will eventually support, potentially orders of magnitude higher than today. New IoT subsystems will continually be added to an organization as new capabilities arise to enable and streamline business processes.

The IoT's matrixed nature also introduces new challenges for security administrators in industrial and corporate deployments. Today, many IoT solutions are already being designed to be leased rather than owned. Consider the example of a leased radiology machine that records the number of scans and permits operations up to a certain number of entitlements. Scans are reported online, that is, the machine opens up a communications channel from the organization to the manufacturer. This channel/interface must be restricted to only allow authorized users (that is, the lessor or its agents), and only allow the specific machine(s) associated with the lessor to connect. Access control decisions can potentially become very complex, even restricted to specific device versions, time of day, and other constraints.

The matrixed nature of the IoT is taken further by the need to share information. This is true not only of sharing data collected by IoT sensors with third-party organizations, but also with sharing access to IoT sensors in the first place. Any IAM system for the IoT must be able to support this dynamic access control environment where sharing may need to be allowed/disallowed quickly and at a very granular level for both devices and information.

Finally, security administrators must take into account personal IoT devices that attach to their networks. This brings about not only security concerns as new attack vectors are introduced, but also significant privacy concerns related to safeguarding personal information. We have, for example, begun to see organizations support the use of personal fitness devices such as Fitbit for corporate health and wellness programs. In 2016, Oral Roberts University introduced a program that required all freshmen to wear a Fitbit and allow the device to report daily steps and heart rate information to the University's computer systems: `http://www.nydailynews.com/life-style/health/fitbits-required-freshmen-oklahoma-university-article-1.2518842`.

At the other end of the spectrum, a valuable OpenDNS report (reference `https://www.opendns.com/enterprise-security/resources/research-reports/2015-internet-of-things-in-the-enterprise-report/`) showed that in some companies, personnel were beginning to bring unauthorized IoT devices including Smart TVs into the enterprise. These devices were often reaching out to Internet services to share information. Smart devices are frequently designed by manufacturers to connect with the vendor's device-specific web services and other information infrastructure to support the device and the customer's use of it. This typically requires an 802.1x type of connectivity. Providing 802.1x-style network access control to IoT devices requires some thought, since there are so many of these devices that may attach to the network. Vendors are currently working on solutions that can fingerprint IP-based IoT devices and determine whether certain types should be granted access through DHCP provisioning of IP addresses. One may do this, for example, by fingerprinting the operating system or some other characteristic of the device.

IoT IAM is one aspect of an overarching security program that must be designed to mitigate this dynamic new environment, where:

- New devices can be securely added to the network at a rapid pace and for diverse functions
- Data and even devices can share not only within the organization but with other organizations
- Privacy is maintained despite consumer data being collected, stored, and frequently shared with others

The following figure shows a holistic IAM program for the IoT:

Integrate the IoT into the existing IAM and GRC	Integration with Physical Access Control System (PACS)	
IoT Identity Management (IDoT)	IoT Identity Relationship Management	IoT Device Password Management
OAuth2.0	802.1x	PKI
IoT Protocols (such as CoAP, REST, DDS,..)		
Security Protocols (TLS, DTLS, OSCOAP, OSCON)		
IPvX (4,6)		

As noted in in the preceding figure, it is important to line up the new IoT Identity and Access Management strategy with the existing governance models and IT systems in your organization. It may also be worthwhile to consider integration of authentication and authorization capabilities for your IoT devices with your **physical access control systems (PACS)**. PACS provide electronic means of enabling and enforcing physical access policies throughout your organization's facilities. Frequently, PACS systems are also integrated with **logical access control systems (LACS)**. LACS systems provide the technology and tools for managing identity, authentication, and authorization access to various computer, data, and network resources. PACS/LACS technologies represent the ideal systems for an organization to begin incorporating new IoT devices in a relatively controlled manner.

The identity lifecycle

Before we begin to examine the technologies that support IAM for the IoT, it is useful to lay out the lifecycle phases of what we call identity. The identity lifecycle for an IoT device begins with defining the naming conventions for the device; it ends with the removal of the device's identity from the system. The following figure provides a view of the process flow:

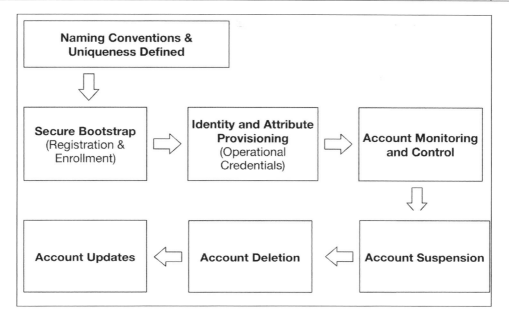

This lifecycle procedure should be established and applied to all IoT devices that are procured, configured, and ultimately attached to an organization's network. The first aspect requires a coordinated understanding of the categories of IoT devices and systems that will be introduced within your organization, both now and in the future. Establishing a structured identity namespace will significantly help manage the identities of the thousands or millions of devices that will eventually be added to your organization.

Establish naming conventions and uniqueness requirements

Uniqueness is a feature that can be randomized or deterministic (for example, algorithmically sequenced); its only requirement is that there are no others identical to it. The simplest unique identifier is a counter. Each value is assigned and never repeats itself. The other is a static value in concert with a counter, for example a device manufacturer ID plus a product line ID plus a counter. In many cases, a random value is used in concert with static and counter fields. Non-repetition is generally not enough from the manufacturer's perspective. Usually, something needs a name that provides some context. To this end, manufacturer-unique fields may be added in a variety of ways unique to the manufacturer or in conformance with an industry convention. Uniqueness may also be fulfilled by using a globally **unique identifier (UUID)** for which the UUID standard specified in RFC 4122 applies.

No matter the mechanism, so long as a device is able to be provisioned with an identifier that is non-repeating, unique to its manufacturer, use, application, or a hybrid of all the above, it should be acceptable for use in identity management. Beyond the mechanisms, the only warning is that the combination of all possible identifiers within a statically specified ID length cannot be exhausted prematurely if at all possible.

Once a method for assigning uniqueness to your IoT devices is established, the next step is to be able to logically identify the assets within their area of operation to support authentication and access control functions.

Naming a device

Every time you access a restricted computing resource, your identity is checked to ensure that you are authorized to access that specific resource. There are many ways that this can occur, but the end result of a successful implementation is that someone who does not have the right credentials is not allowed access. Although the process sounds simple, there are a number of difficult challenges that must be overcome when discussing identity and access management for the numerous constrained devices that comprise the IoT.

One of the first challenges is related to identity itself. Although identity may seem straightforward to you — your name for example — that identity must be translated into a piece of information that the computing resource (or access management system) understands. That identity must also not be duplicated across the information domain. Many computer systems today rely on a username, where each username within a domain is distinct. The username could be something as simple as `<lastname_firstname_middleiniital>`.

In the case of the IoT, understanding what identities — or names — to provision to a device can cause confusion. As discussed, in some systems devices use unique identifiers such as UUIDs or **electronic serial numbers** (ESNs).

We can see a good illustration by looking at how Amazon's first implementation of its IoT service makes use of IoT device serial numbers to identify devices. Amazon IoT includes a Thing Registry service that allows an administrator to register IoT devices, capturing for each the name of the thing and various attributes of the thing. The attributes can include data items such as:

- Manufacturer
- Type
- Serial number
- Deployment date
- Location

Note that such attributes can be used in what is called **attribute-based access control (ABAC)**. ABAC access approaches allow access decision policies to be defined not just by the identity of the device, but also its properties (attributes). Rich, potentially complex rules can be defined for the needs at hand.

The following figure provides a view of the AWS IoT service:

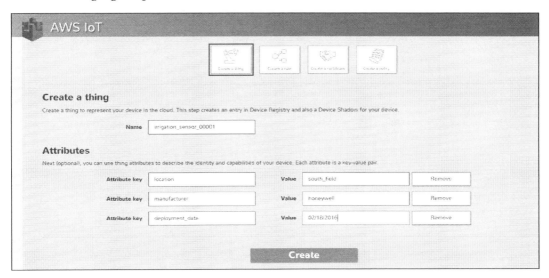

Even when identifiers such as UUIDs or ESNs are available for an IoT device, these identifiers are generally not sufficient for securing authentication and access control decisions; an identifier can easily be spoofed without enhancement through cryptographic controls. In these instances, administrators must bind another type of identifier to a device. This binding can be as simple as associating a password with the identifier or, more appropriately, using credentials such as digital certificates.

IoT messaging protocols frequently include the ability to transmit a unique identifier. For example, MQTT includes a ClientID field that can transmit a broker-unique client identifier. In the case of MQTT, the ClientID is used to maintain state within a unique broker-client communication session.

Secure bootstrap

Nothing is worse for security than an IoT-enabled system or network replete with false identities used in acts of identity theft, loss of private information, spoofing, and general mayhem. However, a difficult task in the identity lifecycle is to establish the initial trust in the device that allows that device to bootstrap itself into the system. Among the greatest vulnerabilities to secure identity and access management is insecure bootstrapping.

Bootstrapping represents the beginning of the process of provisioning a trusted identity for a device within a given system. Bootstrapping may begin in the manufacturing process (for example, in the foundry manufacturing a chip) and be complete once delivered to an end operator. It may also be completely performed in the hands of the end user or some intermediary (such as a depot or supplier), once delivered. The most secure bootstrapping methods start in the manufacturing processes and implement discrete security associations throughout the supply chain. They uniquely identify a device through:

- Unique serial number(s) imprinted on the device.
- Unique and unalterable identifiers stored and fused in device **read-only memory (ROM)**.
- Manufacturer-specific cryptographic keys used only through specific lifecycle states to securely hand off the bootstrapping process to follow-on lifecycle states (such as shipping, distribution, hand off to an enrollment center, and so on). Such keys (frequently delivered out-of-band) are used for loading subsequent components by specific entities responsible for preparing the device.

PKIs are often used to aid in the bootstrapping process. Bootstrapping from a PKI perspective should generally involve the following processes:

- Devices are securely shipped from the manufacturer (via a secure, tamper detection capable shipping service) to a trusted facility or depot. The facility should have robust physical security access controls, record keeping, and audit processes, in addition to highly vetted staff.
- Devices counts and batches are matched against the shipping manifest.

Once received, the steps for each device include:

1. Authenticate uniquely to the device using a customer-specific, default manufacturer authenticator (password or key).
2. Install PKI trust anchors and any intermediate public key certificates (such as those of the registration authority, enrollment certificate authority, or other roots, and so on).
3. Install minimal network reachability information so that the device knows where to check certificate revocation lists, perform OCSP lookups, or other security-related functions.
4. Provision the device PKI credentials (public key signed by CA) and private key(s) so that other entities possessing the signing CA keys can trust the new device.

A secure bootstrapping process may not be identical to that described in the preceding list, but should be one that mitigates the following types of threats and vulnerabilities when provisioning devices:

- Insider threats designed to introduce new, rogue, or compromised devices (that should not be trusted)

- Duplication (cloning) of devices, no matter where in the lifecycle

- Introduction of public key trust anchors or other key material into a device that should NOT be trusted (rogue trust anchors and other keys)

- Compromise (including replication) of a new IoT device's private keys during key generation or import into the device

- Gaps in device possession during the supply chain and enrolment processes

- Protection of the device when re-keying and assigning new identification material needed for normal use (re-bootstrapping, as needed)

Given the security critical features of smart chip cards and their use in sensitive financial operations, the smart card industry adopted rigid enrollment process controls not unlike those described in the preceding list. Without them, severe attacks would have the potential to cripple the financial industry. Granted, many consumer-level IoT devices are unlikely to have secure bootstrapping processes, but over time we believe that this will change depending on the deployment environment and the stakeholders' appreciation of the threats. The more connected devices become, the greater their potential to do harm.

In practice, secure bootstrapping processes need to be tailored to the threat environment for the particular IoT device, its capabilities, and the network environment in question. The greater the potential risks, the more strict and thorough the bootstrapping process needs to be. The most secure processes will generally implement strong separation of duties and multi-person integrity processes during device bootstrap.

Credential and attribute provisioning

Once the foundation for identities within the device is established, provisioning of operational credentials and attributes can occur. These are the credentials that will be used within an IoT system for secure communication, authentication, and integrity protection. We strongly recommend using certificates for authentication and authorization whenever possible. If using certificates, an important and security-relevant consideration is whether to generate the key pairs on the device itself, or centrally.

Some IoT services allow for central (such as by a key server) generation of public/ private key pairs. While this can be an efficient method of bulk-provisioning thousands of devices with credentials, care should be taken to address potential vulnerabilities the process may expose (such as the sending of sensitive, private key material through intermediary devices/systems). If centralized generation is used, it should make use of a strongly secured key management system operated by vetted personnel in secured facilities. Another means of provisioning certificates is through the local generation of the key pairs (directly on the IoT device) followed by the transmission of the public key certificate through a certificate signing request to the PKI. Absent well-secured bootstrapping procedures, additional policy controls will have to be established for the PKI's **registration authority (RA)** in order to verify the identity of the device being provisioned. In general, the more secure the bootstrapping process, the more automated the provisioning can be. The following figure is a sequence diagram that depicts an overall registration, enrollment, and provisioning flow for an IoT device:

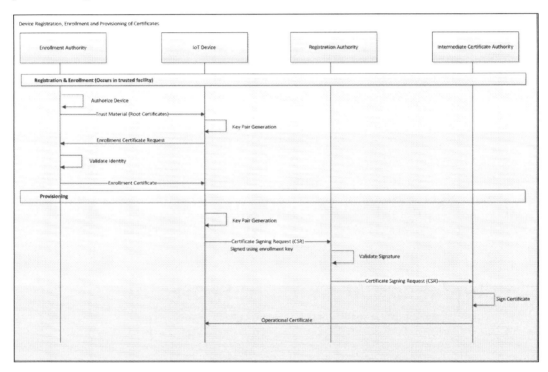

Local access

There are times when local access to the device is required for administration purposes. This may require the provisioning of SSH keys or administrative passwords. In the past, organizations frequently made the mistake of sharing administrative passwords to allow ease of access to devices. This is not a recommended approach, although implementing a federated access solution for administrators can be daunting. This is especially true when devices are spread across wide geographic distances such various sensors, gateways, and other unattended devices in the transportation industry.

Account monitoring and control

After accounts and credentials have been provisioned, these accounts must continue to be monitored against defined security policies. It is also important that organizations monitor the strength of the credentials (that is, cryptographic ciphersuites and key lengths) provisioned to IoT devices across their infrastructure. It is highly likely that pockets of teams will provision IoT subsystems on their own, therefore defining, communicating, and monitoring the required security controls to apply to those systems is vital.

Another aspect of monitoring relates to tracking the use of accounts and credentials. Assign someone to audit local IoT device administrative credential use (passwords, and SSH keys) on a routine basis. Also seriously consider whether privileged account management tools can be applied to your IoT deployment. These tools allow for features such as checking out administrative passwords to aid in audit processes.

Account updates

Credentials must be rotated on a regular basis; this is true for certificates and keys as well as passwords. Logistical impediments have historically hampered IT organizations' willingness to shorten certificate lifetimes and manage increasing numbers of credentials. There is a tradeoff to consider, as short-lived credentials have a reduced attack footprint, yet the process of changing the credentials tends to be expensive and time consuming. Whenever possible, look for automated solutions for these processes. Services such as Let's Encrypt (`https://letsencrypt.org/`) are gaining in popularity to help improve and simplify certificate management practices for organizations. Let's Encrypt provides PKI services along with an extremely easy-to-use plugin-based client that supports various platforms.

Account suspension

Just as with user accounts, do not automatically delete IoT device accounts. Consider maintaining those accounts in a suspended state in case data tied to the accounts is required for forensic analysis at a later time.

Account/credential deactivation/deletion

Deleting accounts used by IoT devices and the services they interact with will help combat the ability of an adversary to use those accounts to gain access after the devices have been decommissioned. Keys used for encryption (whether network or application) should also be deleted to keep adversaries from decrypting captured data at a later point in time using those recovered keys.

Authentication credentials

IoT messaging protocols often support the ability to use different types of credentials for authentication with external services and other IoT devices. This section examines the typical options available for these functions.

Passwords

Some protocols, such as MQTT, only provide the ability to use a username/ password combination for native-protocol authentication purposes. Within MQTT, the CONNECT message includes the fields for passing this information to an MQTT Broker. In the MQTT Version 3.1.1 specification defined by OASIS, you can see these fields within the CONNECT message (reference: `http://docs.oasis-open.org/ mqtt/mqtt/v3.1.1/os/mqtt-v3.1.1-os.html`):

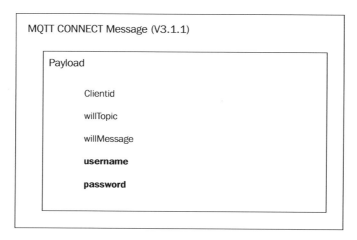

Note that there are no protections applied to support the confidentiality of the username/password in transit by the MQTT protocol. Instead, implementers should consider using the **transport layer security** (**TLS**) protocol to provide cryptographic protections.

There are numerous security considerations related to using a username/password-based approach for IoT devices. Some of these concerns include:

- Difficulty in managing large numbers of device usernames and passwords
- Difficulty securing the passwords stored on the devices themselves
- Difficulty managing passwords throughout the device lifecycle

Though not ideal, if you do plan on implementing usernames/passwords for IoT device authentication, consider taking these precautions:

1. Create policies and procedures for rotating passwords at least every 30 days for each device. Better yet, implement a technical control wherein the management interface automatically prompts you when password rotation is needed.
2. Establish controls for monitoring device account activity.
3. Establish controls for privileged accounts that support administrative access to IoT devices.
4. Segregate the password-protected IoT devices onto less-trusted networks.

Symmetric keys

Symmetric key material may also be used to authenticate, as mentioned in *Chapter 5, Cryptographic Fundamentals for IoT Security Engineering*. **Message authentication codes** (**MACs**) are generated using a MAC algorithm (such as HMAC, CMAC, and so on) with a shared key and known data (signed by the key). On receiving side, an entity can prove the sender possessed the pre-shared key when the its computed MAC is shown to be identical to the received MAC. Unlike a password, symmetric keys do not require the key to be sent between the parties (except ahead of time or agreed on using a key establishment protocol) at the time of the authentication event. The keys will either need to be established using a public key algorithm, input out of band, or sent to the devices ahead of time, encrypted using **key encryption keys** (**KEK**).

Certificates

Digital certificates, public key-based, are a preferred method for providing authentication functionality in the IoT. Although some implementations today may not support the processing capabilities needed to use certificates, Moore's law for computational power and storage is fast changing this.

X.509

Certificates come with a highly organized hierarchical naming structure that consists of organization, organizational unit(s), and **distinguished names (DN)** or **common names (CN)**. Referencing AWS support for provisioning X.509 certificates, we can see that AWS allows for the one-click generation of a device certificate. In the following example, we generate a device certificate with a generic IoT Device common name and a lifetime of 33 years. The one-click generation also (centrally) creates the public/private key pair. If possible, it is recommended that you generate your certificates locally by 1) generating a key pair on the device and 2) uploading a CSR to the AWS IoT service. This allows for customized tailoring of the certificate policy to define the hierarchical units (OU, DN, and so on) that are useful for additional authorization processes:

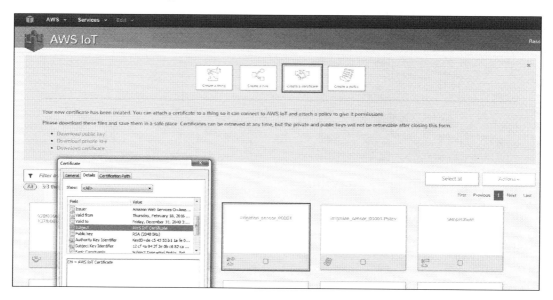

IEEE 1609.2

The IoT is characterized by many use cases involving machine-to-machine communication and some of them involve communications through a congested wireless spectrum. Take connected vehicles, for instance, an emerging technology wherein your vehicle will possess **on-board equipment** (OBE) that can automatically alert other drivers in your vicinity to your car's location in the form of **basic safety messages** (BSM). The automotive industry, **US Dept. of Transportation** (USDOT), and academia have been developing CV technology for many years and it will make its commercial debut in the 2017 Cadillac. In a few years, it is likely that most new US vehicles will be outfitted with the technology. It will not only enable vehicle-to-vehicle communications, but also **vehicle-to-infrastructure** (V2I) communications to various roadside and backhaul applications. The **dedicated short range communications** (DSRC) wireless protocol (based on IEEE 802.11p) is limited to a narrow set of channels in the 5 GHz frequency band. To accommodate so many vehicles and maintain security, it was necessary to 1) secure the communications using cryptography (to reduce malicious spoofing or eavesdropping attacks) and 2) minimize the security overhead within connected vehicle BSM transmissions. The industry resolved to use a new, slimmer and sleeker digital certificate design, the IEEE 1609.2.

The 1609.2 certificate format is advantageous in that it is approximately half the size of a typical X.509 certificate while still using strong, elliptic curve cryptographic algorithms (ECDSA and ECDH). The certificate is also useful for general machine-to-machine communication through its unique attributes, including explicit application identifier (SSID) and credential holder permission (SSP) fields. These attributes can allow IoT applications to make explicit access control decisions without having to internally or externally query for the credential holder's permissions. They're embedded right in the certificate during the secure, integrated bootstrapping and enrollment process with the PKI. The reduced size of these credentials also makes them attractive for other, bandwidth-constrained wireless protocols.

Biometrics

There is work being done in the industry today on new approaches that leverage biometrics for device authentication. The FIDO alliance (www.fidoalliance.org) has developed specifications that define the use of biometrics for both a password-less experience and for use as a second authentication factor. Authentication can include a range of flexible biometric types—from fingerprints to voice prints. Biometric authentication is being added to some commercial IoT devices (such as consumer door locks) already, and there is interesting potential in leveraging biometrics as a second factor of authentication for IoT systems.

For example, voice prints could be used to enable authentication across a set of distributed IoT devices such as **road side equipment (RSE)** in the transportation sector. This would allow an RSE tech to access the device through a cloud connection to the backend authentication server. Companies such as Hypr Biometric Security (`https://www.hypr.com/`) are leading the way towards using this technology to reduce the need for passwords and enable more robust authentication techniques.

New work in authorization for the IoT

Progress toward using tokens with resource-constrained IoT devices has not fully matured; however, there are organizations working on defining the use of protocols such as OAuth 2.0 for the IoT. One such group is the **Internet Engineering Task Force (IETF)** through the **Authentication and Authorization for Constrained Environments (ACE)** effort. ACE has specified RFC 7744 *Use Cases for Authentication and Authorization in Constrained Environments* (reference: `https://datatracker.ietf.org/doc/rfc7744/`). The RFC use cases are primarily based on IoT devices that employ CoAP as the messaging protocol. The document provides a useful set of use cases that clarify the need for a comprehensive IoT authentication and authorization strategy. RFC 7744 provides valuable considerations for authentication and authorization of IoT devices, including:

- Devices may host several resources wherein each requires its own access control policy.

- A single device may have different access rights for different requesting entities.

- Policy decision points must be able to evaluate the context of a transaction. This includes the potential for understanding that a transaction is occurring during an emergency situation.

- The ability to dynamically control authorization policies is critical to supporting the dynamic environment of the IoT.

IoT IAM infrastructure

Now that we have addressed many of the enablers of identity and access management, it is important to elaborate how solutions are realized in infrastructure. This section is primarily devoted to **public key infrastructures (PKI)** and their utility in securing IAM deployments for the IoT.

802.1x

802.1x authentication mechanisms can be employed to limit IP-based IoT device access to a network. Note though that not all IoT devices rely on the provisioning of an IP address. While it cannot accommodate all IoT device types, implementing 802.1x is a component of a good access control strategy able to address many use cases.

Enabling 802.1x authentication requires an access device and an authentication server. The access device is typically an access point and the authentication server can take the form of a RADIUS or some **authentication, authorization, and accounting (AAA)** server.

PKI for the IoT

Chapter 5, Cryptographic Fundamentals for IoT Security Engineering, provided a technical grounding of topics related to cryptographic key management. PKIs are nothing more than instances of key management systems that have been engineered and standardized exclusively to provision asymmetric (public key) key material in the form of digital credentials, most commonly X.509 certificates. PKIs may be isolated to individual organizations, they may be public, Internet-based services, or they may be government-operated. When needing to assert an identity, a digital certificate is issued to a person or device to perform a variety of cryptographic functions, such as signing messages in an application or signing data as part of an authenticated key exchange protocol such as TLS.

There are different workflows used in generating the public and private key pair (the public needing to be integrated into the certificate), but as we mentioned earlier, they generally fall into two basic categories: 1) self-generated or 2) centrally generated. When self-generated, the end IoT device requiring the digital certificate performs a key pair generation function, for example as described in FIPS PUB 180-4. Depending on the cryptographic library and invoked API, the public key may be raw and not yet put into a credential data structure such as X.509 or it may be output in the form of an unsigned certificate. Once the unsigned certificate exists, it is time to invoke the PKI in the form of a **certificate signing request (CSR)**. The device sends this message to the PKI, then the PKI signs the certificate and sends it back for the device to use operationally.

PKI primer

Public key infrastructures are designed to provision public key certificates to devices and applications. PKIs provide verifiable roots of trust in our Internet-connected world and can conform to a wide variety of architectures. Some PKIs may have very deep trust chains, with many levels between an **end entity** (such as an IoT device) and the top-most level root of trust (the root certificate authority). Others may have shallow trust chains in which there is only the one CA at the top and a single level of end entity devices underneath it. But how do they work?

Supposing an IoT device needs a cryptographically strong identity, it wouldn't make sense for it to provision itself with that identity because there is nothing inherently trustworthy about the device. This is where a trusted third party, the PKI certificate authority, comes into play and can vouch for the identity and in some cases the trust level of the device. Most PKIs do not allow end entities to directly interact with the CA, the entity responsible for cryptographically signing end entity certificates; instead they employ another subservient PKI node called a **registration authority** (**RA**). The RA receives certificate requests (typically containing the device's self-generated, but unsigned, public key) from end entities, verifies that they've met some minimum criteria, then passes the certificate request to the certificate authority. The CA signs the certificate (typically using RSA, DSA, or ECDSA signature algorithms), sending it back to the RA and finally the end entity in a message called the **certificate response**. In the certificate response message, the original certificate generated by the end entity (or some other intermediary key management system) is fully complete with the CA's signature and explicit identity. Now, when the IoT device presents its certificate during authentication-related functions, other devices can trust it because they 1) receive a valid, signed certificate from it, and 2) can validate the signature of the CA using the CA's public key trust anchor that they also trust (securely stored in their internal trust store).

The following diagram represents a typical PKI architecture:

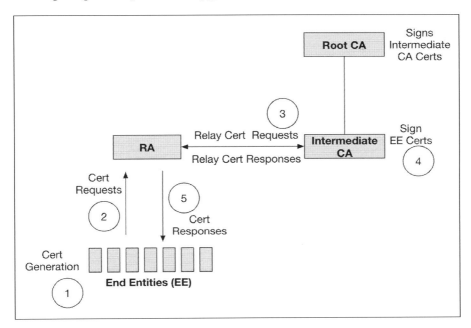

In the preceding diagram, each of the **End Entities (EE)** can trust the others if they have the certificate authority keys that provide the chain of trust to them.

End entities that possess certificates signed by different PKIs can also trust each other. There are a couple of ways they can do this:

- **Explicit trust**: Each supports a policy that dictates that it can trust the other. In this case, end entities only need to have a copy of the trust anchor from the other entity's PKI to trust it. They do this by performing certificate path validation to those pre-installed roots. Policies can dictate the quality of the trust chain that is acceptable to rely on during certificate path validation. Most trust on the Internet today works like this. For example, web browsers explicitly trust so many web servers on the Internet merely because the browser comes pre-installed with a copy of the most common Internet root CA trust anchors.

- **Cross-certification**: When a PKI needs stricter cohesion in the policies, security practices, and interoperability of their domain with other PKIs, they can either directly cross-sign (each becomes an issuer for the other) or create a new structure called a PKI bridge to implement and allocate policy interoperability. The US Federal government's Federal PKI is an excellent example of this. In some cases, a PKI bridge needs to be created to provide a transition time between old certificates' cryptographic algorithms and new ones (for example, the Federal PKI's SHA1 bridge for accommodating older SHA1 cryptographic digests in digital signatures).

In terms of the IoT, many Internet-based PKIs exist today that can provision certificates to IoT devices. Some organizations operate their own on the fly. To become a formally recognized PKI on the Internet can be a significant endeavor. A PKI will require significant security protections and need to meet strict assurance requirements as implemented in various PKI assurance schemes (such as WebTrust). In many cases, organizations obtain service contracts with PKI providers that operate certificate authorities as a service.

Trust stores

We diverge momentarily from infrastructure to discuss where the PKI-provisioned credentials end up being stored in devices. They are frequently stored in internal trust stores. Trust stores are an essential IoT capability with regard to the protection of digital credentials. From a PKI perspective, a device's trust store is a physical or logical part of the IoT device that securely stores public and private keys, often (and better when) encrypted. Within it, both the device's private/public keys and its PKI roots of trust are stored. Trust stores tend to be strongly access-controlled sections of memory, often only accessible from OS kernel-level processes, to prevent unauthorized modification or substitution of public keys or reading/copying of private keys. Trust stores can be implemented in hardware, as in small **hardware security modules** (**HSM**) or other dedicated, secure processors. They can also be implemented solely in software (such as with many instances of Windows and other desktop operating systems). In many desktop-type deployments, credentials can be maintained within **trusted platform modules** (**TPMs**), dedicated chips integrated into a computer's motherboard, though TPMs have not made a large penetration of the IoT market as of yet. Other enterprise-focused mobile solutions exist for secure storage of sensitive security parameters. For example, Samsung Knox provides mobile device secure storage through its Knox workspace container (secure hardware root of trust, secure boot, and other sensitive operational parameters).

IoT devices can depend on PKIs in different ways or not at all. For example, if the device uses only a self-signed credential and is not vouched for by a PKI, it still should securely store the self-signed credential in its trust store. Likewise, if the device has externally provisioned an identity from a PKI, it must maintain and store critical keys pertinent to that PKI and any other PKI that it inherently or indirectly trusts. This is accomplished through the storing of certificate authority public key trust anchors and often the intermediate certificates as well. When deciding to trust an external entity, the entity will present the IoT device with a certificate signed by a certificate authority. In some cases (and in some protocols), the entity will provide the CA certificate or a complete trust chain, along with its own certificate so that it can be validated to a root.

Whether or not an IoT device directly supports PKI, if it uses public key certificates to validate another device's authenticity or presents its own certificates and trust chains, it should do so using digital credentials and trust anchors securely stored in its trust store. Otherwise, it will not be protected from access by malicious processes and hackers.

PKI architecture for privacy

Privacy has many facets and is frequently not a concept directly associated with PKIs. PKIs, by design, are there to provide trusted identities to individuals and devices. When initiating electronic transactions, one usually wants to specifically identify and authenticate the other party before initiating sensitive transactions with them.

Anonymity and the general ability to operate in networks and RF environments without being tracked, however, are becoming increasingly important. For instance, suppose a system needs to provision anonymous trusted credentials to a device so that other entities have the ability to trust it without explicitly knowing its identity. Consider further that the PKI design itself needs to limit insider threats (PKI operators) from being able to associate certificates and the entities to which they are provisioned.

The best example of this is reflected in the emerging trend of anonymous PKIs, one of the best known being the forthcoming **security credential management system (SCMS)** designed for the automotive industry's connected vehicles initiative. The SCMS provides a fascinating look at the future of privacy-protected IoT trust. The SCMS, now in a Proof of Concept phase, was specifically engineered to eliminate the ability of any single node of the PKI from being able to ascertain and associate SCMS credentials (IEEE 1609.2 format) with the vehicles and vehicle operators to which they are provisioned.

1609.2 certificates are used by OBE, embedded devices in the automobile to send out BSM to surrounding vehicles to enable the vehicles to provide drivers with preemptive safety messages. In addition to vehicle use, 1609.2 credentials will be used by networked and standalone **roadside units (RSU)** mounted near traffic signal controllers to provide various roadside applications. Many of the connected vehicle applications requiring enhanced privacy protections are safety-focused, but many are also designed to improve traffic system and mobility performance, environmental emissions reduction, and others.

Given the versatility of so many IoT application use cases, the most sensitive privacy-impacting IoT devices (for example, medical devices) may increasingly begin to make use of no-backdoor, privacy-protecting PKIs, especially when civil liberties concerns are obvious.

Revocation support

When authenticating in a system using PKI credentials, devices need to know when other devices' credentials are no longer valid, aside from expiration. PKIs routinely revoke credentials for one reason or another, sometimes from detection of compromise and rogue activity; in other cases, it's simply that a device has malfunctioned or otherwise been retired. No matter the reason, a revoked device should no longer be trusted in any application or network layer engagement.

The conventional method of doing this is for CAs to periodically generate and issue **certificate revocation lists (CRL)**, a cryptographically signed document listing all revoked certificates. This requires that that end devices have the ability to reach out through the network and frequently refresh CRLs. It also requires turnaround time for 1) the CA to generate and publish the CRL, 2) end devices to become aware of the update, and 3) end devices to download it. During this interval of time, untrusted devices may yet be trusted by the wider community.

OCSP

Given the potential latency and the need to download large files, other mechanisms have evolved to more quickly provide revocation information over networks, most notably the **online certificate status protocol (OCSP)**. OCSP is a simple client/server protocol which allows clients to simply ask a server whether a given public key credential is still valid. The OCSP server is typically responsible for the CA's **Certificate Revocation List (CRL)** and using it to generate an OCSP proof set (internally signed database of proofs). These sets are then used to generate OCSP response messages to the requesting clients. OCSP proof sets can be generated periodically for different time intervals.

OCSP stapling

OCSP stapling resolves some of the challenges of having to perform the latency-inducing, secondary client-server OCSP call just to obtain revocation information. OCSP stapling simply provides a pre-generated OCSP response message, in conjunction with the server's certificate (such as during a TLS handshake). This way, clients can verify the digital signature on the pre-generated OCSP response (no additional handshakes necessary) and make sure the CA still vouches for the server.

SSL pinning

This technique may apply more to IoT device developers that require their devices to communicate with an Internet service (for example, for passing usage data or other information). In order to protect from the potential compromise of the trust infrastructure that provisions certificates, developers can pin the trusted server certificate directly into the IoT device trust store. The device can then check the server certificate explicitly against the certificate in the trust store when connecting to the server. In essence, SSL pinning doesn't place full trust in the certificate's trust chain; it only trusts the server if the received server certificate is identical to the pinned (stored) certificate and the signature is valid. SSL pinning can be used in a variety of interfaces, from web server communications to device management.

Authorization and access control

Once a device is identified and authenticated, determining what that device can read or write to other devices and services is required. In some cases, being a member of a particular **community of interest** (COI) is sufficient, however in many instances there are restrictions that must be put in place even upon members of a COI.

OAuth 2.0

To refresh, OAuth 2.0 is a token-based authorization framework specified in IETF RFC 6749, which allows a client to access protected, distributed resources (that is, from different websites and organizations) without having to enter passwords for each. As such, it was created to address the frequently cited, sad state of password hygiene on the Internet. Many implementations of OAuth 2.0 exist, supporting a variety of programming languages to suit. Google, Facebook, and many other large tech companies make extensive use of this protocol.

The IETF ACE Working Group has created working papers that define the application of OAuth 2.0 to the IoT. The draft document may be promoted to an RFC in the future. The document is designed primarily for CoAP and includes as a core component a binary encoding scheme known as **concise binary object representation** (CBOR) that can be used within IoT devices when JSON is not sufficiently compact.

Proposed extensions to OAuth 2.0 have also been discussed, for example, extending the messaging between an AS and a client to determine how to connect securely with a resource. This is required given that the use of TLS is expected with typical OAuth 2.0 transactions. With constrained IoT devices that employ CoAP, this is not a valid assumption.

The constrained device-tailored version of OAuth 2.0 also introduces a new authorization information format. This allows for access rights to be specified as a list of **uniform resource indicators** (**URIs**) of resources mapped with allowed actions (for example, GET, POST, PUT, and DELETE). This is a promising development for the IoT.

From a security implementation perspective, it's important to step back and keep in mind that OAuth is a security framework. Security frameworks can be something of an oxymoron; the more flexible and less specific the framework is regarding implementation, the wider the latitude to create insecure products. It's a tradeoff we frequently encounter in the world of public standards, where the goals of a new security standard somehow have to be met while satisfying the interests of many stakeholders. Typically, both interoperability and security suffer as a result.

With that in mind, we identify just a few of the many security best practices regarding OAuth2. We encourage readers to visit IETF RFC 6819 for a more thorough treatment of OAuth2 security considerations (`https://tools.ietf.org/html/rfc6819#section-4.1.1`):

- Use TLS for authorization server, client, and resource server interactions. Do NOT send client credentials over an unprotected channel.

- Lock down your authorization server database and the network in which it resides.

- Use high entropy sources when generating secrets.

- Securely store your client credentials: `client_id` and `client_secret`. These parameters are used to identify and authenticate your client application to the API when requesting user account access. Unfortunately, some implementations hard-code these values or distribute them over less protected channels, making them attractive targets for attackers.

- Make use of the OAuth2 state parameter. This will allow you to link the authorization requests with redirect URIs needed for delivery of the access token.

- Don't follow untrusted URLs.

- If in doubt, lean toward shorter expiry times for authorization codes and tokens.

- Servers should revoke all tokens for an authorization code that someone is repeatedly attempting to redeem.

Future IoT implementations that make use of OAuth 2.0 and similar standards greatly need secure by default implementations (library APIs) to reduce developers' exposure to making critical security errors.

Authorization and access controls within publish/subscribe protocols

The MQTT protocol provides a good exemplar for understanding the need for finer-grained access controls. As a publish/subscribe protocol, MQTT allows clients to write and read topics. Not all clients will have permissions to write all topics. Not all clients will have permissions to read all topics either. Indeed, controls must be put in place that restrict the permissions of clients at the topic level.

This can be achieved in a MQTT broker by keeping an access control list that pairs topics with authorized publishers and authorized subscribers. The access controls can take as input the client ID of the MQTT client, or depending on the broker implementation, the username that is transmitted in the MQTT connect message. The broker performs a topic lookup when applicable MQTT messages arrive to determine if the clients are authorized to read, write, or subscribe to topics.

Alternatively, since MQTT is often implemented to operate over TLS, it is possible to configure the MQTT broker to require certificate-based authentication of the MQTT client. The MQTT broker can then perform a mapping of information in the MQTT client X.509 certificate to determine the topics to which the client has permission to subscribe or publish.

Access controls within communication protocols

There are different access control configurations that can be set in other communication protocols as well. For example, ZigBee includes the ability for each transceiver to manage an access control list to determine whether a neighbor is trusted or not. The ACL includes information such as the address of the neighbor node, the security policy in use by the node, the key, and the last **initialization vector (IV)** used.

Upon receiving a packet from a neighbor node, the receiver consults the ACL and if the neighbor is trusted, then the communication is allowed. If not, the communication is either denied or an authentication function is invoked.

Summary

This chapter provided an introduction to identity and access management for IoT devices. The identity lifecycle was reviewed and a discussion on infrastructure components required for provisioning authentication credentials was provided, with a heavy focus on PKI. There was a look at different types of authentication credentials and a discussion on new approaches to providing authorization and access control for IoT devices was also provided.

In the next chapter, we visit the complex ecosystem in which IoT privacy concerns need to be addressed and mitigated. Security controls, such as effective identity and access management discussed in this chapter, represent only one element of the IoT privacy challenge.

7
Mitigating IoT Privacy Concerns

This chapter provides the reader with an understanding of privacy principles and concerns introduced by the IoT through implementation and deployment.

An exercise and guidance in creating a **privacy impact assessment (PIA)** is also provided. PIAs address the causes and fallout of leaking **privacy protected information (PPI)**. We will discuss **privacy by design (PbD)** approaches for integrating privacy controls within the IoT engineering process. The goal of PbD is to integrate privacy controls (in technology and processes) throughout the IoT engineering lifecycle to enhance end-to-end security, visibility, transparency, and respect for user privacy. Finally, we will discuss recommendations for instituting privacy engineering activities within your organization.

This chapter examines privacy in our IoT-connected world in the following sections:

- Privacy challenges introduced by the IoT
- Guide to performing an IoT PIA
- **PbD** principles
- Privacy engineering recommendations

Privacy challenges introduced by the IoT

As your family sits down after dinner and a long day of work, one of the children starts up a conversation with her new connected play doll, while the other begins to watch a movie on the new smart television. The smart thermostat is keeping the living area a steady 22 degrees Celsius, while diverting energy from the rooms that aren't being used at the moment. Father is making use of the home computer's voice control features, while Mother is installing new smart light bulbs that can change color on command or based on variations in the home environment. In the background, the smart refrigerator is transmitting an order for the next-day delivery of groceries.

This setting tells a great story of the consumer Internet of Things in that there are exciting new capabilities and convenience. It also begins to make clear the soon-to-be hyper-connected nature of our homes and environments. If we start to examine these new smart products, we can begin to see the concern surrounding privacy within the IoT.

The privacy challenges with the Internet of Things are enormous, given the gargantuan quantities of data collected, distributed, stored and, ahem, sold every day. Pundits will argue that privacy is dead today. They argue that consumers' willingness to eagerly click through so-called end user privacy agreements compromises their privacy with barely a notion as to what they just agreed to. The pundits are not far off, as privacy concerns are something of a moving target given the fickle nature of consumer sentiment.

Our ability to grasp and find ways of preserving privacy with the IoT represents a monumental challenge. The increased volume and types of data able to be collected and distilled through technical and business analytics systems can produce frighteningly detailed and accurate profiles of end users. Even if the end user carefully reads and agrees to their end user privacy agreement, they are unlikely to imagine the downstream, multiplicative, compromising effect of accepting two, three, or four of them, to say nothing of 30 or 40 privacy agreements. While an improved targeted advertising experience may have been the superficial rationale for agreeing to privacy agreements, it is no understatement that advertisers are not the only entities procuring this data. Governments, organized crime syndicates, potential stalkers, and others can either directly or indirectly access the information to perform sophisticated analytical queries that ascertain patterns about end users. Combined with other public data sources, data mining is a powerful and dangerous tool. Privacy laws have not kept up with the data science that thwarts them.

Privacy protection is a challenge no matter the organization or industry that needs to protect it. Communications within a privacy-conscious and privacy-protecting organization are vital to ensuring that customers' interests are addressed. Later in this chapter, we identify corporate departments and individual qualifications needed to address privacy policies and privacy engineering.

Some privacy challenges are unique to the IoT, but not all. One of the primary differences between IoT and traditional IT privacy is the pervasive capture and sharing of sensor-based data, whether medical, home energy, transportation-related, and so on. This data may be authorized or may not. Systems must be designed to make determinations as to whether that authorization exists for the storage and sharing of data that is collected.

Take, for example, video captured by cameras strewn throughout a smart city. These cameras may be set up to support local law enforcement efforts to reduce crime; however, they capture images and video of everyone in their field of view. These people caught on film have not given their consent to be video-recorded.

As such, policies must exist that:

- Notify people coming into view that they are being recorded
- Determine what can be done with the video captured (for example, do people need to be blurred in images that are published?)

A complex sharing environment

The amount of data actively or passively generated by (or for) a single individual is already large. By 2020, the amount of data generated by each of us will increase dramatically. If we consider that our wearable devices, our vehicles, our homes, and even our televisions are constantly collecting and transmitting data, it becomes obvious that trying to restrict the types and amounts of data shared with others is challenging to say the least.

Now, if we consider the lifecycle of data, we must be aware of where data is collected, where it is sent, and how. The purposes for collecting data are diverse. Some smart machine vendors will lease equipment to an organization and collect data on the usage of that equipment for billing purposes. The usage data may include time of day, duty cycle (usage patterns), number and type of operations performed, and who was operating the machine. The data will likely be transmitted through a customer organization's firewall to some Internet-based service application that ingests and processes the information. Organizations in this position should consider researching exactly what data is transmitted in addition to the usage information, and ascertain whether any of the information is shared with third parties.

Wearables

Data associated with wearables is frequently sent to applications in the cloud for storage and analysis. Such data is already being used to support corporate wellness and similar programs, the implication being that someone other than the device manufacturer or user is collecting and storing the data. In the future, this data may also be passed on to healthcare providers. Will the healthcare providers pass that data on to insurance companies as well? Are there regulations in the works that restrict the ability of insurance companies to make use of data that has not been explicitly shared by the originator?

Smart homes

Smart home data can be collected by many different devices and sent to many different places. A smart meter, for example, may transmit data to a gateway that then relays it to the utility company for billing purposes. Emergent smart grid features such as demand response will enable the smart meter to collect and forward information from the home's individual appliances that consume electricity from the power grid. Absent any privacy protections, an eavesdropper could theoretically begin to piece together a puzzle that shows when certain appliances are used within a home, and whether homeowners are home or not. The merging of electronic data corresponding to physical-world state and events is a serious concern related to privacy in the IoT.

Metadata can leak private information also

A striking report by Open Effect (`https://openeffect.ca/reports/Every_Step_You_Fake.pdf`) documented the metadata that is collected by today's consumer wearable devices. In one of the cases they explored, the researchers analyzed the Bluetooth discovery features of different manufacturers' wearable products. The researchers attempted to determine whether the vendors had enabled new privacy features that were designed into the Bluetooth 4.2 specification. They found that only one of the manufacturers (Apple) had implemented them, leaving open the possibility of the exploitation of the static **media access control** (**MAC**) address for persistent tracking of a person wearing one of the products. Absent the new privacy feature, the MAC addresses never change, creating an opportunity for adversarial tracking of the devices people are wearing. Frequent updates to a device's MAC address limit an adversary's ability to track a device in space and time as its owner goes about their day.

New privacy approaches for credentials

Another worthy example of the need to rethink privacy for the IoT comes from the connected vehicle market. Just as with the wearables discussed previously, the ability to track someone's vehicle persistently is a cause for concern.

A problem arises, however, when we look at the need to digitally sign all messages transmitted by a connected vehicle. Adding digital signatures to messages such as **basic safety messages (BSMs)** or infrastructure-generated messages (for example, traffic signal controller **signal phase and timing (SPaT)** messages) is essential to ensure public safety and the performance of our surface transportation systems. Messages must be integrity protected and verified to originate from trusted sources. In some cases, they must also be confidentiality protected. But privacy? That's needed, too. The transportation industry is developing interesting privacy solutions for connected vehicles:

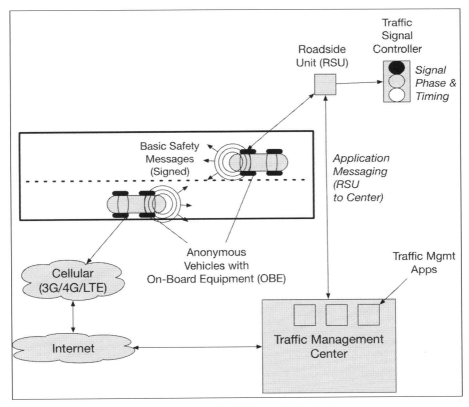

Privacy in connected vehicles and infrastructure

For example, when a connected vehicle transmits a message, there is concern that using the same credentials to sign messages over a period of time could expose the vehicle and owner to persistent tracking. To combat this, security engineers have specified that vehicles will be provisioned with certificates that:

- Have short lifespans
- Are provisioned in batches to allow a pool of credentials to be used for signing operations

In the connected vehicle environment, vehicles will be provisioned with a large pool of constantly rotated pseudonym certificates to sign messages transmitted by **on-board equipment** (OBE) devices within the vehicle. This pool of certificates may only be valid for a week, at which point another batch will take effect for the next time period. This reduces the ability to track the location of a vehicle throughout a day, week or any larger time period based on the certificates it has attached to its own transmissions.

Ironically, however, a growing number of transportation departments are beginning to take advantage of widespread vehicle and mobile device Bluetooth by deploying Bluetooth probes along congested freeway and arterial roadways. Some traffic agencies use the probes to measure the time it takes for a passing Bluetooth device (indicated by its MAC address) to traverse a given distance between roadside mounted probes. This provides data needed for adaptive traffic system control (for example, dynamic or staged signal timing patterns). Unless traffic agencies are careful and wipe any short- or long-term collection of Bluetooth MAC addresses, correlative data analytics can be used potentially to discern individual vehicle (or its owner) movement in a region. Increased use of alternating Bluetooth MAC addresses may render useless future Bluetooth probe systems and their use by traffic management agencies.

Privacy impacts on IoT security systems

Continuing with the connected vehicle example, we can also see that infrastructure operators should not be able to map provisioned certificates to the vehicles either. This requires changes to the traditional PKI security design, historically engineered to provide certificates that specifically identify and authenticate individuals and organizations (for example, for identity and access management) through X.509 distinguished name, organization, domain, and other attribute types. In the connected vehicle area, the PKI that will provision credentials to vehicles in the United States is known as the **security credential management system (SCMS)** and is currently being constructed for various connected vehicle pilot deployments around the country. The SCMS has built-in privacy protections ranging from the design of the pseudonym IEEE 1609.2 certificate to internal organizational separations aimed at thwarting insider PKI attacks on drivers' privacy.

One example of SCMS privacy protections is the introduction of a gateway component known as a **location obscurer proxy** (**LOP**). The LOP is a proxy gateway that vehicle OBEs can connect to instead of connecting directly to a **registration authority** (**RA**). This process, properly implemented with request shuffling logic, would help thwart an insider at the SCMS attempting to locate the network or geographic source of the requests (`https://www.wpi.edu/Images/CMS/Cybersecurity/Andre_V2X_WPI.PDF`).

New methods of surveillance

The potential for a dystopian society where everything that anyone does is monitored is often invoked as a potential future aided by the IoT. When we bundle things like drones (aka SUAS) into the conversation, the concerns are validated. Drones with remarkably high resolution cameras and a variety of other pervasive sensors all raise privacy concerns, therefore it is clear there is much work to be done to ensure that drone operators are not sued due to lack of clear guidance on what data can be collected, how, and what the treatment of the data needs to address.

To address these new surveillance methods, new legislation related to the collection of imagery and other data by these platforms may be needed to provide rules, and penalties in instances where those rules are broken. For example, even if a drone is not directly overflying a private or otherwise controlled property, its camera may view at slant range angles into private property due to its high vantage point and zoom capabilities. Laws may need to be established that require immediate or 'as soon as practical' geospatial scrubbing and filtering of raw imagery according to defined, private-property-aligned geofences. Pixel-based georeferencing of images is already in today's capabilities and is used in a variety of image post-processing functions related to drone-based photogrammetry, production of orthomosaics, 3D models, and other geospatial products. Broad pixel-based georeferencing within video frames may not be far off. Such functionality would provide for consent-based rules to be established so that no drone operator could preserve or post in public online forums imagery containing any private property regions beyond a specific per-pixel resolution. Without such technical and policy controls, there is little other than strong penalties or lawsuits to prevent peeping Toms from peering into backyards and posting their results on YouTube. Operators need specificity in rules so that companies can build compliance solutions.

New technologies that allow law-abiding collectors of information to respect the wishes of citizens who want their privacy protected are needed in our sensor-rich Internet of Things.

Guide to performing an IoT PIA

An IoT PIA is crucial for understanding how IoT devices, within the context of a larger system or system-of-systems, may impact end user privacy. This section will provide you with a reference example of how to perform a PIA for your own deployment, by walking through a hypothetical IoT system PIA. Since consumer privacy is such a sensitive topic, we provide a consumer-level PIA for a connected toy.

Overview

Privacy impact assessments are necessary to provide as complete a risk analysis as possible. Beyond basic safety and security tenets, unmitigated privacy losses can have substantial impacts and result in severe financial or legal consequences to a manufacturer or operator of IT and IoT systems. For example, consider a child's toy fitted with Wi-Fi capabilities, smart phone management, and connectivity to backend system servers. Assume the toy possesses a microphone and speaker, along with voice capture and recognition capabilities. Now consider the security features of the device, its storage of sensitive authentication parameters, and other attributes necessary for secure communication to backend systems. If a device were physically or logically hacked, would it expose any common or default security parameters that could be used to compromise other toys from the same manufacturer? Are the communications adequately protected in the first place through encryption, authentication, and integrity controls? Should they be? What is the nature of the data and what could it possibly contain? Is user data aggregated in backend systems for any analytics processing? Is the overall security of the infrastructure and development process sufficient to protect consumers?

These questions need to be asked in the context of a privacy impact assessment. Questions must address the severity of impact from a breach of information or misuse of the information once it enters the device and backend systems. For example, might it be possible to capture the child's audio commands and hear names and other private information included? Could the traffic be geolocated by an adversary, potentially disclosing the location of the child (for example, their address)? If so, impacts could possibly include the malicious stalking of the child or family members. These types of problems in the IoT have precedence http://fortune.com/2015/12/04/hello-barbie-hack/) and it is therefore vital that a complete PIA be performed to understand the user base, types of privacy impact, their severity, probability, and other factors to gauge overall risk.

Identified privacy risks need to then be factored into the privacy engineering process described later. While the example we provide is hypothetical, it is analogous to one of the hacks elucidated by security researcher Marcus Richerson at RSA 2016 (`https://www.rsaconference.com/writable/presentations/file_upload/ sbx1-r08-barbie-vs-the-atm-lock.pdf`).

This section will utilize a hypothetical talking doll example and make reference to the following system architecture. The architecture will be needed to visualize the flow and storage of private information between the IoT endpoint (the doll), a smartphone, and connected online services. The private information, people, devices, and systems involved will be explored in more detail later, when we discuss privacy by design and the security properties inherent in it:

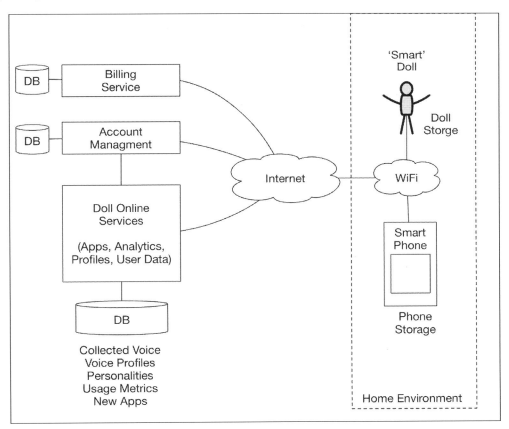

Talking doll IoT system reference architecture

Authorities

Authorities deal with the entities that create and enforce laws and regulations that may impact an organization's collection and use of private information. In the case of the talking doll example, a variety of laws may be at work. For example, the European Union Article 33 rules, the US **Children's Online Privacy Protection Act (COPPA)**, and others may come into play. Under the authorities question, an IoT organization should identify all legal authorities, and the applicable laws and regulations each imposes on the operation. Authorities may also have the ability to issue waivers and allow certain information collection and use based on certain conditions. These should be identified as well.

If your IoT organization, like many IT operations, is operating across international borders, then your PIA should also raise the issue of how data can and might be treated outside of your country. For example, if more lax rules are applied overseas, some data may be more vulnerable to foreign government inspection, regardless of your desired privacy policy in your own country. Or, the foreign rules may be stricter than those mandated by your nation, possibly preventing you from using certain overseas data centers. The process of privacy by design should address the geographical architecture early and ensure that the geographical *design* does not violate the privacy needed for your deployment.

Characterizing collected information

The lifecycle and scope of information pertinent to an IoT device can be narrowly defined or quite broad. In a PIA, one of the first activities is to identify information that will originate, terminate in or pass through the IoT-enabled system. At this point, one should create tables for the different lifecycle phases and the data relevant to each. In addition, it is useful to use at least three different first order ratings to give each information type based on sensitivity. For simplicity, in the following examples we use:

- Not sensitive
- Moderately sensitive
- Very sensitive

Other rating types can be used depending on your organization, industry, or any regulatory requirements. Keep in mind that some types of data, even if marked not sensitive or moderately sensitive, can become very sensitive when grouped together. Such data aggregation risks need to be evaluated whenever pulling together data within application processing or storage environments. The eventual security controls (for example, encryption) applied to aggregated datasets may be higher than what may initially be determined for small sets or single data types.

In the case of the talking doll, once the doll has left the manufacturing environment, it is shipped to wholesalers or retailers awaiting purchase by end users. No end user **personally identifiable information (PII)** has yet entered the system. Once purchased by a parent, the doll is taken home to be bootstrapped, connected to a newly created account, and connected to smartphone applications. Now, PII enters the picture.

Assuming there is a subscription service to download new apps to the doll, we now begin to delineate the PII. The following hypothetical data elements and the lifecycle phases to which they apply are listed to illustrate the data identification process. Each is listed and described; for each the source of the data (application + device) and the consumers of the data are identified so that we understand the endpoint that will have varying degrees of access to the information.

The following example information is identified as being created or consumed during the creation of the doll owner's account:

Account creation			
Parameter	**Description/Sensitivity**	**Origin**	**Consumer/User(s)**
Login	User identifier (not sensitive)	Created by user	User Application server Billing server Smart phone app
Password	User password (high sensitivity)	Created by user (minimum password length/quality enforced)	User App server Billing server Smart phone app
Name, address, phone number	Account holder's (doll owner's) name, address, and phone number	Doll owner	Application server Billing server
Age	Age of child using doll (not sensitive)	Doll owner	Application server
Gender	Account holder's or doll owner's gender (not sensitive)	Doll owner	Application server

Account creation			
Parameter	**Description/Sensitivity**	**Origin**	**Consumer/User(s)**
Account number	Unique account number for this doll owner	Application server	Doll owner Application server Smartphone app Billing server

The following example information is identified as being created or consumed during the creation of the doll owner's subscription:

Subscription creation			
Parameter	**Description/Sensitivity**	**Origin**	**Consumer**
Doll type and serial number	Doll information (low sensitivity)	Packaging	Application server (for subscription profile)
Subscription package	Subscription type and term, expiration, and so on (low sensitivity)	Doll owner selected via web page	Application server
Name	First and last name (high sensitivity when combined with financial information)	Doll owner	Billing server
Address	Street, city, state, country (moderate sensitivity)	Doll owner	Billing server and application server
Credit card information	Credit card number, CVV, expiration date (high sensitivity)	Doll owner	Billing server
Phone number	Phone number of doll owner (moderate sensitivity)	Doll owner	Billing server and application server

The following example information is identified as being created or consumed during the pairing of the downloaded smartphone application that will connect with the talking doll and backend application server:

Attachment to smartphone application			
Parameter	**Description/Sensitivity**	**Origin**	**Consumer(s)**
Account number	Account number that was created by the account server upon doll owner account creation (moderate sensitivity)	Account server via doll owner	Smartphone application Application server
Doll serial number	Unique identifier for the doll (not sensitive)	Doll's packaging from manufacturer	Doll owner Application server Smartphone app
Doll settings and configs	Day-to-day settings and configurations made on the doll via the smartphone application or web client not sensitive, or moderate sensitivity (depending on attributes)	Doll owner	Doll Application server

The following example information is identified as being created or consumed during the normal daily use of the talking doll:

Daily usage			
Parameter	**Description/Sensitivity**	**Origin**	**Consumer**
Doll speech profiles	Downloadable speech patterns and behaviors (not sensitive)	Application server	Doll user
Doll microphone data (voice recordings)	Recorded voice communication with doll (high sensitivity)	Doll and environment	Application server and doll owner via smartphone
Transcribed Microphone Data	Derived voice-to-text transcriptions of voice communication with doll (high sensitivity)	Application server (transcription engine)	Application server and doll owner via smartphone

Uses of collected information

Acceptable use policies need to be established in accordance with national, local, and industry regulation, as applicable.

Use of collected information refers to how different entities (that are being given access to the IoT data) will use data collected from different sources, in accordance with a privacy policy. In the case of the talking doll, the doll manufacturer itself owns and operates the Internet services that interact with the doll and collect its owner's and user's information. Therefore, it alone will be the collector of information that may be useful for:

- Viewing the data
- Studies or analytics performed on the data for research purposes
- Analysis of the data for marketing purposes
- Reporting on the data to the end user
- Selling or onward transfer of the data
- Distillation and onward transfer of any processed metadata that originated with the user's raw data

Ideally, the manufacturer would not provide the data (or metadata) to any third party; the sole participants in using the data would be the doll owner and the manufacturer. The doll is configured by its owner, collects voice data from its environment, has its voice data converted to text for keyword interpretation by the manufacturer's algorithms, and provides usage history, voice files, and application updates to the doll owner.

Smart devices rely upon many parties, however. In addition to the doll manufacturer, there are suppliers that support various functions and benefit from analyzing portions of the data. In cases where data or transcribed data is sent to third parties, agreements between each party must be in force to ensure the third parties agree to not pass on or make the data available for other than agreed-upon uses.

Security

Security is privacy's step-sibling and a critical element of realizing privacy by design. Privacy is not achievable without data, communications, applications, device, and system level security controls. The security primitives of confidentiality (encryption), integrity, authentication, non-repudiation, and data availability need to be implemented to support the overarching privacy goals for the deployment.

In order to specify the privacy-related security controls, the privacy data needs to be mapped to the security controls and security parameters necessary for protection. It is useful at this stage to identify all endpoints in the architecture in which the PII is:

- Originated
- Transmitted through
- Processed
- Stored

Each PII data element then needs to be mapped to a relevant security control that is either implemented or satisfied by endpoints that touch it. For example, credit card information may originate on either the doll owner's home computer or mobile device web browser and be sent to the billing service application. Assigning the security control of confidentiality, integrity, and server authentication, we will likely use the common HTTPS (HTTP over TLS) protocol to maintain the encryption, integrity, and server authentication while transmitting the credit card information from the end user.

Once a complete picture is developed for the security-in-transit protections of all PII throughout the system, security needs to focus on the protection of data-at-rest. Data-at-rest protection of PII will focus on other traditional IT security controls, such as database encryption, access controls between web servers, databases, personnel access control, physical protection of assets, separation of duties, and so on.

Notice

Notice pertains to the notification given to the end user(s) on what scope of information is collected, any consent that the user must provide, and the user's right to decline to provide the information. Notice is almost exclusively handled in privacy policies to which the end user must agree prior to obtaining services.

In the case of our talking doll, the notice is provided in two places:

- Printed product instruction sheet (provided within the packaging)
- User privacy agreement presented by the doll's application server upon account creation

Data retention

Data retention addresses how the service stores and retains any data from the device or device's user(s). A data retention policy should be summarized in the overall privacy policy, and should clearly indicate:

- What data is stored/collected and archived
- When and how the data will be pushed or pulled from the device or mobile application
- When and how data is destroyed
- Any metadata or derived information that may be stored (aside from the IoT raw data)
- How long the information will be stored (both during and after the life of the account to which it pertains)
- If any controls/services are available to the end user to scrub any data they generate
- Any special mechanisms for data handling in the event of legal issues or law enforcement requests

In our talking doll example, the data in question is the PII identified previously, particularly the microphone-recorded voice, transcriptions, metadata associated with the recorded information, and subscription information. The sensitivity of data recorded within one's home, whether a child's musings, captured dialog between parent and child, or a group of children at play, can be exceedingly sensitive (indicating names, ages, location, indication of who is at home, and so on). The type of information the system is collecting can amount to what is available using classic eavesdropping and spying; the sensitivity of the information and its potential for misuse is enormous. Clearly, data ownership belongs to the doll owner(s); the company whose servers pick up, process, and record the data needs to be explicitly clear on how the data is retained or not.

Information sharing

Information sharing, also called **onward transfer** in the US and European Safe Harbor privacy principle, refers to the scope of sharing information within the enterprise that collects it, and with organizations external to it. It is common in business enterprises to share or sell information to other entities (`https://en.wikipedia.org/wiki/International_Safe_Harbor_Privacy_Principles`).

In general, the PIA should list and describe (*Toward a Privacy Impact Assessment (PIA) Companion to the CIS Critical Security Controls; Center for Internet Security, 2015*) the following:

- Organizations with whom information is shared, and what types of agreement either exist or need to be formed between them. Agreements can take the form of contracted adherence to general policies and **service level agreements (SLAs)**.

- Types of information that are transferred to each external organization.

- Privacy risks of transferring the listed information (for example, aggregation risks or risks of combining with publicly available sources of information).

- How sharing is in alignment with the established data use and collection policy.

Note that at the time of writing this, the Safe Harbor agreement between the US and Europe remains invalidated by the **Court of Justice of the European Union (CJEU)**, thanks to a legal complaint that ensued from Edward Snowden's leaks concerning NSA spying. Issues related to data residency—where cloud-enabled data centers actually store data—pose additional complications for US corporations (`http://curia.europa.eu/jcms/upload/docs/application/pdf/2015-10/cp150117en.pdf`).

Redress

Redress addresses the policies and procedures for end users to seek redress for possible violations and disclosure of their sensitive information. For example, if the talking doll owner starts receiving phone messages indicating that an unwanted person has somehow eavesdropped in on the child's conversation with the doll, he/she should have a process to contact the manufacturer and alert them to the problem. The data loss could be from non-adherence to the company's privacy protections (for example, an insider threat) or a basic security flaw in the system's design or operation.

In addition to actual privacy losses, redress should also include provisions for addressing end users' complaints and concerns about documented and disclosed policies affecting their data. In addition, procedures should also be available for end users to voice concerns about how their data could be used for other purposes without their knowledge.

Each of the policies and procedures for redress should be checked when performing the PIA. They will need to be periodically re-evaluated and updated when changes are made either to policies, the data types collected, or the privacy controls implemented.

Auditing and accountability

Auditing and accountability checks within a PIA are to ascertain what safeguards and security controls are needed, and when, from the following perspectives:

- Insider and third-party auditing addresses what organizations and/or agencies provide oversight

- Forensics

- Technical detection of information (or information system) misuse (for example, a host auditing tool detects database access and a large query not emanating from the application server)

- Security awareness, training processes, and supporting policies for those with direct or indirect access to the PII

- Modifications to information sharing processes, organizations with whom information is shared, and approval of any changes to policy (for example, if the doll manufacturer were to begin selling e-mail addresses and doll users' demographics to third-party marketers)

Asking pointed questions about each of the preceding points, and determining the sufficiency and detail of the answers, is necessary in the PIA.

PbD principles

Today's IoT-enabled businesses and infrastructures can no longer afford to incrementally bolt on privacy enforcement mechanisms as a reactionary afterthought. That is why privacy engineering and design has evolved as a necessity and gained significant traction in recent years. This section discusses privacy design and engineering related to the Internet of Things.

Privacy embedded into design

Privacy engineering is driven completely by policy. It ensures that:

- Policy leads to privacy-related requirements and controls

- Underlying system-level design, interfaces, security patterns, and business processes support these

Privacy engineering satisfies the policies (clarified by an organization's legal department) at a technical level in every facet of technical interpretation and implementation. Security engineering and privacy engineering are closely intertwined. One can think of the system and security engineering as implementing the device and system level security functions that satisfy higher-level privacy needs, as specified by privacy policies and laws.

Privacy embedded into design means that there is a concrete mapping between the privacy protected data and the system functions, security functions, policies, and enforcements that enable that data to be protected.

Positive-sum, not zero-sum

The positive-sum principle of privacy engineering and design specifies that privacy improves the functionality (provides full functionality) and security of the system, not the other way around.

A zero-sum privacy approach would result in one of the following:

- No improvement to security and functionality
- Some type of reduction in functionality (or lost business processes)
- Potentially a loss of some type of non-functional business or security need

In other words, a zero-sum approach necessarily means some types of trade-off are taking place, as opposed to a *win-win* approach (`https://www.ipc.on.ca/images/resources/7foundationalprinciples.pdf`).

End-to-end security

End-to-end security is a frequently over-used term, but in the context of privacy it implies that data is protected throughout the lifecycle of the data—generation, ingestion, copying, distribution, redistribution, local and remote storage, archiving, and destruction. In other words, it is not a mere communications-level perspective on end-to-end as in encrypting and authenticating data in transit from one network endpoint to another. Rather, it takes into account the protected data and its treatment in and through all business processes, applications, systems, hardware, and people that touch it. End-to-end security addresses all of the technical and policy controls in place to ensure that the PPI is protected.

Visibility and transparency

Privacy by design implies that any and all stakeholders (whether the system operator, device manufacturer, or affiliates) are operating by the rules, processes, procedures, and policies that they claim to be.

This principle is meant to satisfy any gaps in the auditing and accountability needs raised by the PIA. In essence, how would an end user be able to verify that your IoT privacy objectives or regulatory compliance goals are actually being met? Conversely, how could you as an IoT organization verify that your own affiliate providers' SLAs are being adhered to, especially those concerning privacy? One manner of providing visibility and transparency is for an IoT implementation or deployment organization to subject itself to independent third-party audits, for example, either publishing or making results available to requesters. Industry-specific audits may also satisfy certain facets of visibility and transparency. The old axiom *trust but verify* is the principle at work in this control.

Respect for user privacy

A PbD solution will absolutely have built-in controls that allow respect for user privacy. Respect for user privacy entails providing users with knowledge and control with respect to privacy, notice of privacy policies and events, and the ability to opt out. The following **fair information practices (FIPs)** privacy principles address this topic in detail:

- **Consent**: Consent shows respect for user privacy by ensuring that end users have the opportunity to understand how their data is being used and treated, and provide consent for its use based on that knowledge. The specificity of the consent given needs to be proportionate to the sensitivity of the data being provided. For example, use of medical charts, X-rays, and blood test data will require much greater detail and clarity in the consent notice than just use of one's age, gender, and food preferences.

- **Accuracy**: Accuracy refers to the private information being kept current and accurate for whatever its intended purpose. Part of maintaining this FIP is to ensure that strong integrity controls are being enforced throughout the system. For example, high integrity controls may require digital signatures to be part of the record-keeping process, whereas less sensitive or impactful information may simply require cryptographic integrity in transit or checksums at rest.

- **Access**: The access FIP addresses end users' ability to both access their personal information and ensure its accuracy (and have the ability to correct inaccurate information that has been detected).

- **Compliance**: Compliance deals with how organizations provide the controls and mechanisms to end users to rectify problems in the accuracy or use of their data. For example, does the smart doll manufacturer in the earlier example have a process to:

    - Issue complaints?

    - Appeal any decisions made?

    - Escalate to an external organization or agency?

Privacy engineering recommendations

Privacy engineering is a relatively new discipline that seeks to ensure systems, applications, and devices are engineered to conform to privacy policies. This section provides some recommendations for setting up and operating a privacy engineering capability in your IoT organization.

Whether a small start-up or a large Silicon Valley tech company, chances are you are developing products and applications that will require PbD capabilities built in from the ground up. It is crucial that the engineering processes are followed to engineer a privacy-respecting IoT system from the outset and not bolt the protections on later. The right *people* and *processes* are first needed to accomplish this.

Privacy throughout the organization

Privacy touches a variety of professions in the corporate and government world; attorneys and other legal professionals, engineers, QA, and other disciplines become involved in different capacities in the creation and adoption of privacy policies, their implementation, or their enforcement. The following diagram shows a high-level organization and what concerns each sub-organization has from a privacy perspective:

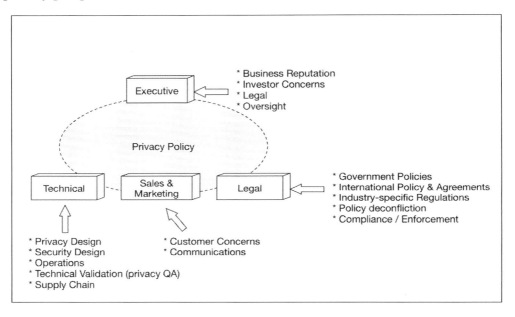

Privacy initiatives and working groups should be established within any organization that develops frontline IoT products and services which collect, process, view, or store any privacy information. The executive level should provide the holistic direction and ensure the different sub-organizations are accountable for their roles. Each department should have one or more privacy champions who put themselves in the shoes of end customers to ensure their interests—not only the dry, regulatory policies—are fully taken into account.

Privacy engineering professionals

For all of the departments involved, the role of the privacy engineer is to understand and participate in both the policy and technical lifecycle of privacy management and implementation. Privacy engineering, a relatively new discipline, requires a different capability set than what is typically found in a single corporate department. We suggest the following attributes for individuals performing privacy engineering:

- They are engineers, preferably ones with a security background. Lawyers and non-technical privacy professionals can and should be available for reference and consulting, but privacy engineering itself is an engineering discipline.

- They ideally have privacy-related qualifications such as an **IAPP (International Association of Privacy Professionals)** certification (`https://iapp.org/certify`).

- They have a strong knowledge of the following:

  - Privacy policy
  - System development processes and lifecycle
  - Functional and nonfunctional requirements, including security functional and security assurance requirements
  - Source code and software engineering practices, in the language(s) the systems are being developed in
  - Interface design (APIs)
  - Data storage design and operations
  - Application of security controls to networks, software, and hardware, as appropriate
  - Cryptography and proper use of cryptographic primitives and protocols, given their importance in protecting PII throughout device and information lifecycles

These are suggestions only; the needs of your organization may impose a number of other minimum requirements. In general, we have found that security engineers who have a development background and have obtained privacy professional training tend to be individuals optimally suited for privacy engineering.

Privacy engineering activities

Privacy engineering in a larger organization should consist of a dedicated department of individuals with the minimum qualifications listed above. Smaller organizations may not have dedicated departments, but may need to improvise by cross-training and adding privacy engineering duties to individuals engaged in other facets of the engineering process. Security engineers tend to be naturally adept at this. Regardless, depending on the size and scope of a project or program, at least one dedicated privacy engineer should be allocated at the inception of program to ensure that privacy needs are addressed. Ideally, this individual or set of individuals will be associated with the project throughout its development.

The assigned privacy engineer should:

- Maintain a strong association with the development team, participating in:
  - Design reviews
  - Code reviews
  - Test activities and other validation/verification steps

- Function as the end user advocate in the development of IoT capability. For example, when performing code reviews with the development team, this individual should ask probing questions about the treatment of each identified PII element (and verify each in code).

- Where did it come from (verify in code)?

- Is the code creating any metadata using the PII that we need to add to our list of PII?

- How was it passed from function to function (by reference, by value) and how and where was it written to a database?

- When a function did not need it anymore, was the value destroyed in memory? If so, how? Was it simply de-referenced or was it actively overwritten (understandably bound to the capabilities of the programming language)?

- What security parameters (for example, used for encryption, authentication, or integrity) is the application or device depending on to protect the PII? How are they being treated from a security perspective, so that they are appropriately available to protect the PII?

- If the code was inherited from another application or system, what do we need to do to verify that the inherited libraries are treating the PII we have identified appropriately?

- In server applications, what type of cookies are we dropping into end users' web browsers? What are we tracking with them?

- Is anything in the code violating the privacy policy we established at the beginning? If so, it needs to be re-engineered, otherwise privacy policy issues will have to be escalated to higher levels in the organization.

This list of activities is by no means exhaustive. The most important point is that privacy engineering activity is a dedicated function performed in conjunction with the other engineering disciplines (software engineering, firmware, and even hardware when necessary). The privacy engineer should absolutely be involved with the project from inception, requirements gathering, development, testing, and through deployment to ensure that the lifecycle of PII protection is engineered into the system, application, or device according to a well-defined policy.

Summary

Protecting privacy is a serious endeavor made even more challenging with the IoT's myriad forms, systems of systems, countless organizations, and the differences in which they are addressed across international borders. In addition, the gargantuan amount of data being collected, indexed, analyzed, redistributed, re-analyzed, and sold provides challenges for controlling data ownership, onward transfer, and acceptable use. In this section, we've learned about privacy principles, privacy engineering, and how to perform privacy impact assessments in support of an IoT deployment.

In our next chapter, we will explore starting up an IoT compliance program.

8
Setting Up a Compliance Monitoring Program for the IoT

The security industry comprises an extremely broad set of communities, overarching goals, capabilities, and day-to-day activities. The purpose of each, in one form or another, is to better secure systems and applications and reduce risks within the ever-changing threat landscape. Compliance represents a necessary aspect to security risk management, but is frequently regarded as a dirty word in security. There is a good reason for this. The term **compliance** invokes feelings of near-zombie-like adherence to sets of bureaucratically derived requirements that are tailored to mitigate a broad set of static threats. That's a mouthful of justifiable negativity.

We'll let you in on a second, dirty, not-so-much-of-a secret in our community: compliance, by itself, fails to actually secure systems. That said, security is only one element of risk. Lack of compliance to an industry, government, or other authority can also increase risks in terms of exposure to fines, lawsuits, and the ever-present negative impacts of degraded public perception within the court of public opinion. In short, to be compliant with mandated compliance regimen, one can potentially improve one's security posture, and certainly reduce other types of risk that are indirectly security-related.

In other words, an organization can find benefits in either case and will frequently not have a choice anyway. With the cynicism behind us, this chapter discusses approaches to building a compliance monitoring program for your IoT deployment that is customized to ensure one's security posture is improved. It also recommends best practices in achieving and maintaining compliance in adherence to applicable cyber security regulations and other guidelines. Vendor tools that will help in managing and maintaining your compliance regimen are also discussed. It accomplishes these goals in the following sections:

- **Describing the challenges that IoT devices introduce for compliance**: We will outline a series of steps to assist organizations with standing up a compliant IoT system.

- **Methods for continuously monitoring compliance and setting up an IoT compliance program**: In this section, we will distinguish traditional versus IoT compliance, as well as identify tools, processes, and best practices for continuously monitoring a system. Included are definitions of roles, functions, schedules, and reports, as well as when and where to introduce penetration testing (and how to go about it).

- **Discussion of IoT impacts to frequently utilized compliance standards**: Here, we discuss changes that may be required to existing compliance guidance programs.

There is never a one-size-fits-all solution for compliance and compliance monitoring, so this section will help you to adapt, build, and tailor your own compliance monitoring solution as the IoT landscape evolves.

IoT compliance

Let's first examine what we mean when we use the term IoT compliance. What we mean by this is that the people, processes, and technologies that make up an integrated and deployed IoT system are compliant with some set of regulations or best practices. There are many compliance schemes, each with a plethora of requirements. If we were to explore what compliance means for a traditional information technology system, for example, we would see requirements such as the financial **payment card industry (PCI)** current **data security standard (DSS)**, an example being PCI DSS 1.4:

> *Install personal firewall software on any mobile and/or employee-owned devices that connect to the Internet when outside the network (for example, laptops used by employees), and which are also used to access the network.*

Even though this requirement is geared toward mobile devices, it is clear that many IoT devices do not have the ability to implement firewall software. How then does an IoT system show compliance when regulatory requirements do not yet take constrained IoT devices into consideration? Today, the commercial industry has not yet evolved a comprehensive IoT-related standards framework, mainly because the IoT is so new, large, and diverse across industries.

Some technical challenges related to IoT systems and compliance include the following:

- IoT systems implement a diverse array of hardware computing platforms
- IoT systems often use alternative and functionally limited operating systems
- IoT systems frequently use alternative networking/RF protocols not typically found in existing enterprises
- Software/firmware updates to IoT components may be difficult to provision and install
- Scanning for vulnerabilities in IoT systems is not necessarily straightforward (again, new protocols, data elements, sensitivity, use cases, and so on)
- There is often limited documentation available for IoT system operations

Over time, existing regulatory frameworks will likely be updated to reflect the new, unique, and emergent characteristics of the IoT. In the meantime, we should focus on how to implement IoT systems in business networks using adaptive compliance practices that reflect risks we know of today. First, we'll lay out a set of recommendations for anyone integrating and deploying an IoT system into their network, and then we will go into detail for setting up a **governance, risk, and compliance (GRC)** program for your IoT.

Implementing IoT systems in a compliant manner

Follow these recommendations as you begin to consider how to integrate your IoT systems into business networks. Earlier chapters in this book described how to securely engineer IoT systems. This section focuses on compliance-specific considerations that will help achieve compliance-oriented risk management benefits in whichever industry you operate.

Here are some initial recommendations:

- It is necessary to document the integration of each IoT system into your network environment. Keep these diagrams ready for regular audits and more importantly, keep them up to date. Leverage change control procedures to ensure that they are not modified without authorization.

- Documentation should include all ports, protocols used, interconnection points to other systems, and also detail where sensitive information may be stored or processed.

- Documentation should include what parts of your enterprise the IoT devices will be allowed to function and from what part of the enterprise (and what portals/gateways may be needed) any management or configuration of the devices will be performed.

- Documentation should also include additional device characterizations such as a) configuration limitations, b) physical security, c) how a device identifies itself (and how authenticated) and is associated to an enterprise user, and d) how a device may or may not be upgradable. Some of these characterizations will be useful in establishing and configuring monitoring solutions.

- Implement a test bed. IoT systems should be set up in a test environment prior to being operationally deployed. This allows rigorous security (and functional) tests to be run against the systems to identify defects and vulnerabilities prior to fielding. It also allows baselining how the devices behave on the network (this may be useful in defining **security incident and event management (SIEM)** detection pattern IDS signatures).

- Establish solid configuration management approaches for all IoT components.

- Plan out the groups and roles that are authorized to interact with the IoT system. Document these and keep as artifacts within your change control system.

- Obtain compliance and audit records from any third-party supplier or partner with whom you share data.

- Establish approval authorities that take responsibility for approving the IoT systems' operation in the production environment.

- Set up regular assessments (quarterly) that review configurations, operating procedures, and documentation to ensure continued compliance. Once scanning solutions are defined and configured, maintain all scan results for audit preparation.

- Set up incident response procedures that dictate how to respond to both natural failure and malicious events.

An IoT compliance program

An IoT compliance initiative will probably be an extension of an organization's existing compliance program. As with any compliance program, a number of factors must be taken into consideration. The following figure provides a view into the activities that should, at a minimum, be included in an IoT compliance program. Each of the activities is a concurrent, ongoing function involving different stakeholders in the organization:

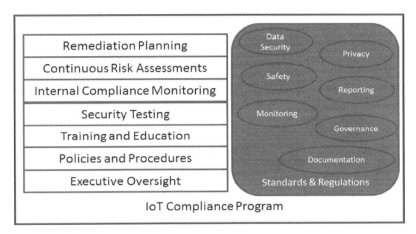

As organizations begin or continue to implement new IoT systems, ensure that each aspect of your IoT compliance program is in order.

Executive oversight

Given its normalization as a critical business function, compliance and risk management requires executive oversight and governance from multiple departments. Organizations that do not have executive-level interest, policy mandates, and monitoring, put their investors and customers at much greater risk when easily prevented breaches occur. The following organizational functions and departments should be included in the governance model for IoT operations:

- Legal and privacy representation
- Information technology/security
- Operations
- Safety engineering

Executive governance—if not already mandated by an industry requirement (for example, PCI DSS)—should include some type of approval authority to operate an IoT system. Any new IoT or IoT-augmented systems should be requested and granted from a designated approval authority within an organization. Without this control, people may bring many potentially high-risk devices into the network. This approval authority should be well versed in the security policies and standards to which the system needs to comply, and have a sufficient degree of technical understanding of the system.

The United States Federal Government implements a comprehensive compliance program that requires packages to be created and maintained that detail the justification for a particular system being added to a federal network. Though this approval function in the government has failed to prevent all breaches, the overall security posture of government systems do benefit from having a designated individual responsible for overall security policy adherence.

US Government Approval Authorities must grant each system or subsystem the right to be used on an agency network and must continue to grant that right each year. Commercial organizations would be wise to adopt and tailor such an approach for vetting and approving IoT systems that are to be added to the corporate network. Having a designated individual responsible for approval reduces inconsistencies in the interpretation and execution of policy. In addition, commercial organizations will need to implement checks and balances such as periodically rotating duties among other individuals/roles. This is particularly important for mitigating certain risks that arise when employees leave an organization.

Policies, procedures, and documentation

Policies and procedures for the safe and secure operation of an IoT system are needed for administrators as well as users of IoT systems. These guidance documents should inform employees how to safeguard data and operate systems securely, in accordance with applicable regulations. They should also provide details on the potential penalties for non-compliance.

An activity for which organizations should consider establishing policies is the introduction of personal IoT devices into the corporate environment. Security engineers should evaluate the ramifications of allowing limited use of personal IoT devices (for example, consumer IoT) in the organization and if so, what limitations should be imposed. For example, they may find they need to restrict the installation of IoT applications on company mobile phones but possibly allow the apps on employee personal phones.

Examples of security documentation artifacts that may be useful include **system security plans (SSPs)**, security CONOPS, cryptographic key and certificate management plans, and continuity of operations policies and procedures. Well-versed security engineers should be able to adopt and tailor these types of plans based on best practices and identified risks.

Training and education

Many users of connected devices and systems will not initially understand the potential impact of misuse for an IoT system. A comprehensive training program should be created and provided to an organization's users and administrators of IoT systems. The training program should focus on a number of details as identified in the upcoming diagram.

Skills assessments

For system administrators and engineers, it is important to identify when there are gaps in knowledge and skills needed to securely design, implement, and operate IoT systems. It may be useful to perform yearly skills assessments for these staff to determine their understanding of the following:

- IoT data security
- IoT privacy
- Safety procedures for IoT systems
- IoT-specific security tools (scanners, and so on)

Topical areas to address in skills assessment and training are indicated in the following diagram:

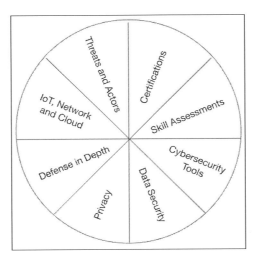

Cyber security tools

From an IoT security perspective, ensure that training is provided on the different tools that are used to routinely scan IoT systems. This can be on-the-job training but the end result is that security administrators understand how to effectively use the tools that will provide regular inputs into the compliance state of IoT systems.

Data security

This is one of the most important aspects of the training needed in IoT compliance programs. Administrators and engineers must be able to securely configure the range of components that make up an IoT system. This includes being able to securely configure the backend, cloud-based data storage, and analytics systems to prevent malicious or even non-malicious leakage of sensitive information. Understanding how to classify information as sensitive or not is also an important part of this training. The diversity of data types and sensitivity levels possible in different IoT devices can introduce unanticipated security and privacy risks.

Defense-in-depth

NIST SP 800-82 defines the principal of defense-in-depth: layering security mechanisms so that the impact of a failure in any one mechanism is minimized (`http://csrc.nist.gov/publications/nistpubs/800-82/SP800-82-final.pdf`). Providing system administrators and engineers with training that reinforces this concept will allow them to help design more secure IoT security systems and IoT implementations.

Privacy

We've already discussed in this book the potential stumbling blocks regarding privacy and the IoT. Incorporate privacy fundamentals and requirements into your IoT training program to help staff safeguard sensitive customer information.

Incorporate details on the basics of IoT into your training regimen. This includes the types of IoT systems that your organization will be adopting, the underlying technology that drives these systems, and the manner in which data is transferred, stored and processed within these systems.

The IoT, network, and cloud

IoT data is very often sent directly to the cloud for processing, and as such, providing a basic understanding of the cloud architectures that support your IoT systems should also be an aspect of your IoT training program. Similarly, as new network architectures are adopted over time (that can better support different IoT deployment paradigms), inclusion of more adaptable, scalable, and dynamically responsive **software defined networking (SDN)** and **network function virtualization (NFV)** capabilities should also be included. New functionality may be needed for supporting dynamic policies with regard to IoT behavior on networks.

Threats/attacks

Keep staff up to date on how researchers and real-world adversaries have compromised IoT devices and systems. This will help to drive responsive and adaptable defense-in-depth approaches to system design as engineers conceptualize the myriad ways that others have broken into these systems.

Sources of information on the latest threats and cybersecurity alerts include the following:

- **Automated Vulnerability Management from NIST**: The National Vulnerability Database (`https://nvd.nist.gov/`)

- **General Cybersecurity Alerts**: **United States Computer Emergency Readiness Team (US-CERT)** (`https://www.us-cert.gov/ncas`)

- **Industrial Control System Threat Information**: The **Industrial Control System Cyber Emergency Response Team (ICS-CERT)** (`https://ics-cert.us-cert.gov`)

- **Medical Device and Health Information Cybersecurity Sharing**: **National Health Information and Analysis Center (NH-ISAC)** (`http://www.nhisac.org`)

- Many of the antivirus vendors provide current Internet threat data through their respective websites

Many other sources that will vary in applicability to your organization or industry can be found in the European Network and Information Security Agency's proactive detection of network security incidents report: `https://www.enisa.europa.eu/activities/cert/support/proactive-detection/proactive-detection-report`.

Certifications

IoT certifications are lacking today, but for example, obtaining **Cloud Security Alliance (CSA) Certificate of Cloud Security Knowledge (CCSK)** and **Certified Cloud Security Professional (CCSP)** certifications may serve as a good starting point to understanding the complex cloud environment that will power most IoT implementations. Also consider certifications focused on data privacy, such as the **Certified Information Privacy Professional (CIPP)** from **International Association of Privacy Professionals (iAPP)**: `https://iapp.org/certify/cipp/`.

Testing

It is vital to test IoT implementations prior to deploying them into a production environment. This requires the use of an IoT test bed.

Functional testing of IoT device deployments requires the ability to scale to the number of devices that would typically be deployed in an enterprise. It may not be feasible to physically implement these numbers during initial test events. As such, a virtual test lab solution is required. Products such as Ravello (`https://www.ravellosystems.com/`) provide the ability to upload and test virtual machines in a realistic, simulated environment. When applied to the IoT, leverage the use of containers (for example, Docker) to support the creation of baselines of the environment that can be tested with both functional and security tools.

In addition, higher assurance IoT deployments should include rigorous safety (failsafe) as well as security regression tests to validate proper device and system response to sensor error conditions, security-or safety-related shutoffs, error state recoveries, as well as basic functional behavior.

Internal compliance monitoring

Determining that your IoT systems are compliant with security regulations is an important first start, but the value of performing the assessment activity diminishes over time. In order to be vigilant, organizations should mandate a continuous assessment methodology to evaluate the real-time security posture of systems. If you haven't already begun a move towards continuous monitoring of your systems, the adoption of IoT-integrated deployments is certainly good time to begin. Keep in mind that continuous monitoring should not be confused with network monitoring. Network monitoring is just one element of an automated policy-based audit framework that should comprise a continuous monitoring solution.

The United States **Department of Homeland Security (DHS)** defines a six-step process for continuous diagnostics and monitoring (`https://www.dhs.gov/cdm`):

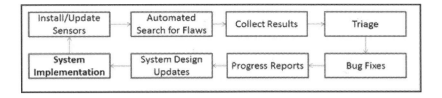

These six steps are a good process to adopt for commercial enterprises implementing IoT systems. They provide the means for large organizations to continuously identify new security issues while prioritizing resources against the most pressing issues at any given time. The adaptation for handling within an IoT system warrants exploration.

An additional step has been added here that focuses on understanding the cause of the failure and updating the system design and associated implementation accordingly. A continuous feedback loop between the identification of flaws and the potential architectural update of system designs is required for an effective security management process.

Install/update sensors

Sensors in the traditional IT sense may be host-based monitoring agents installed on enterprise computers (for example, that collect host logs for backend audit) or IDS/IPS-enabled network sensors. In the IoT, putting agents on the constrained edge things within a system is not straightforward, and in some cases may simply not be feasible. That does not mean that you cannot instrument your IoT system, however. Let's examine an architectural fragment:

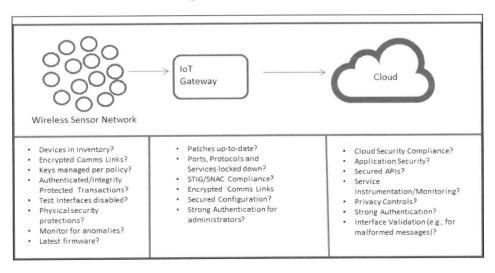

We can evaluate collected security-relevant data by considering an IoT architectural model of WSN endpoints transmitting data to a protocol gateway, then that gateway passing the data to the cloud. Once in the cloud, we can leverage the capabilities of the **cloud service provider (CSP)** to capture data between application endpoints supporting the IoT sensors. For example, within Amazon we can leverage AWS CloudTrail to monitor API calls to the cloud.

The protocol gateway is likely to have the processing power and storage that is sufficient for installing traditional IT endpoints security tools. These components can send back data on a scheduled or on-demand basis to support continuous system monitoring from either a cloud-based or on-premises support structure.

WSNs (wireless sensor networks) frequently consist of highly constrained, resource-limited IoT devices. Such devices may lack the processing, memory, or operating system support needed to be instrumented with security and audit agents. Even so, the wireless sensors can play an important part in the holistic security posture of the system; therefore, it is worthwhile to examine what security features we can leverage and derive from them.

Keep in mind that many such devices do not persistently store at all, instead passing it on via the gateway to backend applications. We therefore need to ensure that basic integrity protections are applied to all of the data-in-transit. Integrity will ensure that no tampering of the data has occurred upstream of the gateway and that data arriving at the gateway is legitimate (though not authenticated). Many wireless protocols will support at minimum basic checksums (for example, 32-bit **cyclic redundancy check (CRC)**), though hashes are more secure. Better yet, are those that include a keyed **message authentication code (MAC)** as described in *Chapter 5, Cryptographic Fundamentals for IoT Security Engineering*. AES-MAC, AES-GCM, and others can provide rudimentary edge-to-gateway integrity and data-origin authentication on both sent as well as received messages. Once at the gateway (the IP network edge for some IoT devices), attention can focus on capturing other data needed to monitor for IoT security anomalies.

Automated search for flaws

It's important to note that some IoT devices can exhibit much greater functionality. Some may include components such as simple web servers to support configuration of the device. Think of your home router, printer, and so on. Many home and business appliances are built out of the box ready for network-based configuration. Web interfaces can also be used for security monitoring; for example, most home Wi-Fi routers support rudimentary email-based notification (configured through the web interface) of security-related events pertinent to your network. Web interfaces and notification systems can provide a capability in some IoT devices to indicate flaws, misconfigurations, or even just out-of-date software/firmware information.

Non-web interfaces may be found in other devices, for example, the myriad endpoints that support the **simple network management protocol (SNMP)**. SNMP-enabled devices speak the SNMP protocol to set, get, and receive notifications on managed data attributes that conform to device-and industry-specific **management information bases (MIBs)**.

 If your IoT device supports SNMP, ensure that it is SNMPv3 and that endpoint encryption and authentication is turned on (SNMPv3 user security model). In addition, 1) change SNMP passwords on a routine basis, 2) use difficult-to-predict passphrases, 3) closely track all `snmpEngineIds` and their associated network addresses, and 4) do not use usernames on multiple devices if it can be helped.

Source:

```
https://smartech.gatech.edu/bitstream/handle/1853/44881/lawrence_
nigel_r_201208_mast.pdf
```

The diverse ecosystem of IoT devices should be searched automatically for flaws using whatever protocols are available on the endpoints. This includes mobile applications, desktop applications, gateways, interfaces, web services hosted in the cloud that support the growing amount of data collection, analysis, and reporting that characterizes the IoT. Even seemingly non-security-relevant data such as miscellaneous event times, temperatures, and other features of the device can be exploited for improved security hygiene. Network-based tools such as Splunk are invaluable for collecting, aggregating and automatically sifting through enormous quantities of IoT data, whether from basic connected devices to full-scale industrial control systems. Using software agents at gateways, protocol brokers, and other endpoints, Splunk can ingest MQTT, COAP, AMQP, JMS, and a variety of industrial protocols for custom analysis, visualization, reporting, and record keeping. If an IoT edge device has the requisite OS and processing capabilities, it may also be a candidate for running a Splunk agent. Custom rules can be designed in Splunk to automatically identify, analyze, and report on combined non-security-, security-, and safety-related items of interest in your deployment.

There are a number of tools that administrators can use to search for vulnerabilities in IoT network gateways. Within the US Federal Government, the **Assured Compliance Assessment Solution (ACAS)** suite of tools integrated by tenable is used extensively. ACAS includes Nessus, **Passive Vulnerability Scanner (PVS)**, and a console.

Other vulnerability scanning tools, some of which are open source, can be used at different stages of the system or software development lifecycle as well as in operational environments (as during penetration testing exercises). Examples include the following (`http://www.esecurityplanet.com/open-source-security/slideshows/10-open-source-vulnerability-assessment-tools.html`):

- OpenVAS
- Nexpose
- Retina CS community

Fostering basic risk management, organizations that are developing in-house IoT products need to incorporate a feedback loop in the vulnerability assessment and development lifecycle. As vulnerabilities are identified within fielded products, development and patching backlog entries should be made that can be prioritized for quick remediation. Organizations developing in-house smart IoT products should also make use of tools that support static and dynamic code analysis as well as fuzzing. These tools should be run on a regular basis, preferably as part of a fully featured **Continuous Integration** (**CI**) environment. SAST and DAST tools are often expensive but can now be leased on a cost-effective basis. The OWASP Firmware Analysis Project also lists some device firmware security analysis tools that may be useful in evaluating the firmware security of your IoT devices (`https://www.owasp.org/index.php/OWASP_Internet_of_Things_Project#tab=Firmware_Analysis`).

Collect results

The tools used in the search for flaws should provide reports that allow for triage. These reports should be saved by the security team to use during compliance audits.

Triage

The severity of the findings will dictate what resources are assigned to each flaw and in what order each flaw needs to be remediated. Assign a severity rating to each flaw based on the security impact to the organization and prioritize the high-severity findings to be fixed first. If your organization uses Agile development tools such as the Atlassian suite (Jira, Confluence, and so on), you can also track these defects as "Issues", assign specific lifecycle structures to them, and make judicious use of the different labels you can attach to them.

Bug fixes

Bug fixes should ideally be handled in the same manner that other features are handled within the development cycle. Input DRs into the product backlog (for example, Jira issues) and prioritize them to the next sprint. In severe cases, exceptions can be made to stop new feature development and focus solely on closing a critical security flaw.

Incorporate regression testing after each DR is completed to ensure that unintentional flaws are not introduced during the fix of the DR.

Reporting

Security vendors have developed dashboards for reporting compliance. Make use of those dashboards for providing reports to executive management. Each compliance tool has its own reporting capabilities.

System design updates

When security flaws are discovered in IoT systems and devices, it is important to hold retrospectives focused on determining whether there are design or configuration changes that must be made to the systems and networks, or whether the devices should be allowed to operate on them at all. At least quarterly, review the flaws discovered during the preceding three months and focus on identifying any changes to baselines and architectures that are required. In many cases, a severe vulnerability in a particular device can be mitigated by a simple configuration change in the network.

Periodic risk assessments

Perform periodic risk assessments, ideally using third parties to validate that the IoT system is not only compliant but also meets its minimum security baseline. Perform black box penetration testing least every six months and perform more focused testing (white box) at least every year. The testing should focus on the IoT systems as a whole and not just the devices themselves.

A comprehensive penetration test program should be established by organizations deploying IoT solutions. This should include a mix of black box and white box testing as well as fuzz testing against well-known IoT application protocols in use.

Black box

Black box assessments can be conducted for a relatively low cost. These assessments are aimed at attempting to break into a device with no a priori knowledge of the technology that the device implements. As funding permits, have third parties perform black box tests against devices as well as the infrastructure that supports the devices. Perform these assessments at least yearly for each IoT system and more often if systems change more frequently (for example, through updates). If your systems wholly or partially reside in the cloud, perform at least the application penetration testing against representative VMs that you have deployed in the cloud containers. Even better, if you have a test infrastructure mock-up of the deployed system, penetration testing against it can yield valuable information.

Ideally, black box assessments should include a characterization of the system in order to help understand what details can be identified by someone without authorization. Other aspects of black box assessments are identified in the following table:

Activity	Description
Physical security evaluation	Characterize the physical security needs relative to the intended deployment environment. For example, are there any unprotected physical or logical interfaces? Does the sensitivity of the data processed or stored in the device justify tamper protections such as a tamper-evident enclosure, embedded protection (for example, hard resin or potting around sensitive processors and memory devices), or even a tamper response mechanism that wipes memory in the event of physical intrusion?
Firmware/software update process analysis	How is firmware or software loaded into the device? Does the device periodically poll a software update server, or are updates performed manually? How is initial software loaded (by whom and where)? If factory software images are loaded over a JTAG interface, is that interface still easily accessible in the field? How is the software/firmware protected at rest, during download, and loading into memory? Is it integrity protected at the file level? Is it digitally signed (even better) and therefore authenticated? Can software patches be downloaded in chunks, and what occurs if the download/install process is halted for some reason?

Activity	Description
Interface analysis	Interface analysis identifies all exposed and hidden physical interfaces and maps all device application and system services (and related protocols to each one). Once this has been accomplished, the means of accessing each service (or function) needs to be determined. Which function calls are authenticated? Is the authentication on a per call basis, or is only a single authentication required when initializing a session or otherwise accessing the device? What services or function calls are not authenticated? What services require additional steps (beyond authentication) for authorization prior to performing the service? If anything sensitive can be performed without authentication, is the device's intended environment in a highly secure area only accessed by authorized individuals?
Wireless security evaluation	A wireless security evaluation first identifies what wireless protocols are in use by the device and any known vulnerabilities with the protocols. Does the wireless protocol use cryptography? If so, are there default keys in use? How are keys updated? In addition, wireless protocols frequently have default protocol options configured. Some options may be less suited for certain operating environments. For example, if your Bluetooth module supports rotating MAC addresses and it is not a default configuration in your IoT application, you may want to activate it by default. This is especially true if your intended deployment environment is more sensitive to device tracking and other privacy concerns.
Configuration security evaluation	Configuration evaluation focuses on the optimal configuration of IoT devices within a system to ensure that no unnecessary services are running. In addition, it will check that only authorized protocols are enabled. Least privilege checking should also be evaluated.
Mobile application evaluation	Most IoT devices can communicate with either mobile devices or gateways; therefore, an evaluation of the mobile devices must also be conducted. During black box testing, this should include attempts to characterize the mobile application features, capabilities, and technologies, as well as attempts to break the interfaces that connect with the IoT devices, either directly or through web service gateways. Investigation of alternative methods to override or replace trust relationships between the mobile applications and IoT devices should also be investigated.

Activity	Description
Cloud security analysis (web services security)	At this stage, an investigation into the communication protocols used by either an IoT device or mobile application and cloud-hosted services should occur. This includes analyzing whether secured communications (for example, TLS/DTLS) are employed and how a device or mobile application authenticates to the cloud service. Whether on-premises or cloud, the infrastructure the endpoint is communicating with must be tested. Certain web servers have known vulnerabilities, and in some cases the management applications for these servers are public-facing (not a good combination).

White box assessments

White box (sometimes called glass box) assessments differ from black box in that the security testers have full access to design and configuration information about the system of interest. The following are some activities and descriptions that can be performed as part of white box testing:

Activity	Description
Staff interviews	Evaluators should perform a series of interviews with development and/or operational IT staff to understand the technologies used within the implementation, integration and deployment points, sensitive information processed, and critical data stores.
Reverse engineering	Perform reverse engineering of IoT device firmware when possible, to identify whether new exploits can be developed based on the current state of device firmware.
Hardware component analysis	From a supply chain perspective, determine whether the hardware components in use can be trusted. For example, some organizations may go so far as to fingerprint devices in proprietary ways to ensure that hardware components are not clones or emanate from unknown sources.
Code analysis	For any software that the IoT system includes, perform both SAST and DAST to identify vulnerabilities.
System design and configuration documentation reviews	Review all documentation and system designs. Identify areas of inconsistencies and gaps in documentation. Leverage the documentation review to create a security test plan.

Activity	Description
Fault and attack tree analysis	Many companies in diverse industries should develop, adopt, and maintain comprehensive fault and attack tree models.
	Fault trees provide a model-based framework from which to analyze how a device or system can fail from a set of unrelated leaf node conditions or events. Each time a product or system is engineered or updated, fault tree models can be updated to provide up-to-date visibility into the safety risk posture of the system.
	Related but quite different to fault trees are attack trees, which address device or system security. Attack trees should be created as a normal risk management white box activity to understand how an attacker's sequenced activities can compromise the security of an IoT device or system.
	Higher assurance communities such as those developing safety-of-life IoT deployments (for example, avionics systems and life-critical medical systems) should perform combined fault and failure tree modeling to better understand the combined safety and security posture. Note that some security controls can reduce safety, indicating the complex trade-offs between safety and security.

Fuzz testing

Fuzz testing is a specialized, advanced field in which attackers attempt to exploit an application through abnormal protocol usage and manipulation of its states. The following table identifies some fuzz testing activities:

Activity	Description
Power on/power off sequences/state changes	Perform in-depth analysis to identify how IoT devices respond to different (and unexpected) inputs in various states. This might include sending unexpected data to the IoT device during certain state changes (for example, power on/power off).
Protocol tag/length/value fields	Implant unexpected values in the protocol fields for IoT communications. This could include non-standard lengths of field inputs, unexpected characters, encodings, and so on.
Header processing	Implant unexpected fields in the headers or header extensions (if applicable) of IoT communication protocols.
Data validation attacks	Send random input or improperly formatted data to the IoT endpoints, including its gateways. For example, if the endpoints support ASN.1 messaging, send messages that do not conform to the ASN.1 message syntax, or application-acceptable message structures.

Activity	Description
Integrate with analyzer	The most efficient fuzz testing will use various automated fuzzers that have an analysis engine on the endpoint's behavior as it's being fuzzed. A feedback loop is created that observes the fuzzed application's responses to various inputs; this can be used to alter and devise new and valuable test cases that may, at the least, disable the endpoint, and at the most, fully compromise it (for example, a buffer overflow with subsequent, direct memory access).

A complex compliance environment

As a security professional, you are responsible for being compliant with security standards that have been published for the industries within which you operate. Many organizations are faced with meeting regulatory standards that span multiple industries. For example, a pharmacy may be responsible for being compliant with HIPAA as well as PCI regulations because it must protect both patient data as well as financial transactions. These concepts still apply to the IoT—some of the *things* are new, but the information types and protection mandates have been around for some time.

Challenges associated with IoT compliance

IT shops have traditionally had to track compliance with cybersecurity and data privacy regulations and standards. The IoT introduces new aspects of compliance. As embedded compute and communications capabilities are introduced into organization's physical assets, the need to focus on compliance with safety regulations must also come into play.

The IoT also blurs the line between many regulatory frameworks, a particular challenge for IoT device manufacturers. In some cases, device developers may not even realize that their products are subject to oversight from particular agencies (`http://www.lexology.com/library/detail.aspx?g=753e1b07-2221-4980-8f42-55229315b169`).

Examining existing compliance standards support for the IoT

As your organization begins to deploy new IoT capabilities, you will likely be able to leverage existing guidance you're already familiar with to demonstrate some of the security controls needed for the IoT. The challenge is that these guidance documents have not kept up with the changing pace of technology, and as such some tailoring of the controls to suit new IoT setups may be required.

In addition, there are currently gaps in coverage for various aspects of IoT standards. The IoT Study Group and **Interational Organization for Standardization (ISO)/ International ElectroTechnical Commission (IEC) Joint Technical Committee (JTC)** JTC 1 SC 27 recently detailed a set of IoT standards gaps that included the following:

- Gateway security
- Network function virtualization security
- Management and measurement of IoT security (that is, metrics)
- Open source assurance and security
- IoT risk assessment techniques
- Privacy and big data
- Application security guidance for IoT
- IoT incident response and guidance

Underwriters Laboratory IoT certification

Addressing the enormous gap in IoT compliance and certification, the well-known **Underwriters Laboratory (UL)** has recently introduced an IoT certification regimen (`http://www.ul.com/cybersecurity/`) into its **Cybersecurity Assurance Program (CAP)**. Based on its UL 2900 series of assurance requirements, the process involves a thorough examination of a product's security; UL intends the process to be used and tailored for a broad cross-section of industries, from consumer smart home appliances all the way to critical infrastructure (for example, energy, utilities, and healthcare).

NIST CPS efforts

NIST has been very active in the IoT security standards realm, particularly with regard to the **cyber-physical systems** (**CPS**) subset of the IoT. In late 2015, the NIST CPS Public Working Group (founded in mid-2014) released its first draft of its draft framework for cyber-physical systems, a conceptual framework from which CPS-related industries can derive development and implementation compliance standards and requirements related to cyber-physical systems. The working group was set up *"to bring together a broad range of CPS experts in an open public forum to help define and shape key characteristics of CPS, so as to better manage development and implementation within and across multiple smart application domains, including smart manufacturing, transportation, energy, and healthcare"*. (`https://blog.npstc. org/2015/09/22/cyber-physical-systems-framework-issued-by-nist-for- public-comment/`).

We point this out because there has been, so far, very little work in the realm of cross-industry standardization of cyber-physical system concepts and terms. IoT-related organizations may need to look for definitional guidance and framework support to develop their own tailored sets of compliance regimen both in development and deployment of new IoT paradigms. The NIST CPS framework is valuable because it addresses three distinct facets related to development and deployment of CPS, namely:

- Conceptualization
- Realization
- Assurance

In addition, the framework is fully cognizant of the distinctions between traditional cybersecurity needs and those of industrial control system. For example, the stability and control of physical system state and its dependence on timing information for critical state estimation and control functions. The resilience of inner control system functions depends on such attributes. Even if not for an industrial control system usage, the IoT is replete with examples that involve physical sensors and actuation; most of these meld the cyber and the physical domains in ways implementers may not be fully aware of. Across the three CPS facets identified above, the draft framework explicitly identifies and defines the following aspects of a CPS:

- Functional
- Business
- Human
- Trustworthiness

- Timing
- Data
- Boundaries
- Composability
- Lifecycle

While the NIST CPS framework is still in its infancy, it will likely become a significant source of structure and definitional knowledge needed for cross-industry modernization of CPS systems, standards, and risk management approaches.

NERC CIP

NERC CIP is the **North American Electric Reliability Corporation's Critical Infrastructure Protection (NERC CIP)** standards series that apply to the US's electrical generation and distribution systems. Organizations developing or deploying CPS, IoT, and other cybersecurity-related systems in the electrical industry should be well versed in NERC CIP. These standards address the following sub-topics for bulk electric systems:

- Cyber system categorization
- Security management controls
- Personnel and training
- Electronic security perimeters
- Physical security of **bulk electric system (BES)** cyber systems
- System security management
- Incident reporting and response planning
- Recovery plans for BES cyber systems
- Configuration change management and vulnerability assessments
- Information protection

Conformance aspects related to categorizing the sensitivity of components, integrating the correct controls, and overall assurance of the integrated electrical system must be addressed for those organizations in the electrical industry adopting and deploying new IoT systems.

HIPAA/HITECH

Health organizations will face additional challenges associated with the transition to connected medical devices and other smart healthcare equipment. Recent successful attacks on health organizations (for example, ransomware attacks on hospitals and critical patient data, `http://www.latimes.com/business/technology/la-me-ln-hollywood-hospital-bitcoin-20160217-story.html`) shows that either organizations are failing to meet compliance requirements or there are already serious gaps in standards and practices. Ransoming critical, protected patient data is serious; formulating and delivering real-life attacks on medical devices is much worse, however. Evolving technologies and future attacks may make today's problems pale in comparison.

Reference:

`http://www.business.com/technology/internet-of-things-security-compliance-risks-and-opportunities/`

PCI DSS

Payment Card Industry (PCI) Data Security Standard (DSS) has been the primary regulation to which industry stakeholders that process payments must adhere. PCI DSS is published by the PCI Security Standards Council (`https://www.pcisecuritystandards.org/`), an organization focused on protecting financial accounts and transactional data. The latest PCI DSS is version 3.1, published April 2015.

In order to understand the impact of the IoT on payment processors' abilities to safeguard information, let's first examine the 12 high-level PCI DSS requirements. The following table outlines the 12 requirements per the latest standard (`https://www.pcisecuritystandards.org/documents/PCI_DSS_v3-1.pdf`):

Domain	Item	Requirement
Build and maintain a secure network and systems	1	Install and maintain a firewall configuration to protect cardholder data
	2	Do not use vendor-supplied defaults for system passwords and other security parameters
Protect cardholder data	1	Protect stored cardholder data
	2	Encrypt transmission of cardholder data across open, public networks

Domain	Item	Requirement
Maintain a vulnerability management program	1	Protect all systems against malware and regularly update antivirus software or programs
	2	Develop and maintain secure systems and applications
Implement strong access control measures	1	Restrict access to cardholder data by business need to know
	2	Identify and authenticate access to system components
	3	Restrict physical access to cardholder data
Regularly monitor and test networks	1	Track and monitor all access to network resources and cardholder data
	2	Regularly test security systems and processes
Maintain an information security policy	1	Maintain a policy that addresses information security for all personnel

If we examine the retail industry as an exemplar for discussing possible IoT impacts to the PCI, we have to consider the types of changes the IoT may bring about in the retail world. We can then determine whether 1) PCI DSS applies to new IoT system implementations in the retail environment or 2) whether other regulations apply to IoT implementations in retail establishments.

There will be many types of IoT device implementations and system deployments in the retail industry. Some of these include the following:

- Mass implementation of RFID tagging for inventory control
- Consumer ordering technologies that support automated delivery of products
- Automated checkout
- Smart fitting rooms
- Proximity advertising
- Smart vending machines

Examining such use cases, we can see that many of them (for example, automated checkouts and smart vending machines) include some aspect of financial payment. In these cases, the supporting IoT systems must adhere to existing PCI DSS requirements.

Consumer ordering technology is another interesting aspect of the IoT from a compliance perspective. Technologies such as Amazon's Dash button (`http://www.networkworld.com/article/2991411/internet-of-things/hacking-amazons-dash-button.html`) allows easy, rapid ordering of products. Although the devices do not process credit card information, they interconnect with Amazon's systems to submit orders for products. Devices that sit on the periphery of financial transactions will need to be evaluated to determine applicability of certain financial industry standards.

NIST Risk Management Framework (RMF)

NIST Special Publication 800-53 is a mainstay of security risk management controls and control categories. It is best viewed as a security control meta-standard because it is intended to be tailored for each organization based on a comprehensive set of system definition and risk modeling exercises. While statically defined, the controls themselves are comprehensive and well thought-out. The continuous and iterative steps of the RMF are depicted in the following image:

> The RMF Process
>
> 1. Categorize
> 2. Select
> 3. Implement
> 4. Assess
> 5. Authorize
> 6. Monitor

The RMF process makes use of 800-53 security controls but takes a step back and calls for a series of continuous risk management activities that should be followed by all system implementations. These include the following:

- Categorizing the system based on the importance of the system to mission operations and the sensitivity of the data processed
- Selecting the appropriate security controls
- Implementing the selected security controls
- Assessing the implementation of the security controls
- Authorizing the system for use
- Continuously monitoring the system security posture

This process is flexible and at a high level can be applied and adapted to any IoT system implementation.

Summary

The IoT is still in its infancy, and while compliance is certainly a dicey subject, the most important, overarching goal in setting up a compliance program is to ensure that it is effective and cost-effective overall. In this chapter, you were introduced to a variety of compliance programs unique to certain industries. In addition, you were provided some important best practices for setting up your own program. While there are still many gaps with regard to IoT standards and frameworks, there are significant developments among standards bodies today that are beginning to close those gaps.

In the next chapter, we will explore cloud security concepts regarding the IoT.

Cloud Security for the IoT

9

This chapter provides a view into cloud services and security architectures designed to support the Internet of Things. Using cloud services and security best practices, organizations can operate and manage cross-organizational, multi-domain IoT deployments across trust boundaries. We examine **Amazon Web Services (AWS)** cloud and security offerings, components offered by Cisco (Fog Computing), as well as Microsoft Azure.

Closely bound to cloud and cloud security are big data aspects of the IoT that require security. We will delve into IoT data storage, data analytics, and reporting systems along with best practices on how to secure these services. Securing the various facets of IoT in the cloud also requires us to address what elements of security are the responsibilities of the customer versus the cloud provider.

This chapter addresses IoT cloud services and cloud security through the following sections:

- **Cloud services and the IoT**: In this section we will define the cloud as it relates to and benefits the IoT. In addition, we will identify unique requirements that IoT levies on the cloud. In this section, we will also identify and review IoT-related security threats both internal and external to the cloud before delving into cloud-based security controls and other offerings.

- **Exploring cloud service provider (CSP) IoT offerings**: We will explore a few CSPs and their software/security-as-a-service. We address Cisco's Fog Computing, Amazon's AWS, and Microsoft's Azure.

- **Cloud IoT security controls**: We examine the security functionality needed from the cloud to build out an effective IoT enterprise security architecture.

- **Tailoring an enterprise IoT cloud security architecture**: This section utilizes available cloud security offerings to mix and match into an effective, overall IoT cloud security architecture.

- **New directions in cloud-enabled IoT computing**: We step back from the cloud security discussion here to briefly explore new computing paradigms that the cloud is well poised to deliver.

Cloud services and the IoT

In terms of B2B, consumer and industrial IoT deployments, nothing connects devices, device data, individuals, and organizations together more than cloud-based IoT supporting services. Gateways, applications, protocol brokers, and a variety of data analytics and business intelligence components reside in the cloud for convenience, cost, and scalability. In terms of supporting billions of IoT devices, cloud-based services offer the most compelling environment for new or legacy companies to deploy services. In response, CSPs have begun to offer more and more features to support connecting IoT products in a secure way. Developer-friendly IoT cloud-based starter kits are entering the stage to help IoT product and service companies cloud deploy with minimal effort. Organizations that go the route of standardizing on these cloud connectivity solutions should perform due diligence to ensure that they understand the security controls built into each offering.

As an example, ARM recently worked with Freescale and IBM to create a cloud-enabled IoT starter kit (`http://www.eetimes.com/document.asp?doc_id=1325828`). The kit includes an MCU that automatically streams data to a website on the Internet. Although the kit is geared towards training developers how to easily weave the cloud into IoT solutions, it is important that developers understand that doing so in production is very different and requires a security engineering process.

This section provides a discussion on some of the cloud services that are beginning to stand up in support of IoT systems. With organizations soon to deploy millions of IoT products across diverse systems, the cloud is the optimal mechanism for tracking the location and state of these devices. There will be other cloud services that spring up to support device provisioning, firmware updates, and configuration control as well. Given the ability to directly influence the functional and security state of an IoT device, the security of these services is paramount. Attackers will probably target these services, which, if compromised, would offer the ability to make large-scale changes to the state of many devices at once.

Asset/inventory management

One of the most important aspects of a secure IoT is the ability to track assets and inventories. This includes attributes of the devices as well. The cloud is a great solution for enabling enterprise asset/inventory management, providing a view into all devices that have been registered and authorized to operate within the organizations' boundaries.

Service provisioning, billing, and entitlement management

This is an interesting use case as many IoT device vendors will offer their devices to customers as a service. This requires the ability to track entitlements, authorize (or remove authorization for) device operations, as well as prepare billings in response to the amount of usage. Examples include subscription services for camera and other sensor-based monitoring (for example, DropCam cloud recording), wearables monitoring and tracking (for example, FitBit device services), and many others.

Real-time monitoring

Cloud applications used in support of mission-critical capabilities, such as emergency management, industrial control, and manufacturing may provide real-time monitoring capabilities. Where possible, many organizations are beginning to port industrial control system, industrial monitoring and other functions to the cloud to reduce operational costs, make the data more available and open up new B2B and B2C services. As the number of IoT endpoints proliferates, we will see devices such as **programmable logic controllers (PLCs)** and **remote terminal units (RTUs)** become direct connected to the cloud, supporting the ability to monitor systems more efficiently, and effectively.

Sensor coordination

Machine-to-machine transactions offer enhanced abilities to coordinate and even autonomously conduct service negotiations. Over time, workflows will become more automated, increasingly driving humans out of the transaction loop. The cloud will play a central role in enabling these automated workflows. As an example, cloud services will emerge that IoT devices can query to gather the latest information, restrictions, or instructions. The publish/subscribe protocols that drive many IoT implementations (for example, MQTT) as well as RESTful communications are both ideal for enabling these new use cases.

Customer intelligence and marketing

One of the powerful features of the IoT is the ability to tailor marketing to customers. Salesforce has created an IoT cloud aimed heavily at beacons and other smart devices. The cloud includes Thunder, which introduces a new real-time event engine. This system provides customers with the ability to automatically trigger messaging or send alerts to sales personnel. One good example is the concept of smart local advertisements. In these instances, customers are identified through some mechanism as they walk through a store or shopping center, for instance. Once identified, their purchase history, preferences or other characteristics are reviewed and tailored messaging is provided. From a privacy perspective, it is interesting to think through how either the tracking mechanism or the dossier collected can be used against a customer by a malicious party.

Other types of IoT customer intelligence includes energy efficiency improvements that benefit the environment. For example, home appliances can share usage data with cloud backend systems as part of a smart grid approach; device usage can be modulated based on need and price. By aggregating IoT appliance data that includes time and frequency of use, energy consumed, and current electrical market pricing, devices and users can respond by altering usage patterns to save energy costs and reduce environmental impact.

Information sharing

One of the primary benefits of the IoT is that it allows the sharing of information across many stakeholders. For example, an implantable medical device may provide information to a medical office, and that medical office may then provide that information to an insurance provider. The information may also be kept resident with other information gathered on a patient.

Information sharing and interoperability services of the cloud are mandatory prerequisites to enabling powerful IoT analytics. Given the diversity of IoT hardware platforms, services, and data structures, providers such as wot.io aim to provide middleware-layer data exchange services for the myriad data vendors' sources and sinks. Many IoT applications and supporting protocols are publish/subscribe-based, lending themselves naturally to middleware frameworks that can translate between the various data languages. Such services are critical to enabling data B2B, B2I, and B2C offerings.

Message transport/broadcast

The cloud and its centralized, adaptable, elastic capabilities is the ideal environment for implementing large scale IoT message transaction services. Many of the cloud services support HTTP, MQTT, and other protocols that, in various combinations, can transport, broadcast, publish data, subscribe to data or move data around in other necessary ways (centrally or at the network edge). One of the enormous hurdles with IoT data processing is the management of scale. Put plainly and simply, the IoT requires the cloud's architectural ability to elastically scale its data services—hence message transport/broadcast services—to meet unprecedented and growing demands.

Examining IoT threats from a cloud perspective

Many targeted threats to cloud-based infrastructures are identical or similar to those against non-cloud IT systems. The following threat profiles, among many others, are important to consider:

Threat area	Targets/Attacks
Cloud system administrators and users	Harvesting and use of administrator passwords, tokens and/or SSH keys to log into and wreak havoc on an organization's virtual private cloud (imagine the compromise of a corporation's AWS root account).
	Web browser cross-site scripting on user/manager host machines.
	Malicious payloads (for example, JavaScript-based) from web browsing or e-mail attachments (rooted administrator computers offer an attractive attack vector to compromise an organization's cloud-based enterprise, too).
Virtual endpoints (VMs, containers)	VM and other container vulnerabilities
	Web application vulnerabilities
	Insecure IoT gateways
	Insecure IoT brokers
	Misconfigured web servers
	Vulnerable databases (for example, SQL injection) or databases misconfigured for proper access controls

Threat area	Targets/Attacks
Networks	Virtual networking components
	Denial of service flooding of any endpoint
Physical and logical threats to IoT devices that connect to the cloud	Insecure IoT edge gateways (not in the cloud)
	Tampering and sniffing traffic or accessing data
	Tampering and injecting malicious payloads into the IoT communication protocol traffic between devices, edge gateways, and cloud gateways
	IoT device endpoint spoofing (communication redirects or lack of proper authentication/authorization)
	Lack of encryption/confidentiality
	Poor ciphersuites
	Lack of perfect-forward-secrecy
	Insecure database (plaintext or poor access control) storage on device
	Theft of IoT devices

The preceding list is just a small sample of security topics that need to be addressed when migrating to or making use of IoT infrastructures to the cloud. Fortunately, major cloud providers or their partners have answers to most of the above threats, at least those that exist within the CSP's trust boundary. Cloud-based security controls cannot, however, supplant device vendors' responsibilities for hardening IoT devices and ensuring their virtualized applications and Virtual Machine internals are hardened. These are challenges that deployment organizations must face.

In terms of the relative magnitude of cloud-based risks, in most cases the automated **infrastructure-as-a-service** (**IaaS**) capabilities of the cloud can likely lower the security risks to an organization operating IoT devices and systems. With relatively few exceptions, the security offerings available for hosted cloud infrastructure and services necessitate fewer cybersecurity professionals and can reduce high maintenance, on-premises security costs. Cloud-provisioned IaaS services are more likely to have consistently applied, secure-by-default configurations to VMs and networks, benefiting client organizations through security practice economies of scale. Before delving into cloud security for the IoT, we will first explore some of the IoT business offerings and benefits available in the cloud today.

Exploring cloud service provider IoT offerings

Cloud-based security offerings, also called **security-as-a-service (SECaaS)**, represent a rapidly growing cloud-enabled business, and these offerings are ripe for supporting the IoT. Not only are SECaaS offerings scalable, but they also help organizations cope with the ever-worsening, limited supply of security engineering resources. Most companies today lack the people and knowledge needed to perform security integration, keep up with the latest security threats, architect security operations centers, and perform security monitoring. CSPs offer some solutions.

AWS IoT

Amazon is poised to be a leading enabler of cloud-based IoT services, and in many cases will be the IoT cloud service provider's cloud provider. In Amazon's own words:

> *"AWS IoT is a managed cloud platform that lets connected devices easily and securely interact with cloud applications and other devices. AWS IoT can support billions of devices and trillions of messages, and can process and route those messages to AWS endpoints and to other devices reliably and securely."*

Source: `http://aws.amazon.com/iot/`

Amazon's AWS IoT is Amazon's framework that allows IoT devices to communicate with the cloud using a variety of protocols (HTTP, MQTT, and so on). Once in the cloud, IoT devices can speak with each other and services via application brokers. AWS IoT integrates with a variety of other Amazon services. For example, you can utilize its real-time data streaming and analytics engine, Kinesis. Kinesis Firehose operates as the ingestion platform accepting data streams and loading it into other Amazon domains: **Simple Storage Service (S3)**, Redshift (data warehousing), and Amazon **Elastic Search (ES)**. Once in the appropriate data platform, a variety of analytics can be performed using Kinesis Streams and the forthcoming Kinesis Analytics. Amazon Glacier (`https://aws.amazon.com/glacier/`) provides scalable, long-term data archiving and backup for less frequently accessed data.

In terms of supporting IoT applications and IoT development, AWS IoT integrates well with Amazon Lambda, Kinesis, S3, CloudWatch, DynamoDB, and a variety of other Amazon-provisioned cloud services:

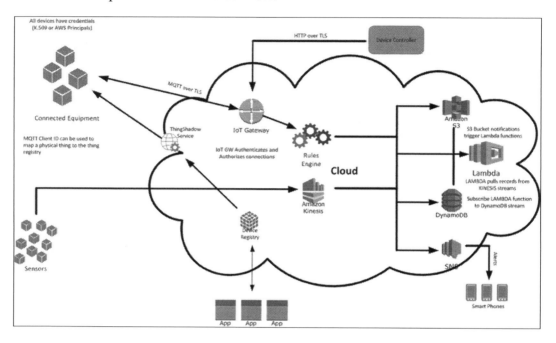

A variety of industries have begun to engage the Amazon IoT platform, including healthcare. For example, Philips has partnered to make use of the AWS IoT services as the engine for its HealthSuite Digital platform. This platform is designed to allow medical service providers and patients to interact in transformative new ways using IoT healthcare devices, traditional data sources, analytics, and reporting. Many other IoT-related companies are beginning to leverage or partner with AWS in their IoT portfolios.

CSP IoT services such as AWS IoT offer the ability to preconfigure IoT devices and then upload the configurations to the physical devices when they are ready to bring online. Once operational, AWS IoT offers a virtual Thing Shadow that can maintain the state of your IoT device even when offline. The configuration state is kept in a JSON document stored in the cloud. So, for example, if a MQTT-enabled light bulb is offline, a MQTT command can be sent to the virtual things repository to change its color. When the lightbulb comes back online, it will change its color appropriately:

The AWS Thing Shadow is an intermediary between a controlling application and the IoT device. Thing shadows leverage the MQTT protocol with predefined topics that can be used to interact with the service and devices. MQTT messages that are reserved for the Thing Shadow service begin with `$aws/things/thingName/shadow`. The following are the reserved MQTT topics that can be used to interact with the shadow (`https://docs.aws.amazon.com/iot/latest/developerguide/thing-shadow-mqtt.html`):

- `/update`
- `/update/accepted`
- `/update/documents`
- `/update/rejected`
- `/update/delta`
- `/get`
- `/get/accepted`
- `/get/rejected`
- `/delete`
- `/delete/accepted`
- `/delete/rejected`

Things can either update or get the Thing Shadow. AWS IoT publishes a JSON document for each update and responds to each update and get request with status of `/accepted` or `/rejected`.

From a security perspective, it is important that only authorized endpoints and applications are able to publish to these topics. It is also imperative that the administrative console be locked down sufficiently to keep unauthorized actors from gaining access to directly configure IoT assets.

To illustrate some of the AWS IoT data processing workflow, let's explore an additional use case for a connected farm that leverages the data processing capabilities of the AWS cloud. Special thanks to Steve Csicsatka for assistance with this diagram:

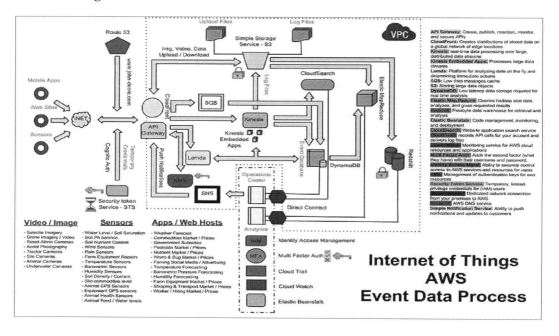

In this use case, there are a number of endpoints that are injecting data into the AWS cloud. Data enters AWS through a number of potential front doors:

- Kinesis
- Kinesis Firehose
- MQTT broker

Once inside AWS, the AWS IoT rules engine functions as the decision point to determine where data should be routed and any additional actions to take on the data. In many instances, data will be sent to a database—for example, S3 or DynamoDB. Redshift can also be employed and should be used to preserve records over time, as well as for long-term data storage.

Within the AWS IoT suite, one can take advantage of the integrated log management features through CloudWatch. CloudWatch can be configured directly within AWS IoT to log process events on messages flowing from devices to the AWS infrastructure. Message logging can be set to errors, warnings, informational, or debug. Although debug provides the most comprehensive messages, these also take up additional storage space:

Amazon CloudTrail should also be leveraged for an AWS-based IoT deployment. CloudTrail supports account-level AWS API calls to enable security analysis, analytics, and compliance tracking. There are many third-party log management systems, such as Splunk, AlertLogic, and SumoLogic that integrate directly with CloudTrail.

Microsoft Azure IoT suite

Microsoft has also taken a big leap into the IoT cloud space with its Azure IoT Hub.

Azure boasts some powerful IoT device management features for IoT implementers, including device software/firmware updating and configuring. Beyond IoT device management, Azure provides features that allow IoT deployers to organize and group devices within their operational domains. In other words, it enables IoT device-level topology management as well as per-device configuration, a prerequisite to establishing group-level management, permissions, and access control.

Azure's group management service is provided through the device group API, while its device management features, software versioning, and provisioning, and so on, are provided through its device registry management API (`https://azure.microsoft.com/en-us/documentation/articles/iot-hub-devguide/`). Centralized authentication is provided using the existing Azure Active Directory authentication framework.

The Azure IoT Hub supports IoT-related protocols such as MQTT, HTTP, and AMQP to enable device-to-cloud and cloud-to-device communication. Given the inevitable variety of communication standards, Azure provides cross-protocol fusion capabilities to developers via a generic IoT Hub message format. The message format consists of a variety of system and application property fields. If needed, device-to-cloud communications can leverage Azure's existing event hub APIs, but if per-device authentication and access control are needed, the IoT Hub will support this.

Per-device authentication and access control in Azure are enabled through the use of IoT Hub security tokens that map to each device's access policy and credentials. Token-based authentication allows authentication to take place without transmitting sensitive security parameters across the wire. Tokens are based upon a unique Azure-generated key that is generated using the accompanying manufacturer or implementer-provided device ID.

To illustrate some of the Azure IoT data processing workflow, let's return to our connected farm IoT system and examine the backend configuration within Azure. As with AWS, there are various entry points into the cloud for connected devices. Data can be ingested into Azure through the API gateway or through the IoT services, which support REST and MQTT. Data can then be sent to blob storage or to DocumentDB. Also note that the Azure **Content Delivery Network (CDN)** is a good tool for distribution of firmware updates to your IoT device inventory:

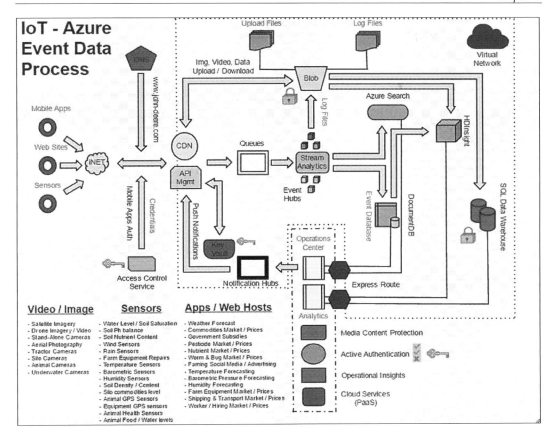

Cisco Fog Computing

Cisco's IoT strategy for the cloud addresses the fact that the vast majority of IoT devices operate at the network edge versus in a region close to centralized cloud processing. Hence, the term **fog**, visible moisture at the ground (edge) versus central cloud (sky) represents Cisco's rebranding of the well-known concept of edge computing. The sheer scale of the IoT, Cisco is betting, will require much more powerful functional and security resources integrated into network and application stacks at organizations' network edges. The benefits of keeping data and processing as edge-central as possible include the following:

- **Reduced latency**: Many data-intensive edge applications for the IoT are real-time because they involve vast amounts of sensor data, localized decision making, and response

- **Data and network efficiency**: Data volumes that comprise the IoT are enormous and there are many cases where porting the data makes no sense in terms of clogging networks just to move it around for application and security treatment

- Policies can be locally managed and controlled based on local edge conditions

- Reliability, availability, and security at the IoT edge are improved based on local needs

The preceding benefits are perhaps most tangible to the industrial IoT where central-only cloud processing just won't do. Time-sensitive sensor streams, controllers, and actuators, monitoring and reporting applications and voluminous datasets associated with the industrial IoT make Fog Computing an appealing model.

Cisco's Fog Computing, though early in its lifecycle, is already implemented in the IOx (`https://developer.cisco.com/site/iox/technical-overview/`), a middleware framework that sits between hardware and applications running directly on edge equipment.

The basic IOx architecture consists of the following:

- **Fog nodes**: These represent the devices (for example, routers and switches) that comprise edge networks and provide host resources to the Fog framework.

- **Host OS**: Sitting on Fog nodes is the Host OS that supports the following:
  - **Cisco Application Framework (CAF)** for local application management and control
  - **Applications** (of many possible types)
  - **Network and middleware services**

- **Fog director**: Connected to the CAF's northbound APIs, the Fog director provides the centralized application management and repositories for apps running on all of Fog nodes. Administration via the Fog director is accessed through the Fog portal.

IoT Fog Computing development is supported by Cisco DevNet Software Development Kits. IoT organizations can also make use of existing Cisco cybersecurity solutions such as Cisco NetFlow, TrustSec, and **identity services engine (ISE)**.

IBM Watson IoT platform

IBM Watson barely needs an introduction. The world became intimately familiar with its capabilities back in 2010 when the Watson cognitive computing platform began to beat the best champions on the famous game show Jeopardy. Watson's cognitive computing ability to learn and solve problems from gargantuan ingested datasets is being put to good use in a variety of industries, such as healthcare. Today, IBM is augmenting Watson's processing domain by applying it to the Internet of Things. IBM's foundational IoT APIs are available through the IBM Watson IoT Platform Development Center (`https://developer.ibm.com/iotfoundation/` and `https://developer.ibm.com/iotfoundation/recipes/api-documentation/`) and include IoT interfacing capabilities such as the following:

- Inventory and viewing of an organization's IoT devices
- Registering, updating, and viewing devices
- Operating on historical, ingested datasets

MQTT and REST interfaces

IoT device transactions and communications are facilitated by the platform's support of MQTT and REST communication protocols (`https://docs.internetofthings.ibmcloud.com/devices/mqtt.html`), allowing IoT developers to build powerful data ingestion, cognitive analytics, and data output capabilities.

The Watson IoT platform's MQTT API allows unencrypted connections on port 1883 and encrypted communications on ports 8883 or 443. It is good to note that the platform requires TLS 1.2. The IBM recommended ciphersuites are as follows:

- ECDHE-RSA-AES256-GCM-SHA384
- AES256-GCM-SHA384
- ECDHE-RSA-AES128-GCM-SHA256
- AES128-GCM-SHA256

Registration of devices requires the use of the TLS connection, as the MQTT password is transmitted back to the client protected by the TLS tunnel.

When MQTT is used for device connectivity to the cloud, the option exists to use a token instead of an MQTT password. In this case, the value `use-token-auth` is provided in place of the password.

The REST interface is secured with TLS 1.2 as well. The allowable port is 443 and the application API key serves as the username, while an authentication token is used as the password, in support of HTTP basic authentication.

Cloud IoT security controls

Given the variety of cloud-based services that support IoT deployments, each cloud and stakeholder endpoint plays a vital role in securing the multitude of transactions. This section provides a brief listing of recommended IoT security controls and services that your organization should consider. Basic controls such as authentication and encryption to the cloud are supported by all of the CSPs, but you should carefully review and consider your CSP based on their offerings in other areas.

Most CSPs bundle the services in different ways. Your organization can either directly or indirectly obtain and benefit from these services based on unique package offerings. These services can be combined in different ways to build powerful, transitive trust relationships throughout your virtualized infrastructure.

Authentication (and authorization)

Considering authentication security controls, your organization will need to handle most or all of the following:

1. Verify administrator authenticity for individuals accessing administrative functions and APIs (multi-factor authentication is preferred here, given the enormous sensitivity of administrative controls on your virtual infrastructure).

2. Authenticate end users to cloud applications.

3. Authenticate cloud applications (including IoT gateways and brokers) from one to the other.

4. Directly authenticate IoT devices (that have the requisite security and functional resources) to gateways and brokers.

5. Proxy-authenticate end users from application provider to another.

A variety of authentication mechanisms are supported by CSPs. Amazon AWS and Microsoft Azure are described in the following sections.

Amazon AWS IAM

The AWS IAM authentication service supported by the Amazon cloud is a multi-featured authentication platform that supports federated identity, multi-factor authentication, user/role/permission management, and full integration with other Amazon services.

The AWS multi-factor (for example, token-based) authentication (MFA) service of the IAM supports a variety of MFA form factors to suit either your organization's new or existing authentication framework. Hardware tokens, key fobs, access cards, and virtualized MFA devices (for example, those that may run on a mobile device) are supported by Amazon. MFA can be used both by your virtual private cloud administrators as well as by your end users.

Transitive trust authorization flows between multiple web applications (especially from browsers) can be obtained by using OAuth2.0 (RFC6749), an open standard for authorization that allows secure, delegated access to third-party web services. OAuth2 provides authorization access only, however. Authentication functionality can be obtained by utilizing an **OpenID Connect** (**OIDC**) service that is built on OAuth2. OIDC makes use of identification tokens acquired via the OAuth2 transaction to support authorization for users.

Azure authentication

As stated earlier, Microsoft Azure provides centralized and federated identity authentication as well through its Azure **Active Directory** (**AD**) authentication framework.

Microsoft Azure also offers both OAuth2 and OpenID Connect identity-as-a-service within its Azure AD offering. Amazon AWS offers this capability as well as part of its identity and access management offering. If your chosen cloud provider does not offer OpenID Connect but does offer OAuth2, you may also be able to integrate the OAuth2 service from provider 1 with the OpenID Connect service (for authentication tokens) from provider 2, though this may not be as seamless as coming from a single provider.

Software/firmware updates

An enormous number of vulnerabilities in software and firmware execution stacks can be mitigated by quick, easy, and highly automated patching frameworks. We strongly recommend you implement an automated, secure firmware/software update capability to end devices. Fresh executables or executable chunks (patches) should be digitally signed within your DevOps environment by a hardened software signing service. In terms of the end devices, you should ensure that software and firmware updates propagating to end IoT devices are capable of being validated by those end devices.

Some CSPs support software/firmware services such as Azure CDN and so on.

End-to-end security recommendations

Consider the following end-to-end security recommendations in your IoT cloud deployment:

- Ensure that security is not lost at the gateway. Ideally, end-to-end authentication and integrity protections should persist from the CSP to the IoT devices with the gateways simply acting as pass-throughs. Although this is not always possible, take alternate defensive actions when deployed sensor nodes rely upon the gateway to validate the authenticity and integrity of firmware updates and commands.

- Apply the rigor of secure software development practices to the web services and databases that serve the IoT devices.

- Sufficiently protect the cloud applications that support the analysis and reporting workflows.

- Apply secure configurations to the databases that feed the analysis and reporting applications.

- Apply integrity protections to the IoT device data. This requires the use of integrity protections on data transmitted from the IoT device to the gateway as well as the gateway to the cloud.

- Leased devices will operate within the customer environment and service providers will not want to inadvertently infect their customer networks with malware (and vice versa). Segregation of these devices on customer networks should be enforced when possible. This use case opens up potential for fraud and/or theft from stealing services, and as such it is important to design the devices in a manner that prevents tampering. This can be accomplished using tamper-evident or tamper-responsive protections that are described in resources such as NIST FIPS 140-2.

- Protect against denial of service attacks by using robust, properly configured load balancing application gateways (a number of superb industry solutions exist for this now).

- Provide assurances that the data being transmitted to the IoT devices (or gateways) is authenticated by the devices themselves.

- Encrypt the data when needed.

- Transactions and messaging between devices themselves (M2M) must be authenticated (and integrity protected)

- In all cases, service providers should be able to track the privacy controls associated with information generated by a person or by a device that can be tied to a person. In the case of the medical device, has the patient been notified and authorized the use of not only the data generated while in medical offices, but also for any data that is uploaded to the cloud by connected devices? Notifications should also include any organization that the data may be shared with.

- Maintaining control of data through to destruction is not possible when the data may have been passed on to potentially many other organizations; however, service providers should make attempts to obtain privacy agreements with peer organizations. Additionally, assess the adequacy of the security controls implemented by those other organizations.

- Implement flexible access controls (use attribute-based access controls for higher resolution access decisions).

- Tag data for privacy protections.

- Provide notifications on data use.

Maintain data integrity

How can you assure the integrity of data that will be used for myriad purposes and by potentially many stakeholders? In the context of an enterprise IoT system, the ability to trust the data collected is critical. This drives a need for the following:

- Authentication and integrity controls applied to the IoT devices to ensure rogue devices cannot transmit data into the cloud.

- Secure configuration of gateway devices. Gateway devices may be installed on-site or operate in the cloud, but these gateways devices process large quantities of data and as such should be secured via:

    ◦ Security logging and analysis in a SIEM.

    ◦ Secure configurations (operating system, database, application).

    ◦ Firewall protection.

    ◦ Encrypted communications on each interface. This requires the use of encrypted communication on the cloud-facing interface. This is typically accomplished with Transport Layer Security (TLS) and an appropriate ciphersuite. On the sensor-facing interface, encrypted RF communications is strongly recommended.

    ◦ Strong authentication using PKI certificates if possible.

- Software security measures for the web service that interfaces with and collects data from the gateways or devices.

- Secure infrastructure configurations (for example, web server) supporting the IoT web service.

Secure bootstrap and enrollment of IoT devices

In order to have confidence in the credentials used by a particular device to authenticate to services and gateways, care must be taken during the initial provisioning of trust to devices. Depending on the criticality of a particular device, bootstrap can occur at the vendor, or in-person by a trusted agent. Completing bootstrap and enrollment results in the ability to provision operational certificates to devices in a secure manner (and over a network).

Security monitoring

IoT gateways/brokers should be configured to look for suspicious behavior of the endpoints. As an example, MQTT brokers should capture messages from publishers and subscribers that may signal malicious behavior. The MQTT Specification Version 3.1.1 provides examples of behaviors to report:

- Repeated connection attempts
- Repeated authentication attempts
- Abnormal termination of connections
- Topic scanning
- Sending undeliverable messages
- Clients that connect but do not send data

 Note that tuning an SIEM to identify potential misuse of IoT systems requires thought. An understanding of how the behavior of a specific IoT device can be correlated with events occurring in other parts of the overall system is required.

Tailoring an enterprise IoT cloud security architecture

There are many architectural aspects and options for cloud-enabling an IoT system. CSPs, IoT service providers, and enterprise adopters must examine the capabilities being provided to focus the appropriate security controls in an architecturally supportive framework.

The following diagram is a genericized virtual private cloud from a cloud service provider that offers basic functional and security services to protect endpoint-to-endpoint data transactions. It shows typical, virtualized services available for general IT as well as IoT-enabled deployments. Not all IoT deployers will need to make use of all the cloud capabilities available, but most will require a minimal cross-section of the above services, and require them to be well protected:

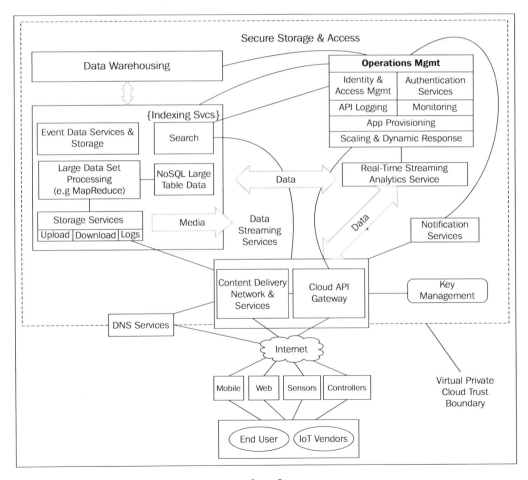

Faced with building out a security architecture against the above system, one must remember that tailoring an enterprise IoT cloud security architecture is really about assembling the primitive security architecture constructs and services **already available** from your CSP (for your own use) than inventing or adapting everything from scratch. That said, the following activities—some of which have been discussed in detail in this book (thus are not listed in as much detail here)—are strongly advised:

1. Conduct a detailed threat model by first characterizing your system and security starting point:

    1. Identify all existing IoT device types, protocols, and platforms.

    2. Identify and categorize based on sensitivity and privacy all IoT data originating from the IoT devices at the network edge.

    3. Determine the nearby and distant data producers, consumers of the sensitive data.

    4. Identify all system endpoints, their physical and logical security characteristics, and who controls and administers them.

    5. Identify all organizations whose people interact with the IoT services and datasets and/or manage, maintain, and configure devices. Ascertain how each is enrolled into the system, obtains permissions, accesses it, and is (as needed) tracked or audited.

    6. Determine data storage, reuse, and protections needed at rest and in transit.

    7. Based on risks, determine what data types need to be protected point-to-point (also identifying those points) and which need to be protected end-to-end so that the end consumer or data sink can be guaranteed of the data's origin, integrity, and (if needed) confidentiality.

    8. If a field gateway is required, examine the South and North protocols required by that platform to 1) communicate with the field devices (for example, ZigBee) and 2) coalesce and transmit those communications to the cloud gateway (for example, HTTP coupled with TLS).

    9. Finalize a risk and privacy assessment against the data to ascertain necessary controls that may currently be lacking from the CSP.

2. (Cloud-specific) Formulate a security architecture from the following:

    1. Security provisions directly available from the CSP.

    2. Add-on cloud-based security services that are available from the CSP's partners or through compatible, interoperable third-party services.

3. Develop and adapt policies and procedures:

    1. Data security and data privacy treatment.

    2. User and admin roles, services, and security requirements (for example, identify where multi-factor authentication is needed in protecting certain resources).

4. Adopt and implement your own security architecture into the frameworks and APIs supported by the CSP.

5. Integrate security practices (the NIST Risk Management Framework addresses this well).

New directions in cloud-enabled IOT computing

Before closing out this chapter, we thought it worthwhile to list both some additional IoT-enabling characteristics of the cloud as well as some new, potential future directions and use cases of the cloud-connected IoT.

IoT-enablers of the cloud

The cloud has many characteristics, some described above, that make it an attractive, adaptive, and enabling technology stack from which to envision, build, and deploy new IoT services. This section provides just a few.

Software defined networking (SDN)

SDNs emerged as next-generation network management capabilities to simplify and reduce the amount of work to reconfigure networks and manage policy-based routes. In other words, they were created to make the network itself more programmable and dynamic, an absolute necessity for the enormous scale and flexibility needed to manage our world's IoT traffic. SDN architectures function by decoupling network control from the forwarding functions. They are comprised of SDN controllers that implement 1) a northbound API or bridge that connects to network applications, and 2) a Southbound API that connects the network controllers to the fielded network devices that perform traffic forwarding.

IoT architectures that leverage large cloud services already benefit from SDN. Large virtualization systems that host management servers, brokers, gateways to the fielded IoT devices, and other IoT architectural elements are built into Amazon, Google, and other cloud providers. Over time, we expect to see much more fine-grained capabilities emerge in the ability to create, adapt, and dynamically customize one's own IoT network. SDNs are being used today by security vendors tackling **distributed denial of service (DDOS)** challenges and enterprises should look to tailor their implementations to support that functionality.

Data services

Given the gargantuan quantities of data, data sources, and data sinks in the IoT, the cloud environment provides capable tools for managing and structuring this data. For example, Amazon's DynamoDB offers extremely scalable, low-latency, NoSQL database capabilities for powering various IoT data storage, sharing, and analytics services. Through an easy-to-use web frontend, developers create and manage tables, logs, access, and other data control features. A benefit to IoT organizations of any size is that pricing models are proportionate to the quantity of data actually used.

Data security, authentication, and access control can be implemented on a per-table basis in DynamoDB, leveraging the AWS identity and access management system. This means that a single organization can perform a variety of analytics, produce derivative data populated in distinct tables, then selectively make that data available via an application to its many unique customers.

Container support for secure development environments

One of the challenges faced in IoT development environments is the diverse nature of IoT hardware platforms. A variety of platforms come with different software development kits, APIs, and drivers. The programming languages used across different hardware also vary, from C to embedded C to Python and many others. A reusable development environment that can be shared across a development team will need to be flexible enough to support these scenarios.

One approach to supporting a highly flexible IoT development environment is through the use of container technology. Using this technology, containers can be built with the libraries and packages required to develop the current device type. These containers can be replicated and shared across the development team as a development baseline. As new types of IoT devices are developed by the team, new baselines can be created for use that add new software library stacks.

Containers for deployment support

Using Docker (`http://www.docker.com/`) as a development tool provides a valuable advantage for storing, deploying, and managing the workflow of IoT device images. Docker was designed with the capability of enabling developers and system administrators to deploy software/firmware images directly to IoT hardware. This approach has two additional benefits:

- Device images can be updated (not just initially deployed) through Docker.

- Docker can be integrated with a test system such as Ravello for full testing of the IoT system. Ravello Systems (`https://www.ravellosystems.com`) offers a powerful framework for deploying and testing VMWare/KVM applications virtually in self-contained cloud capsules running in AWS or Google cloud.

While Docker offers a powerful ability to deploy containers, another technology, Google's open source Kubernetes, leverages Docker to allow organizations to manage large clusters of containers. The distributed computing ability of large, easily managed clusters of containers is an enormous IoT enabler.

Microservices

Microservices are a renewed concept of modularizing large, monolithic enterprise applications (web UI and REST APIs, database, core business logic, and so on) into small, bite-sized services much like a **service oriented architecture (SOA)**. The technology provides an approach to simplifying and mitigating the complexity of enterprise applications that tend to grow and snowball in response to changing requirements. While conceptually similar to SOA, microservice architectures decompose large system needs into separately virtualized, self-contained application VMs. Each typically comes with its own business logic, data backend, and APIs connecting to other microservices. In the microservice architecture, each individual microservice is virtually-instantiated into the container type (for example, Docker, VMWare) of choice.

Microservice architectures can not only simplify long-term development and maintenance of small- or large-scale cloud applications, they also lend themselves naturally to cloud elasticity. If you have an enterprise consisting of a dozen microservices and two of them (perhaps account registration or a notification service) are in demand, the cloud architecture can spin up new microservice containers for just the impacted services.

Businesses are enabled to dream up new IoT enterprise applications that leverage the IoT's data-rich environment; using microservices, they can quickly assemble new services and dynamically scale them in response to data and processing ebbs and flows. In addition, Agile development processes are much easier to maintain as each Agile team can tightly focus on one or two individual microservices.

The move to 5G connectivity

While the US, Europe, and Asia reconcile their differences in the formulation of the as-yet-to-be-defined 5G standard, a number of its salient features promise to revolutionize and boost the number of things, use cases, and applications that leverage the Internet. Ubiquitous networking through 5G will be a key enabler of the Internet of Things in its ability to support orders of magnitude more devices at significantly higher data rates (~10x) than LTE networks. Thus far, competing views on the specification of 5G have agreed on the following (`http://www.techrepublic.com/article/does-the-world-really-need-5g/`):

- Data rates should start at 1 GB/s, and evolve to multi-GB/s
- Latency should be brought under 1 ms
- 5G equipment should be much more energy efficient than its predecessors

Given the IP address space of IPv6 and the near-future of 5G (and beyond) connectivity, it is no wonder that many forward-thinking companies are investing heavily and preparing for unimaginable growth for the IoT.

Cloud-enabled directions

This section provides just a few examples, based on the above cloud enablers, of what is possible using centralized and distributed cloud processing to push the IoT in amazing new directions.

On-demand computing and the IoT (dynamic compute resources)

The so-called sharing economy has ushered in services such as Uber, Lyft, Airbnb, home-based solar energy redistribution to the electric grid, and other business paradigms that allow resource owners (of cars, apartments, solar panels, and so on) to offer up spare cycles in exchange for something. **On-demand computing** (ODC) is still relatively new and in its infancy, but it is leveraged significantly in cloud-based elastic architectures. Compute resources are scheduled, delivered, and billed on-demand based on a dynamically changing client demand.

The enormous benefits of the cloud to the IoT may be surpassed by its inverse. Enabled with 5G, the IoT in its sheer quantity of edge devices and available compute resources may benefit cloud-based applications in their ability to make available latent compute resources to various edge applications. Imagine a computing-intensive edge application that cannot possibly process on a single device. Now imagine that device is able to make use of the processing capacity of surrounding edge devices owned by other users. Dynamic, on-demand local clouds that are supported by things for things will require 5G networks and enable yet-to-be-imagined applications. In addition to the network support, IoT-facilitated ODC will require evolving to new application architectures such as microservices and their fine-grained execution units described earlier.

From a security perspective, secure, trusted computing domains within IoT devices will be a basic requirement for IoT-provisioned ODC. Imagine profiting by allowing your vehicle to provide computing cycles to a nearby business, a remote individual or process, or even a cloud provider itself. On-demand, executable uploads and processing of untrusted code on your vehicle will have to be domain-separated with a high degree of assurance, otherwise your personal applications and data could easily be put at risk of compromise from temporary guest processes. ARM, TrustZone, and other technologies of today represent only the beginnings of enabling this type of cross-domain computing for the IoT.

New distributed trust models for the cloud

Addressed in earlier chapters, digital credentials and PKI are used extensively to secure today's cloud-based client and service endpoints. Maintaining federated trust across different trust domains is not a simple or necessarily efficient exercise today. To that end, in May 2016, the Apache Foundation adopted into its incubator program a new project called Milagro (`http://milagro.apache.org/`). Milagro is interesting in that it leverages pairing-based cryptography and multiple, independent **distributed trust authorities** (DTAs) to independently generate multiple, private key shares to clients and servers. The consuming endpoints construct the final crypto variables to enable mutual authentication and key agreement in or across whatever cloud environment is needed. The basic idea is that DTAs can be operated by any number of independent organizations, each providing a partial **SECaaS** solution for end parties. The distributed nature of this model improves upon today's monolithic trust hierarchies by requiring attackers to compromise all of the DTAs involved in generating an end user's key material. If Milagro succeeds through incubation, some interesting new open source distributed trust models may very well emerge for the cloud and dependent IoT deployments.

Cognitive IoT

IBM's Watson and its new IoT interfaces are only the beginning of cognitive data processing for our Internet of Things. In general, the IoT is too large to group all potential cognitive processing use cases into a small set; however, the list below represents just a small fraction of what is just around the horizon with IoT systems and data coupled with cognitive analytics:

- **Predictive health monitoring**: Massive health monitoring bio-datasets coupled with various patient metadata will allow cognitive systems to predict with much greater clarity the probability of disease conditions or other health maladies before they appear. Most historical studies evaluate risk factors based on very limited information. With IoT health monitoring, wearables, data fusion services, and other private and public data sources, cognitive systems will have orders of magnitude greater dataset resolutions with which to work and identify health risks. IoT systems will be the backbone of these capabilities.

- **Collaborative navigation techniques**: Enabling swarms of small UAS that are operating in GPS-denied environments to collectively understand their environment in order to more effectively navigate.

Summary

In this chapter, we discussed the cloud, cloud service provider offerings, the cloud's enablement of the IoT, security architectures, and how the cloud is spawning new, powerful directions for connectivity and support of the Internet of Things. In our final chapter, we will explore incident management and forensics for the IoT.

10
IoT Incident Response

Incident management is an enormous topic and many excellent and thorough volumes have been written about its utility and execution in the traditional IT enterprise. At its core, incident management is a lifecycle-driven set of activities that range from planning, detection, containment, eradication, and recovery, to ultimately the learning process about what went wrong and how to improve one's posture to prevent similar future incidents. This chapter provides guidance for organizations—corporate or otherwise—who plan to integrate IoT systems into their enterprises and who need to develop or update their incident response plans to suit.

Incident management for IoT systems follows the same frameworks that are already familiar to us. There are simply new considerations and questions to answer when trying to plan for effectively responding to compromised IoT-related systems. To distinguish the IoT from conventional IT, we postulate the following incidents:

- In the near future, a utility company purchases a fleet of connected vehicles to enhance driver safety and increase savings related to fuel consumption and liability (for example, guarding against aggressive driving). One day, one of the utility vehicles crashes into another car, causing damage and injury. When speaking with the driver, it was noted that the vehicle simply stopped responding to their controls.

- A heart patient with an implanted pacemaker and diseased heart dies suddenly. The coroner notes that the patient had a pacemaker, but also notes that it was supposedly operating correctly. The case is ruled a myocardial infarction, death by natural causes.

Both of these device types—connected vehicles and pacemakers—will be supported by different types of enterprises, some on-premises and some in the cloud. Both also demonstrate the blurred lines between a potential IoT security incident and normal, everyday occurrences. This drives a need to examine incident management in a manner that focuses on the underlying business/mission processes of the IoT devices and systems, to understand how attackers might use the guise of everyday happenstance to mask their malicious intent and actions. This should be accomplished by making sure the security engineers charged with the operational protection of IoT systems have a fundamental understanding of the threat models that underlie those systems.

IRPs will vary for different enterprise types. For example, if your organization has no intent to operate industrial IoT systems, but has recently adopted a bring your own IoT device policy, your IRP may stop at the point that a compromise has been identified, contained, and eradicated. It may not in this case extend into deep, intrusive forensics on the nature of the IoT device vulnerability (you can simply ban the device type from your networks going forward). If, however, your enterprise utilizes consumer and industrial IoT devices/apps for routine business functions, your IRP may need to include more sophisticated forensics after containing and eradicating the compromise.

Threats both to safety and security

Ideally, misuse cases will be created during the upfront threat modeling process. Many specific misuse patterns can then be generated for each misuse case. Misuse patterns should be low-level enough that they can be decomposed into signature sets applicable to the monitoring technology (for example, IDS/IPS, SIEM, and so on) that will be used both on-premises and in your cloud environment. Patterns can include device patterns, network patterns, service performance, and just about anything that indicates potential misuse, malfunction or outright compromise.

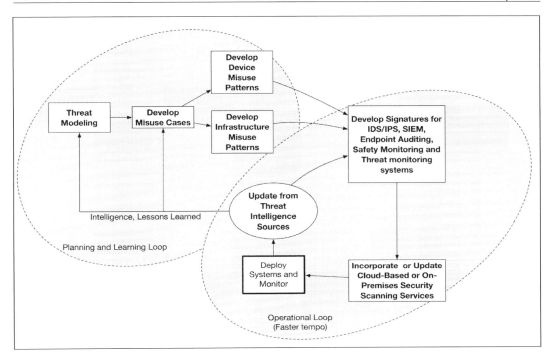

In many IoT use cases, SIEMs can be telemetry-enhanced. We say *telemetry-enhanced* SIEMs, because physically interacting IoT devices have many additional properties that may be monitorable and important for detecting misbehavior or misuse. Temperature, time of day, event correlation with other neighboring IoT device states: almost any kind of available data can be envisioned to enable a power, detection, containment, and forensic posture beyond traditional SIEM use.

In the case of the connected utility vehicle incident described in the introduction, the culprit may have been a disgruntled employee who instigated a remote attack against the connected vehicle subsystems responsible for controlling the braking system (for example, injecting ECU communications into the network-connected CAN bus). Without proper forensics capabilities, it may be difficult or impossible to identify this individual. What is even more concerning is that in most cases, the insurance investigators would not even know that they should consider exploring the possibility of a security-compromised system!

In the case of the pacemaker patient, the culprit may have been a former employee trying to force the victim to pay money by adapting and packaging an attack learned on the Internet—the delivery of ransomware to close-range medical devices that have a specific microcontroller and interface set. Without an understanding that this is even a possible attack vector, there is no in-depth investigation. Moreover, the ransomware can be designed to self-wipe right after the event to destroy any evidence of the malfeasance.

These scenarios show that IoT incident management takes a few twists and turns from conventional IT enterprises, as follows:

- The physical nature of the networked things, their locations, and who owns or operates them. The cyber-physical aspects of incident response may include a safety factor—even life and death—especially for medical, transportation, and other industrial IoT use cases.

- The cloud aspects of managing the physical things (as per the previous chapter), including the fact that many of the direct incident response activities may be out of the immediate control of one's organization.

- The ease with which attackers can mask their intentions and actions by disguising the results in the noise of everyday happenings. The timing of an attack puts defenders at a serious disadvantage. The goals of an IoT attack, especially against cyber-physical systems, can often be as simple as crashing a car or causing traffic lights to stop working. A skilled attacker may be able to pull these types of attacks off relatively quickly to meet their end goals, leaving defenders with limited ability to stop the attacks.

- The possibility that other seemingly unrelated IoT things that are connected to common hubs and gateways in the proximity of the compromise may provide interesting new datasets contributing to incident detection and forensics.

The example situations also illustrate the need to be able to perform comprehensive incident management and forensics on deployed IoT products in order to understand and respond when there is a potential ongoing campaign against an IoT system or a class of IoT product. Forensics can also be leveraged to determine and assign liability for IoT product malfunctions (whether malicious or not), and bring to justice those that would cause adverse effects within IoT systems. This is even more important in CPS, whether medical devices, industrial control, smart home appliances, or others that involve physical-world detection and actuation.

This chapter focuses on building, maintaining, and executing an incident response plan for your organization so that you may promote improved situational awareness and response to the various operational IoT hazards (ranging from low-level incidents to full-scale compromises). This is accomplished in the following subsections:

- **Defining IoT incident response and management**: Here we will define and establish the goals of IoT incident response and what it needs to accommodate.

- **Planning and executing IoT incident response**: In this section, we will explore how to incorporate the right facets of incident response into your organization as a structured plan. We will detail how to categorize and plan for different incidents/events, as well as plan for triage and forensics operations (as per an IRP). Within forensics, we will discuss how to acquire forensic firmware images of the IoT devices. Lastly, we will provide some practical instruction in operationalizing and executing your incident response plan. The IoT aspects of executing incident response may also pertain to your cloud provider (assuming you support CSP-hosted subsystems). Using your incident response plan addresses methods of detecting compromises and other incidents, executing post-incident forensics, and, very importantly, integrating lessons learned into your security lifecycle.

Planning and executing an IoT incident response

IoT incident response and management can be broken into four phases:

- Planning
- Detection and analysis
- Containment, eradication, and recovery
- Post-incident activity

The following figure provides a view into the processes and how they relate to each other:

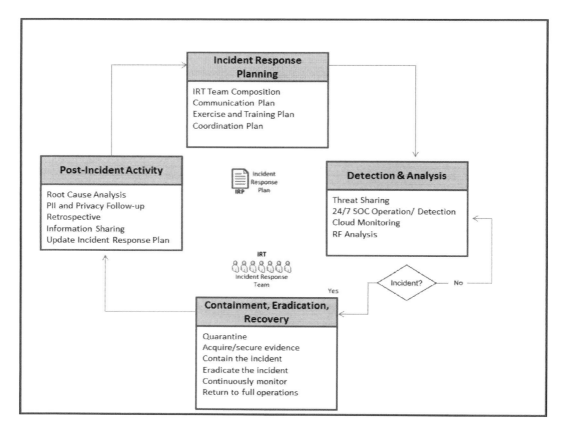

Any organization should have, at a minimum, these processes well documented and tailored for its unique system(s), technologies, and deployment approaches.

Incident response planning

Planning (sometimes called **incident response preparation**) is composed of those activities that are, figuratively speaking, designed to keep you from behaving like a deer in headlights when disaster strikes. If your company were to experience a massive denial of service attack that your load balancers and gateway couldn't keep up with, do you know what to do? Does your cloud provider handle this automatically, or are you expected to intervene by escalating services? If you find evidence that some of your web servers have been compromised, do you simply take them down and refresh them with golden images? What do you do with the compromised images? Who do you give them to, and how? What about record-keeping, rules, who gets involved and when, how to communicate, and so on? These and many other questions should be answered with the utmost precision in a detailed incident response plan.

NIST SP 800-62r2 provides a template and discussion of the contents of an **incident response plan (IRP)** and procedures. This template can be augmented for IoT-specific characteristics, such as determining what additional data should be collected (for example, physical sensor data in concert with specific message sets and times) in response to incidents ranging from erroneous behavior to full-scale compromise. Having a plan in place allows you to focus on critical analysis tasks during an incident, such as identifying the types and severity of the compromise.

IoT system categorization

The act of categorizing systems is strongly emphasized in the federal government space to identify whether specific systems are mission critical and to identify the impact of compromised data. From an enterprise IoT perspective, it is useful to categorize your systems, when possible, in a similar manner. The categorization of IoT systems allows for the tailoring of response procedures based on the business/mission impact of an incident, the safety impacts of an incident, and the need for near-real-time handling to stop imminent damage/harm.

NIST FIPS 199 (http://csrc.nist.gov/publications/fips/fips199/FIPS-PUB-199-final.pdf) provides some useful approaches for the categorization of information systems. We can borrow from and augment that framework to help us categorize IoT systems. The following table is borrowed from FIPS 199 to show the potential impact on the security objectives of confidentiality, integrity, and availability:

Security Objective	POTENTIAL IMPACT		
	LOW	MODERATE	HIGH
Confidentiality Preserving authorized restrictions on information access and disclosure, including means for protecting personal privacy and proprietary information. [44 U.S.C., SEC. 3542]	The unauthorized disclosure of information could be expected to have a **limited** adverse effect on organizational operations, organizational assets, or individuals.	The unauthorized disclosure of information could be expected to have a **serious** adverse effect on organizational operations, organizational assets, or individuals.	The unauthorized disclosure of information could be expected to have a **severe or catastrophic** adverse effect on organizational operations, organizational assets, or individuals.
Integrity Guarding against improper information modification or destruction, and includes ensuring information non-repudiation and authenticity. [44 U.S.C., SEC. 3542]	The unauthorized modification or destruction of information could be expected to have a **limited** adverse effect on organizational operations, organizational assets, or individuals.	The unauthorized modification or destruction of information could be expected to have a **serious** adverse effect on organizational operations, organizational assets, or individuals.	The unauthorized modification or destruction of information could be expected to have a **severe or catastrophic** adverse effect on organizational operations, organizational assets, or individuals.
Availability Ensuring timely and reliable access to and use of information. [44 U.S.C., SEC. 3542]	The disruption of access to or use of information or an information system could be expected to have a **limited** adverse effect on organizational operations, organizational assets, or individuals.	The disruption of access to or use of information or an information system could be expected to have a **serious** adverse effect on organizational operations, organizational assets, or individuals.	The disruption of access to or use of information or an information system could be expected to have a **severe or catastrophic** adverse effect on organizational operations, organizational assets, or individuals.

The impact is then analyzed in terms of impact on organizations or individuals. In FIPS 199, we can see that the impact on organizations and individuals can be low, medium, or high depending on the effect of confidentiality, integrity, or availability loss.

With IoT systems, we can continue to use this framework; however, it is also important to understand the impact of time and how time can drive the critical need for a response such as in safety-impacting systems. Looking back at our earlier examples, if we identify that someone has been attempting unsuccessfully to access an automotive fleet's systems, some potential responses may seem overly drastic. But given the potentially catastrophic nature of the compromise, combined with the motivation and intent of the attacker (for example, crashing a car), drastic responses may well be warranted. For example, the incident response plan may call for the manufacturer to temporarily disable all of the connected vehicle systems or comprehensively check the integrity of other electronic control units in the entire fleet.

The question to ask is whether there is the potential for imminent danger to employees, customers, or others if an identified attack pattern against IoT assets becomes known. If a company's security leadership is aware that someone was actively trying to compromise their fleet's connected IoT system, and yet the company continued to let those systems operate with a resulting injury/death, what are the potential liabilities and resultant legal claims against the organization?

IoT incident response procedures

The **European Union Agency for Network and Information Security (ENISA)** recently examined threat trends (`https://www.enisa.europa.eu/publications/ strategies-for-incident-response-and-cyber-crisis-cooperation/at_ download/fullReport`) in emerging technology areas. The report noted growth trends that have some bearing on the Internet of Things, namely:

- Malicious code: worms/Trojans
- Web-based attacks
- Web application attacks/injection attacks
- Denial of service
- Phishing
- Exploit kits
- Physical damage/theft/loss
- Insider threat
- Information leakage
- Identity theft/fraud

Organizations need to be ready to respond to each of these types of threats. The incident response plan will lay out the procedures that must be followed by various roles within the organization. These procedures may be tailored slightly depending on the impact of a compromise to the business or stakeholders. At a minimum, the procedures should outline when to escalate the identification of an incident to more senior or specialized personnel.

Procedures should also detail when to notify stakeholders of a suspected compromise of their data and what exactly to tell them as part of that notification. They should also specify whom to communicate with during the response, the steps to take to reach a compromise, and how to preserve an evidence chain of custody during the ensuing investigation. With respect to chain of custody, if there is a third-party cloud service provider involved, the cloud service plan (or SLA) needs to specify how that provider will support maintaining a chain of custody during incidents (in compliance with local or national laws).

The cloud provider's role

Chances are you are leveraging at least one cloud service provider to support your IoT services. Cloud SLAs are extremely important in your incident response plan; unfortunately, Cloud SLA objectives and contents are not well streamlined across the industry. In other words, be aware that some CSPs may not provide adequate IR support when it's most needed.

The Cloud Security Alliance's *Security Guidance for Critical Areas of Focus in Cloud Computing V3.0* (`https://cloudsecurityalliance.org/guidance/csaguide.v3.0.pdf`, Section 9.3.1) states that the following aspects of IR should be addressed in your cloud provider's SLA:

- Points of contact, communication channels, and availability of IR teams for each party

- Incident definitions and notification criteria, both from provider to customer and to any external parties

- CSP support to customers for incident detection (for example, available event data, notification about suspicious events, and so on)

- Definition of roles/responsibilities during a security incident, explicitly specifying support for incident handling provided by the CSP (for example, forensic support via collection of incident data/artifacts, participation/ support in incident analysis, and so on)

- Specification of regular IR testing carried out by the parties to the contract and whether results will be shared

- Scope of post-mortem activities (for example, root cause analysis, IR report, integration of lessons learned into security management, and so on)

- Clear identification of responsibilities around IR between provider and consumer as part of the SLA

IoT incident response team composition

Finding the right technical resources to staff an incident response team is always a challenge. Carnegie Mellon's CERT organization (`http://www.cert.org/incident-management/csirt-development/csirt-staffing.cfm`) notes that team staffing depends on a number of factors, including:

- Mission and goals
- Available staff expertise
- Anticipated incident load
- Constituency size and technology base
- Funding

Typically, an incident manager will be chosen to bring together a number of team members, based on the scope of the incident and the response required. It is crucial to keep a cadre of staff well trained in incident response and ready to assist as necessary when an incident does occur. The incident manager must be fully versed in the local IR procedures, as well as the cloud provider's SLAs.

Proper planning up front will enable the right pairing of staff with the specifically required roles needed for each incident. Teams responding to IoT-related incidents will need to include some unique skill sets driven by the specific IoT implementations and deployment use cases involved. In addition, staff need to have a deep understanding of the underlying business purpose of the compromised IoT system. Keep an emergency **point of contact** (**POC**) list for each type of incident within your organization.

Communication planning

The act of responding to an incident is often confusing and fast-paced; details can quite easily be overlooked in the *fog of war*. Teams need a pre-created communication plan to remember to involve the appropriate stakeholders and even partners. The communication plan should detail when to elevate the incident to higher-tier engineering staff, management, or executive leadership. The plan should also detail what should be communicated, by whom, and when, to outside stakeholders such as customers, government, law enforcement, and even the press when necessary. Finally, the communication plan should detail what information can be shared with different information-sharing services and social media (for example, if making announcements via Twitter, Facebook, and others).

From an internal response perspective, the communication plan should include POCs and alternatives for each IoT system in the organization, as well as POCs at suppliers, such as CSPs or other partners with whom you share IoT data. For example, if you support data-sharing APIs with analytics companies, it is possible that an IoT data breach could result in privacy-protected data unknowingly traversing those APIs, that is, unwanted onward transfer of PII.

Exercises and operationalizing an IRP in your organization

All potential IRT members should learn the incident response plan. The plan should be integrated into the organization with executive buy-in and oversight. Roles and responsibilities should be established and exercises should be conducted that include engagement with third parties, such as CSPs. Training should be provided, not only on the technical aspects of the systems being supported, but also on the business and mission objectives of the systems.

Regular exercises should be conducted to validate not only the plan but the organization's efficiency and skill in executing it. These exercises will also help ensure that the incident response plan is kept up to date and that the staff involved are well versed and can act competently in a real incident. Finally, make sure that systems are fully documented. Knowing where sensitive data resides (and when it resides there) will substantially improve the reliability and confidence in findings from the incident response team.

Detection and analysis

Today's **security information and event management (SIEM)** systems are powerful tools that allow correlation between any type of observable event to flag possible incidents. These same systems can of course be configured to monitor the infrastructure that supports IoT devices; however, there are considerations that will affect the ability to maintain a sufficient degree of situational awareness across a deployed IoT system:

- IoT systems are heavily dependent on cloud-hosted infrastructures
- IoT systems may include highly constrained (that is, limited processing, storage, or communication ability) devices that often lack the ability to capture and forward event logs

These considerations drive a need to architect the monitoring infrastructure to capture instrumentation data from CSPs that support the system, as well as anything that is possible from the devices themselves.

Although there are limited options available in this regard, some small start-up companies are attempting to close the gap. Bastille (`https://www.bastille.net/`) is an example of a company that is working toward a comprehensive RF-monitoring solution for the IoT. Their product monitors the RF spectrum from 60 MHz to 6 GHz, covering all of the major IoT communication protocols. Most importantly, Bastille's wireless monitoring solution integrates with SIEM systems to allow proper situational awareness in a wireless, connected IoT deployment.

Routine scanning (along with SIEM event correlations) should also be employed, as well as cloud-based or edge-situated behavioral analytics (appropriate for device gateways, for example). Solutions such as Splunk are good for these types of activities.

Any discussion on the types of tools needed for IoT-specific **digital forensics and incident response (DFIR)** needs to begin with an understanding of the types of incidents that can be encountered by an organization. Again, tools such as Splunk are effective in looking for such patterns and indicators. Possible indicators may include the following:

- We may see rogue sensor data injected to try and cause confusion within analytics systems
- We may see attempts at using rogue IoT devices to exfiltrate data from enterprise networks in which they are situated

- We may see attempts at compromising privacy controls to determine where individuals are located and what they are doing at any given time

- We may see attempts at injecting malware into control systems by exploiting trust relationships between individuals and organizations, or between connected devices and control system networks

- We may see attempts to disrupt business operations by launching denial of service attacks against IoT infrastructure

- We may see attempts at causing damage through unauthorized access to IoT devices (physical or logical)

- We may see attempts at compromising the confidentiality of data that flows across the entire IoT system by compromising device, gateway, and cloud-hosted cryptographic modules and key material

- We may see attempts to take advantage of trusted autonomous transactions for financial gain

It becomes clear when responding to possible incidents in an IoT deployment that the ability to understand whether an IoT device has been compromised becomes vitally important. These devices often possess trusted credentials that support interactions with upstream infrastructure, and in many cases interactions with other devices. The compromise of a trusted relationship such as this can lead to horizontal, pivoted movement throughout a system, as well as the ability to access virtualized, supporting infrastructure in the data center/cloud. Absent sophisticated monitoring capabilities for relevant system endpoints, these movements can be accomplished very quietly.

This tells us that by the time an analyst detects an incident underway, the perpetrator may have already established widespread hooks into important subsystems throughout the enterprise. This understanding should drive the incident response process to focus heavily on immediately analyzing other devices, compute resources, and even other systems to determine whether they are still operating according to an established secure baseline. Unfortunately, today's tools for quickly determining the security status of thousands or even millions of connected devices during an incident response is lacking.

Although there are gaps in the tools available for an optimal IoT-based incident response action, there are still standard tools that teams should have available to them.

Analyzing the compromised system

The first step toward being able to successfully analyze an incident is having good, current knowledge of the latest threats and indicators. Effective threat intelligence tools and processes are capabilities that responders should have in their arsenal. As enterprise IoT systems become increasingly attractive targets, these platforms will undoubtedly share indicators and defensive patterns with their membership. Some examples of today's threat-sharing platforms include:

- DHS **Automated Indicator Sharing (AIS)** initiative: Today, this focuses on the energy and technology sectors (`https://www.us-cert.gov/ais`)
- Alienvault **Open Threat Exchange (OTX)** (`https://www.alienvault.com/open-threat-exchange`)
- IBM X-Force Exchange: This is a cloud-based threat intelligence service (`http://www-03.ibm.com/software/products/en/xforce-exchange`)
- Information technology **Information Sharing and Analysis Center (ISAC)**

ISACs that lean more toward mission-specific threat intelligence exist as well. Examples include:

- **Industrial Control System (ICS)** ISAC (`http://ics-isac.org/blog/home/about/`)
- Electricity sector ISAC
- Public transportation/surface transportation ISAC
- Water ISAC

Once a possible incident is identified, additional analysis is performed to begin determining the scope and activity of the suspected compromise. Analysts should begin to assemble a timeline of activities. Keep this timeline handy and update it as new information is found. The timeline should include the presumed start time, and document any other significant times in the investigation. One can use audit/log data to correlate the activities that occurred. Something to consider in this regard is the need to keep and propagate an accurate source of time. Utilization of the **network time protocol (NTP)**, when available for IoT systems, can help. The timeline is created and elaborated as the team identifies the actions that the adversary may have performed.

Analysis can also entail activities that include attempts at attribution (that is, identifying who is attacking us). Tools that are useful for these activities would usually include the WHOIS databases from the various Internet registries that provide the ability to look up owners of IP address blocks. Unfortunately, there are easy-to-use methods that can be employed against IoT and any other IT systems, which provide anonymity for attackers. If one inserts a rogue IoT device into a network to transmit bogus readings, identifying the IP address of the device does little to help the analysis, because the device rides on the victim network. Even worse, the device may not have an IP address. Attacks from outside the organization can make use of command and control servers, botnets and just about any compromised host, VPN, Tor network, or some combination of mechanisms to mask the true source and source address of the attacker. Dynamic pivoting and rapid clearing of one's tracks is the norm whether it's a nation state, criminal organization (or both), or script kiddie that is attacking. The latter just may not be quite as skilled in how to thwart the forensics capabilities of their adversary.

A more thorough examination of the compromised device is in order to try and determine the characteristics of the attacker based on the files loaded, or even lifting fingerprints from the device itself. In addition, IoT Incident response may include forensic analysis of device gateways—gateways may be located at the network edge, or centrally within a CSP. Typically, a response team would capture images of the compromised systems for offline evaluation. This is where infrastructure tools that can be adapted and applied to IoT systems can become very useful.

Comparison between good behavioral and security baselines and compromised systems is valuable for identifying malicious artifacts and aiding in investigations. Tools that support the offline configuration of IoT devices can be used for this. For example, Docker images, when used to deploy IoT devices, can provide the good baseline example needed for a comparison.

If authentication services are set up for IoT device authentication, the logs from those authentication servers should also provide a valuable data source for an investigation. One should be diligent in looking for failed logins to systems and devices, as well as suspicious successful logins and authorizations from abnormal source IPs, times of day, and so on. Enterprise SIEM correlation rules will provide this functionality based on the use of threat intelligence feeds and reputational databases.

Another aspect of an investigation is determining what data has actually been compromised. Identifying exfiltrated data is the first step, but then you also must understand whether that exfiltrated data has been protected (at rest) using strong cryptographic measures. Exfiltration of gigabytes of ciphertext doesn't benefit the attacker unless he also acquires the cryptographic private key needed for the decryption. If your organization is unable to know the state of data (plaintext or ciphertext) at every point in the system, every host, every network, application, gateway, and so on, you will have a difficult time ascertaining the extent of the data breach. An accurate characterization of the data breach is crucial for informing the investigation as to whether data breach notifications need to be made, as per legal and regulatory mandates.

Forensic tools are also needed to help piece together information on the attack. There are a number of tools available that can be leveraged, such as:

- GRR
- Bit9
- Mastiff
- Encase
- FTK
- Norman Shark G2
- Cuckoo Sandbox

Although these tools are often used in terms of a traditional forensics effort, they have some gaps when dealing with actual IoT devices. Researchers (Oriwoh, et al. *Internet of Things Forensics: Challenges and Approaches*, `https://www.researchgate.net/publication/259332114_Internet_of_Things_Forensics_Challenges_and_Approaches`) outline a Next Best Thing approach to IoT forensics evidence collection. They argue convincingly that often the devices themselves will not provide sufficiently useful information and that instead one must look to the devices and servers to which data is sent within a system. For example, an MQTT client may not actually store any data, but instead may automatically send data to upstream MQTT servers. In this case, the server will most likely provide the next best thing to analyze.

Analyzing the IoT devices involved

In cases where the devices themselves may yield critical data in the investigation, IoT devices may need to be reversed to extract firmware for analysis. Given the enormous variety of potential IoT devices, the specific tools and processes will vary. This section provides some example methods of extracting and analyzing firmware images of devices that may have been compromised or were otherwise involved in an incident and may yet yield clues by analyzing memory. In practice, organizations may need to outsource these activities to a reputable security firm; if this is the case, find firms that have a firm background in forensics and have a good working knowledge of, and policies regarding, chain of custody and chain of evidence (should the data become necessary in courts of law).

Embedded devices can be challenging to analyze. Many commercial vendors provide USB interfaces to memory, but frequently restrict what areas of memory can be accessed. If the embedded device does support a *nix type of OS kernel, and the analyst is able to get a command line to the device, a simple dd command may be all that is necessary to extract the device's image, specific volumes, partitions, or master boot record to a remote location.

Absent a convenient interface, you'll likely need to extract memory directly, and that's typically through a JTAG or UART interface. In many cases, security-conscious vendors go to great lengths to mask or disable JTAG interfaces. To get physical access, it might be necessary to cut, grind or find some other method of removing a physical layer from the connector. If the JTAG test access ports are accessible and there's a JTAG connector already there, tools such as Open On-Chip Debugger (http://openocd.org/) or UrJTAG (http://urjtag.org/) can be useful in communicating with flash chips, CPUs and other embedded architectures and memory types. It may also be necessary to solder a connector to the ports to gain access.

Absent an accessible JTAG or UART interface, more advanced chip-off (also called **chip de-capping**) techniques may be in order to extract data. Chip-off forensics is generally destructive in nature, because the analyst has to physically remove the chip by de-soldering or chemically removing adhesives, whatever the manufacturer used to attach the chip in the first place. Once removed, chip programmers can be used to extract the binary data from the memory type that was employed. Chip-off is generally an advanced process performed by specifically outfitted laboratories.

Whatever procedure was used to access and extract the full memory of the device, the next step involves the analysis of the binary. Depending on the chip or architecture in question, a number of tools are available for performing raw binary analysis. Examples include:

- **Binwalk** (`http://binwalk.org`): Very useful for scanning a binary for specific signatures related to files, filesystems, and so on. Once identified, files can be extracted for downstream inspection and analysis.

- **IDA-Pro** (`https://www.hex-rays.com/products/ida/index.shtml`): Used by many security researchers (and anyone looking to find and exploit vulnerabilities in well-known OS architectures), IDA is a powerful disassembly and debugging tool that can target a variety of operating systems for reverse engineering.

- **Firmwalker** (`https://github.com/craigz28/firmwalker`): A script-based tool for searching files and filesystems in firmware.

Escalate and monitor

Know how and when to perform incident escalation. This is where good threat intelligence becomes especially valuable. Compromises are usually not single events, but rather small pieces of a larger campaign. As new information is learned, the methods of detection and response need to escalate and adapt to handle the incident.

Finally, something to consider is that cybersecurity staff deploying IoT systems in industries such as transportation and utilities should keep an eye on national and international threats above and beyond the local organization. This is the normal course of business for US and other national intelligence-related agencies. Nation-state, terrorist, organized crime and other international-related security considerations can have direct bearing on IoT systems in terms of nationalistic or criminal attack motivations, desired impacts, and the possible actors who may carry out the actions. This type of awareness tends to be more applicable to critical energy, utilities, and transportation infrastructure, but targeted attacks can come from anywhere and target just about anything.

There is a significant need for information to be shared between operational and technology teams even within organizations. In terms of public/private partnerships that facilitate such information sharing, one is InfraGard:

> "*InfraGard is a partnership between the FBI and the private sector. It is an association of persons who represent businesses, academic institutions, state and local law enforcement agencies, and other participants dedicated to sharing information and intelligence to prevent hostile acts against the U.S.*"

Source: `https://www.infragard.org/`

Another valuable information-sharing resource is the **High Tech Crime Investigation Association (HTCIA)**. HTCIA is a non-profit that hosts yearly international conferences and promotes partnerships with public and private entities. Regional chapters exist in many parts of the world.

Other more sensitive partnerships, such as the US **Department of Homeland Security's (DHS) Enhanced Cybersecurity Services (ECS)**, exist between government and industry to improve threat intelligence and sharing across commercial and government boundaries. These types of programs typically invoke access to classified information outside the realm of most non-government contracting organizations today. We may very well see such programs undergo significant enhancement over the years to better accommodate IoT-related threat intelligence, given the large government and military interest in IoT-enabled systems and CPS.

Containment, eradication, and recovery

One of the most important questions to answer during an incident response is the level at which systems can be taken offline without disrupting critical business/ mission processes. Often within IoT systems, the process of swapping out a new device for an old device is relatively trivial; this needs to be taken into account when determining the right course of action. This is not always the case, of course, but if it is feasible to quickly swap out infected devices then that path should be taken.

In any case, compromised devices should be removed from the operational network as quickly as possible. The state of those devices should be strictly preserved so that the devices can be further analyzed using traditional forensics tools and processes. Even here though, there are challenges, as some constrained devices may overwrite data important to the analysis (`https://www.cscan.org/openaccess/?id=231`).

More complicated issues arise when an IoT gateway has been compromised. Organizations should keep on hand preconfigured spare gateways ready to be deployed should a gateway be compromised. If possible, a re-flashing of all IoT devices may also be in order if the gateway is compromised. Today, this can be quite a challenge, unfortunately. Automated software/firmware provisioning services (not unlike the Microsoft **Windows Server Update Services (WSUS)** application) represent an enormous gap in today's IoT. The ability to patch any device, anywhere, over the wire or over the air, is definitely needed, and it's a capability that needs to function regardless of who owns a device and whether or how it is transferred to other owners, other cloud-based provider services, and so on.

Infrastructure compute platforms must also be considered. Remove servers or server images (cloud) from the operational network and replace them with new, baselined images to keep services up and running (much easier and faster in a cloud deployment). An incident response plan should include each of the discrete steps to do this. If you utilize a cloud management interface, include the specific management URI at which to perform the action, the specific steps (button presses), everything. Determine by what means IoT images in your system can be acquired. Isolate the infected images to begin forensics analysis, where you will attempt to identify the malware and the vulnerability/vulnerabilities that the malware is attempting to exploit.

One thing to note is that it is always desirable to track what an adversary is doing on your network. If the required resources are available, it would be beneficial to set up logical rules gateway devices that, upon command or pattern, segment off compromised IoT devices to make an attacker or malware unaware of the discovery. Dynamically reconfiguring these devices to talk to a parallel dummy infrastructure (either at the gateway or in the cloud) can allow for closer observation and study of the actions being taken by the malicious actor(s). Alternatively, you can re-route traffic for the affected device(s) to a sandbox environment for further analysis.

Post-incident activities

Sometimes called recovery, this phase includes steps for performing root cause analysis, after-incident forensics, privacy health checks, and a determination of which PII items, if any, were compromised.

Root cause analysis should be used to understand exactly how the defensive posture failed and determine what steps should be taken in order to keep the incident from reoccurring. Active scanning of related IoT devices and systems should also occur post-incident, to proactively hunt for the same or similar intruders.

It is important to employ retrospective meetings for sharing lessons learned among team members. This can be explicitly stated in your incident response plan by calling for one-day, one-week, and one-month follow-up meetings with the entire IR team. Over the course of that time, many details from follow-up forensics and analysis will shed new light on the source of the incident, its actors, the vulnerabilities exploited, and, equally important, how well your team did in the response. Retrospective meetings should be handled like group therapy—no pointing fingers, blame, or harsh criticism of individuals or processes, just an honest assessment of 1) what happened, 2) how it happened, 3) how well or poorly your response went (and why), and 4) how you can respond better next time. The retrospectives should have a moderator to ensure that things flow well, time is not wasted, and that the most salient lessons learned are captured.

Finally, all of the lessons learned should be evaluated for:

- Necessary changes to the IRP plan
- Necessary changes to the **network access control (NAC)** plan
- Any need for new tools, resources, or training required to safeguard the enterprise
- Any deficiencies in the cloud service provider's IR plan that would have helped in the incident response (indeed, you may need to determine if you need to migrate to a different cloud provider, or add additional services with your current one)

Summary

This chapter provided guidance on building, maintaining, and executing an incident response plan. We defined IoT incident response and management, and discussed the unique details related to executing IoT incident response activities.

The safe and secure implementation of IoT systems is a difficult challenge to undertake given the unique characteristics of these systems, their ability to impact events in the physical world, and the diverse nature of IoT implementations. This book has attempted to provide practical advice for designing and deploying many types of complex IoT system. We hope that you are able to tailor this guidance to your own unique environments, even as the pace of change in this high-potential technology area continues to increase.

Index

ThingWorx **94**
threats
  defining **36**
threats/attacks
  defining **233**
  references **233**
threat-sharing platforms
  examples **295**
threats, vulnerability and risks (TVR)
  defining **34**
Transmission Control Protocol (TCP) 27
transport layer security (TLS) 146, 185
trust center link keys (TCLK) 165
trusted platform modules (TPMs) 192

U

Uniform Resource Indicators (URIs) 25
universal serial bus (USB) ports 91
University of San Diego,
    California (UCSD) 52
Unmanned Aerial Systems (UAS) 16
unmanned aircraft systems (UAS) 17
US Dept. of Transportation (USDOT) 187
User Datagram Protocol (UDP) 28

V

vehicle-to-infrastructure (V2I)
    communications 187
vehicle-to-vehicle (V2V)
    communications 120
vulnerability
  defining **36, 37**

W

White box
  assessments **242, 243**
Windows Server Update
    Services (WSUS) 300
WSNs (wireless sensor networks) 236

X

Xively 94
XMPP
  URL **26**
XMPP-IoT
  URL **26**

Z

zeroization 159, 160
zero-sum approach
  reference link **217**
ZigBee
  about **163**
  URL **163**
ZigBeeAlliance09 114
ZigBee-based IoT network online
  reference **114**
ZigBee Home Automation Public
    Application Profile (HAPAP) 114
ZigBee Light Link Profile (ZLL) 114
ZWave
  references **29**